LONDON

The Synfulle Citie

English bawds, c. 1610, unknown Flemish painter.

*Their Brestes alle bare embusk'd
and paynted bee, on hire.*
Thomas Nashe

The woman in the background is most probably Elizabeth Holland of
Hollands Leaguer *fame.*

LONDON

The Synfulle Citie

E. J. Burford

ROBERT HALE · LONDON

Robert Hale Limited
Clerkenwell House
Clerkenwell Green
London EC1R 0HT

Photoset in Linotron Palatino by
Rowland Phototypesetting Limited, Bury St Edmunds, Suffolk
Printed in Great Britain by
St Edmundsbury Press Limited, Bury St Edmunds, Suffolk
and bound by WBC Bookbinders Limited, Bristol and Maesteg

Contents

List of Illustrations

List of Illustrations

The Courtauld Institute: *Frontispiece*. The Museum of London: 1–3, 8. The Wellcome Institute: 5–6, 43. Statens Historika Museum, Stockholm: 9. The Bishopsgate Institute: 10. The Bodleian Library: 13. The British Museum: 14, 53–4, 59, 61–2, 65. John B. Freeman: 16, 38, 42, 44. The Guildhall Library: 23–4, 29, 31, 37, 45–6, 48, 50, 52. GLC: 27, 56–7. Dorotheum, Vienna: 36. All other illustrations from the collection of the author.

THE VALEDICTION

for my beloved Nancy, a woman of great beauty, intelligence and courage, my boyhood sweetheart and my cherished wife for sixty-three years: always my inspiration and mainspring. She died, as she lived, with courage and dignity.

'I never had but this one true love.'

Acknowledgements

I should like to express my sincere thanks and appreciation to all those who have helped with information and advice in the compilation of this book, not forgetting that wonderfully ubiquitous chronicler Anon spread over the centuries, details of whose work are to be found in the bibliography. Among the most seminal works is that of Henry Thomas Riley MA, compiler and Editor of the *Liber Albus* which contains a wealth of facts and figures relating to the laws and regulations of the earliest years of the City of London. A worthy present-day successor on whom I have leaned heavily is James R. Sewell MA, City Archivist. I am also greatly indebted to Richard Bowden, the Archivist of the Marylebone Library and John Fisher, Deputy Keeper of Prints in the Guildhall Library as well as John Phillips, Keeper of Prints at the Greater London Council's Record Office. To David Webb, Librarian at the Bishopsgate Institute, I owe the data on London's earliest Saint, whose tiny church nestles in Bishopsgate to this day; and to David Davies MLL, Dean of the Faculty of Law at the City Polytechnic data on various arcane legal tangles. Nor must I forget to thank the many assistants in various libraries for the trouble which they took to rout out many of the anecdotes needed to enliven the narrative. I am sure that the readers will join with me in this appreciation.

E. J. Burford
London, 1989

Introduction

This book is quite different from all others dealing with London. It deals with the *real* City of London – the so-called 'Square Mile' – which lived for more than a thousand years within the shadow of its massive Roman walls. It is the fascinating story of the lives, loves and lusts of the inhabitants of changing racial origins who eventually emerged as *Homo londoniensis* – the Londoner.

It deals with the seemingly never-ending attempts by the mayor and aldermen to solve the intractable problem of those forms of sexual recreation known as fornication and sodomy, as practised timeously throughout the City's evolution in buildings which were called in turn 'lupanars', 'bagnios', 'stewes' and, eventually, 'whore-houses' and 'Mollies-houses'. Ordinances demanding punishments such as whipping, ducking, dragging at the cart-arse, the pillory, the stocks, the *thew* and imprisonment, and eventually expulsion from their beloved city into 'assigned places' outside the walls – all were to no avail. This 'plague of lust' could never be entirely eradicated: in any case, sexual activity was too noisy, raucous and drunken to be hidden from neighbours who objected rather to the disturbance than the copulation.

Simultaneous with this attempt to 'cleanse' the city morally were the equally unavailing attempts to cleanse it physically of the dirt and filth. Dunghills and open latrines contributed to the variegated 'stingles', helped by the citizens' persistence in fouling their own nest in 'pyssynge alleys' and 'shite-bournes' lanes.

This book will describe, unexpurgated, the lively, lovely, bustling, noisy, cheerful, rowdy but dirty city and its inhabitants, coarse in speech and manners, with their dress and dwellings in different generations. In describing its unique form of government, it will disclose some hitherto unknown aspects of the City's rulers – the mayors, sheriffs and aldermen – those pedlars who became plutocrats, plebeians who became pseudo-aristocrats, the

Earliest Londinium as rebuilt after Boudicca's onslaught in AD 61. Painting by Alan Sorrell.

godly and the sinners who became philanthropists and philistines – but all united in one worthy aim: to make their City greater and, above all, richer. Richness was all! He who aspired to be Lord Mayor had to be immensely rich – many an alderman had to decline the office of sheriff because the cost of the eventual mayoralty was ruinous.

A glimpse will be given into the City's power base following the 'quiet revolution' in 1189 when a commune was set up – the forerunner of today's Common Council; and how poor religious craft fraternities became rich, powerful guilds which in the end could and did stand up to kings – when they were not fawning upon them.

Finally it will explain how the ward of Farringdon Without became 'that greate estate of lecherie' and produced sophisticated brothelry under such *entrepreneuses* as Priss Fotheringham and the even more famous 'Mother' Elizabeth Cresswell, friend to king and commoner alike with her principle of 'No Money! No Cunny!'

1 Roman Revels

This is the story of how it came about that a couple of tiny prehistoric hamlets inhabited by simple savages, whose only covering in summer was a dye of blue woad and in winter the skins of wild animals, grew to become the capital city of a great nation and of an even greater empire.

These two settlements of wattle-and-daub huts lay where two streams entered a wide *tamasa*, the pre-Celtic word meaning a 'dark river'. Their background was a huge, thick forest with uplands inhabited by wild bears and wolves and other predators, and wild cattle which they hunted for their meat and hides. Westward the land was fair and fertile; to the north and east lay the great marshes which helped to protect them from human enemies.

Their pursuits were simple: simple tilling of their fields, simple eating and drinking, simple fighting for women, simple raids on richer or unfriendly tribes and, of course, simple carnal copulation, sometimes *in more caninus*, encouraged by a simple 'phallic-vulvic' religion. This religion included a water god who doubled as a war god, and a goddess much later known as a *sheila-na-gig*. In his history of the Celts, Jan Filip records their belief that certain trees were 'possessed of divine power' and hence worshipped. The ancient name for a god of the trees or wood was 'Guidgen', a word that also refers to alders. The name of '*sheila-na-gig*' would therefore have been 'Lady or Goddess of the Alder or Wood'. The phallic god's name was Lug, and the little *dun* – a settlement – at the westernmost river's edge, corresponding to the later Fleet river, became known as Lug-dun, the Romans calling it Lugdunum and thus immortalizing the god's name. The easternmost *dun* was at the confluence of the river and the smaller stream, later known as the Wallbrook; as Waelsbroc – the brook of the Welsh (by which name the Saxons called the ancient Britons) – it enters history. Cruel fate has since reduced both streams to underground sewers.

3

The villagers' religion required the use of simple phallic figures, matched by simple vulvic figurines. The latter survived in Ireland until well into the Christian era, many being extra-mural ornaments to primitive churches. One of the simple sacrifices entailed the use of a large wicker cage containing phallic statuettes which were immersed in the river – on occasion a man might thus be drowned.

The coming, about 400 BC of the first Belgic Celts did not much disturb such activities, the conquerors being only more aggressive and much better organized, with some pretensions to culture picked up piecemeal during their centuries-long sojourn in Europe. Their religious practices were similar, and they would have been astounded to be told that their simple and natural ceremonies and sexual activities would later be regarded as 'sinful' – a word that had no existence in their vocabularies.

With the coming of the Romans, this idyllic life-style ended.

In 54 BC Julius Caesar invaded Britain in a punitive expedition against the British Celts for helping their Gallic cousins against the expansion of his Roman territories. He came with five legions and 2000 cavalry, and they had a hard fight against the Kantware (men of Kent) all the way up from their landing-place at Rutupiae (Richborough, near Deal) before reaching the marshy banks of the River Tamesis at the point now known as Southwark. At this place, some forty miles from the sea, Caesar wrote in his *De Bello Gallico*, '. . . the river could only be forwarded at one place' – at low tide it was only five feet deep. He established a base camp at Southwark, threw a pontoon bridge across the river to open supply lines and sent his cavalry across to help his struggling soldiers treading on the hidden stakes in the river. 'The defenders then took to flight.'

Caesar could have erected a much more substantial bridge – he had built a strong wood-piled bridge across the much wider Rhine in ten days on a previous campaign, but he was in a hurry to get back to Gaul to deal with other pressing matters. The departing legions also left behind a useful crop of bilingual bastards and the much less agreeable legacy of venereal disease, which some legionaries had picked up in the eastern campaigns.

Almost a century later, in AD 43, the Divine Emperor Claudius decided to add Pritania to his empire. He sent General Aulus Plautius with four legions, cavalry, engineers and camp-followers, together with four – or maybe six – elephants to frighten the natives, although the principal British tribes, the Catuvellani and the Trinovantes, were wary of the Roman might and were in temporary alliance to meet the threat.

Caesar's legions wading across the shallow River Tamesis in the teeth of fierce opposition from the British tribal forces. Painting by R. Sorrell.

Aulus Plautius's troops, according to the chronicler Dio Cassius, had difficulty in crossing the river because of the marshy ground: '. . . his German auxiliary troops swam over . . . the others by a bridge a little way downstream . . .' The general had to wait for his 'divine' master to reach Pritania for his Triumph. The engineers had time to build a very substantial wooden bridge over which Claudius, his Praetorian Guard and his elephants could pass in glory. Once over, they spread fire and destruction all the way to the Trinovantan capital, Camulodunum (Colchester in Essex), which they then detroyed. When rebuilt, it remained the capital of Roman Britain throughout the whole occupation.

Londinium was then a small trading-place of no great import-ance, but by AD 60 (*vide* Tacitus) it had grown into a town 'with many great merchants and traders'. However, it was only a *civitates* – a settlement whose main function was to pay taxes and maintain the military roads. These first Londoners were Roman officials and well-to-do Gaulish merchants as well as detribalized Britons and

Aulus Plautius's legionaries building the first London Bridge: note the temporary pontoon bridge on the left, which was too fragile to accommodate the weight of the Emperor Claudius' Triumph in AD 43 which included several elephants. Painting by Alan Sorrell.

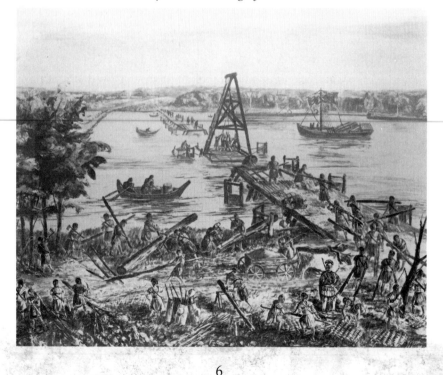

numerous slaves. Their habitations clustered around the riverside wharves, since the main business was in imports for the interior and exports of British meat and grain. A very important export was flaxen-haired, blue-eyed women slaves – in great demand in Rome. They may have looked like angels to Pope Gregory but they were by no means angelic in temper and behaviour – British women were accustomed to fight side-by-side with their men.

These merchant denizens could not have realized the hatred Roman rule had engendered in the countryside, so that the bloody events that were to ensue were a ghastly surprise. Roman rule was harsh, and their exactions were immense; moreover, many officials were corrupt and viciously sadistic, because their power was absolute. As an example, Plautianus, head of the Praetorian Guard (who had spent some time in Britain) and a favourite of the Emperor Severus (*vide* Dio Cassius), '. . . had a hundred free-born Roman citizens, some married men, castrated' so that his daughter, who had married the Emperor's son Caracalla, '. . . might be attended to by a train of eunuchs worthy of an eastern Queen . . .'. Plautinus was eventually murdered by one of his victims.

When, in AD 61, the procurator Decius Catus seized the property of the dead chieftain of the Iceni, Prasutag (who had been a Roman 'client'), he had the widow Boudicca flogged and her daughters raped in her presence. These women were not, however, delicate shrinking violets – they were tough characters. Boudicca mobilized her Iceni and called upon all the East Anglian tribes to join her. A huge horde swept down on Camulodunum, slaughtered the small Roman garrison and every Roman 'client' and sympathizer, sacked and looted the city and then burned it to the ground. Then they turned towards Londinium. The procurator, realizing what a cataclysm he had unleashed, quietly and quickly slipped abroad with his family and his loot.

The governor, Suetonius Paulinus, was in Anglesey in Wales, rooting out the Druids. He had only Legion XIV Gemini and a cohort of Legion XX Victoria and the handful of cavalry who had escaped from Camulodunum. By a forced march he reached Londinium just ahead of Boudicca's vengeful horde. Deciding that he could not defend Londinium with such a small force, and awaiting the reinforcements which he had called for, he had to abandon Londinium: '. . . neither the tears nor the entreaties of the stricken citizens could bend him from his purpose . . .'.

Boudicca swooped down on the unwalled undefended settlement, sparing nothing and nobody: 'Death by the sword and the gibbet was the fate of those who remained, regardless of age or sex. Men, women and children were nailed to trees. All buildings were systematically destroyed by fire . . . .' The ashes of this conflagration were many feet deep: centuries afterwards thousands of skeletons from this massacre were exhumed just outside Bishopsgate.

The horde swept on to Verulamium (St Albans), which met the same fate. Meanwhile Suetonius's reinforcements had arrived, and when Boudicca's host encountered them at Battle Bridge (thought to be near King's Cross), they were in turn decimated and systematically slaughtered all the way back to Norfolk – no prisoners were taken. Boudicca poisoned herself.

The lesson was learnt: a fortified enclave was built in the north-west corner of the rebuilt town, where Cripplegate now stands. A permanent and substantial garrison was lodged there. Londinium quickly recovered and in the next few years was extended eastward along the riverside and a considerable distance northwards. The bridge was the focal point, the main highway going thence northwards through the gate – the later Bishopsgate. The rebuilding conformed to the regular Roman pattern: a forum as the centre for bankers, money-changers and big-businessmen, a large oblong basilica with alcoves and colonnades as a residence for the principal magistrate and as law courts, and an important government residence (recently excavated) for a very high official, at Huggin Hill. There were temples to essential male gods such as Hermes and Pan; that of the soldiers' god Mithras can be seen today at Bucklersbury. The agricultural god Sylvanus with his enormous phallus would have been much in evidence. There would have been fine temples for the great goddesses: the *Bona Dea*, Isis and Venus. Along the roads radiating from the forum were open-fronted shops for all kinds of merchandise, local and imported, and a great many inns and taverns. As the population surged, apartment blocks of considerable height were built to accommodate the poorer inhabitants, the ground floors of brick and the upper storeys of wood. They were grossly overcrowded, and there was an ever-present danger of fire.

The riverside was lined with wharves and warehouses and customs houses. The streets were very noisy, with traffic day and night over the bridge to and from the ports to the inland centres. Along the riverside were the slave markets – open spaces known as 'Romelands' up to the time of Henry VIII. There was never any lack of slaves: they came from all over the empire. Young girls from Syria were in great demand as 'adepts on the harp' – they were also sold to the brothels. Male Greek slaves were in demand because

Plaques from a Roman temple: a priestess makes a sacrifice to Hermes, who dedicates a statuette by a wreath.

usually they were literate and numerate. In the market, foreign slaves had their feet chalked white to distinguish them from local slaves, the *vernae*: after some years in slavery the chalk permeated the skin.

During the following fifty years there were many uprisings in the country, so that sometime after AD 120 a substantial brick-and-stone wall was built around the town, fronted by a deep and wide ditch, outside which was a wide open ground called a *pomerium* – although there were no apple or any other trees planted, affording no cover for any potential enemies. The north-western fort was now enclosed within the wall, having a postern allowing rapid movement of troops. There were four main gates in the wall through which the main roads led to the provincial 'capitals'.

The walled town now became a *municipium* in which Roman citizens were allowed to reside, together with enfranchised immigrants, and carry on their avocations under the watchful eye of an *aedile* – an official supervisor – who ensured that Rome's laws were carried out and Rome's taxes diligently collected. His palace was adjacent to the fort, the street being known probably as the Via Aedilium – hence today's Addle Street.

At this point Londinium was a well-governed, calm and orderly provincial town, physically clean, with public latrines emptying into stone *cloacae* (sewers) flushed twice daily by the Thames' tidal flow, as well as by *thermae* (hot baths). Moral health was guaranteed by a large number of registered *lupanaria* (high-class brothels) and *fornixes* (proletarian whorehouses); their inhabitants were also subjected – at least notionally – to health inspections from time to time.

It was a busy, bustling, pagan city, with plenty of 'bread and circuses' to keep the populace diverted, if not happy. There were the great festivals, celebrated with great licence. In the Lupercalia, the feast of the wolf-goddess, naked maidens ran about the streets being whipped on by naked youths, waving garlands, exchanging small phallic ornaments and copulating publicly.

In the Floralia, the Feast of Flowers celebrated annually between 28 April and 3 May, '. . . custom sanctioned unusual sexual freedom for actresses and prostitutes', and immense wooden phalluses were carried high during the procession. At the annual festival for the *Bona Dea* – a fertility cult celebration in honour of the daughter of the satyr god Faunus – women of all classes partici-

Scene outside a brothel in Roman times. A man is being importuned. The Lena stands by the door, on which the sign Occupata can be seen.

PRIAPE

Scene at the great 'Festival of Priapus'. A donkey, the god's symbol because of its legendary sexual powers, has been slaughtered as a sacrifice. The god's phallus is being garlanded to the sound of music. (Bernard de Montfauçon, 1719.)

pated under huge images of the phallus and the vulva, ending in a public copulatory free-for-all.

In the Saturnalia every December, the god Saturn was paraded about in full-frontal glory, inciting everybody to every kind of lubricity; it was the only festival in which slaves were given time off to participate in their owners' sexual antics. In the subsequent drunken spree many an old score would have been settled, evidencing the epigram *'Quot servi tot hostes'* ('You have as many enemies as you have slaves').

On the day of the festival to the great goddess Isis women devotees could perform any kind of sexual excess in public with any passer-by. Most popular was the Bacchanalia in honour of the drunken god Priapus, on which day every woman seen outside her home was deemed to be a bacchante and available for copulation in circumstances of indescribable lubricity. There was also the temple

11

of the vestal virgins in which sexual licence could be enjoyed by everyone except the vestal virgins themselves, since unchaste ones were buried alive! In all these festivals the phallic symbol was overpowering in evidence: in the primitive pagan mind no distinction was made between the god and his symbol; the image acted as the god, much as today bread and wine are accepted as the flesh and blood of Christ.

There was the very ancient idol Mutinus (originating in Modena in Italy), a man-size effigy seated with a very realistic erect phallus: women were encouraged to sit on it in simulated intercourse *in more caninus* (in the manner of dogs). No odium was attached to such behaviour – indeed, any virgin whose hymen had thus been perforated was esteemed for this sacrifice to the god. Later an irate Christian divine condemned it as a god 'in whose lap shameful brides do sit!'.

In the local amphitheatre, there would be gory entertainment, including crucifixions and flayings of victims of some emperor's whim, or the same being savaged and eaten by bears and wolves (local animals ready available and much cheaper than imported lions) and gladiatorial contests like those in Rome, albeit on a smaller scale but no less enjoyable to spectators and bookies alike.

Less bloodthirsty entertainments were to be found in the *thermae*, the hot baths open to men, women and children. Children under ten were admitted free, but while men paid a *quadra* (a farthing), women had to pay double. The larger of these amenities (one was uncovered in Cheapside) were luxurious places of social resort. They had boutiques selling jewellery, perfumes, dresses and bric-à-brac. There would be an art gallery where poets would gather to spout their verses while importuning the rich to engage them as 'clients' to sing their praises in exchange for free meals. There might be a reading room for *literati*, and scribes to attend the wants of both poets and illiterates. There were bathing cubicles, often used as an overnight hotel in which a young *venusia* could be enjoyed. There were restaurants and bars which witnessed true patrician behaviour, such as guzzling immense quantities of food and drink and the use of a feather to tickle the throat to vomit it out and start all over again. It was quite permissible to compete with one's guests by pissing in a chamberpot held by a naked female slave – much fêted was he who hit either target squarely!

Erotic pictures were on the walls, and the utensils used in the repasts were shaped like penises or vulvae; the phallic bread rolls were called *colyphae*, and the same shape was used for the marzipan sweets and cakes, as well as the table-lamps and even the candelabrae – nothing was left to the imagination. Surrounding the building was the *palaestra* – the promenade which (*vide* Juvenal) '. . . was much frequented by sodomites'.

There were also the *pervigiles popinae*, the all-night bars (literally 'the keep-awake bars') mostly owned by freedmen – manumitted slaves or slaves who had bought their freedom, '. . . coarse, clever, thrusting ex-slaves, Greeks and Jews . . . not suffering from upper-class morality or conventions . . . cashing in on their masters' disdain for commerce and industry . . .'. In fact, many were literate and cultured men captured in some Roman war; by superior knowledge and talent they were so useful to their masters that they became indispensable and could be made freedmen. Very often they served as a front for some patrician's commercial activities. Many became rich and powerful, but they would always harbour deep resentment: indeed, Horace in his *Amores* remarks:

> Never look down upon an ex-slave with money;
> What matters if his feet were covered with white chalk?

An added amenity of these all-night bars was the availability of lovely Syrian prostitutes, almost all of them someone's slave.

With wealth, many of these freedmen aspired to become *equestri* – knights, a badge of nobility which cost a mere 300,000 sesterces. This by then much debased patrician status enabled them to enter the ranks of public administrators, hitherto reserved for Romans. In a polyglot provincial town this title commanded respect and, more importantly, influence and power. Nevertheless, Londinium, greatest and richest settlement in all Pritania, never achieved the accolade of *Colonia*, a self-governing free entity.

Over and above all, the *lupanar* brothels were the greatest attraction to the male citizenry. They were not difficult to find: at almost every street corner stood a *Herm* – a short stone pillar of Hermes furnished with a large, erect penis with the prepuce painted a brilliant red. This would be touched, fondled or kissed by a great many passing women and girls – even garlanded at festival time. It brought good luck to all: a husband for a virgin, a child for the barren, though it was also regarded as merely a good-luck token. An even more ancient signpost was a black palm-imprint on an adjacent wall. Fornication was not a crime: the *lupanar* was intended to keep the gilded youth away from sodomy. The *Lex Julia de Adulteriis* of 18 BC stated that adultery was not a crime if a married man copulated with a licensed prostitute, but if she was not registered, it was a *stuprum*, a filthy vice.

Indeed, to swell its treasury the empire had the *Lenonium Vectigal de Meretricium et Exsoletorum* (Tax on Whorehouses, Prostitutes and Mercenary Catamites) which was regularly renewed until the reign of Emperor Severus (who died in York in AD 220). He directed the immense revenues to the repair of the theatres, circuses and amphitheatres, all focal points of prostitution, and the residue to the imperial treasury.

The best *lupanars* were large villas with gardens with fountains for relaxation before and after copulation. The walls of the rooms would be painted with lewd erotica, as at Pompeii. All the accoutrements were of gold or silver, and the cuisine was of the very best. The élite of the town patronized them, and the very pick of womanhood was there to serve.

At the other end of the scale were the *fornixes*, originally situated under the arches along the colonnades of great public buildings. The word *fornix*, an arch, also had the meaning of 'filthy' – and indeed these were mere dirty shacks by the roadside. Any sexual intercourse could be seen by the passers-by: hence this sort of quick, casual copulation became known as 'fornication'.

Any woman who wanted to become a prostitute had to apply to the *aedile*, giving her name and status, date of birth and the name under which she wished to trade. (At one time even ladies of high rank were applying, since the earnings of courtesans were very great.) The *aedile* would first try to persuade the applicant against entering such a profession but, if she persisted, had then to issue a *licencia stupro*. This stated, *inter alia*, her business name and address and charges and had to be posted at the door of her residence or of the brothel. This gave her the right to sue any client who tried to bilk her. In AD 30 Caligula re-enacted the *Lenonium Vectigal*: its immense revenues were known as *chrysargia* because they had to be paid in gold or silver coin.

No shame was attached to the customers. Horace sums it up in his *Amores*:

> Hired intercourse earns no gratitude
> Payment frees the client from all commitment –
> He owes you nothing for being obliging . . .

but he also said that '. . . even the prostitute earning a bare living, compliant to everyone at a price, curses the ponce she is forced to obey'.

Independent whores were the *meretrices* (money-earners), the poorest being the *prostibulae* who used the *fornixes*, often only sheds with wooden bunks. For a small extra sum, a blanket or a

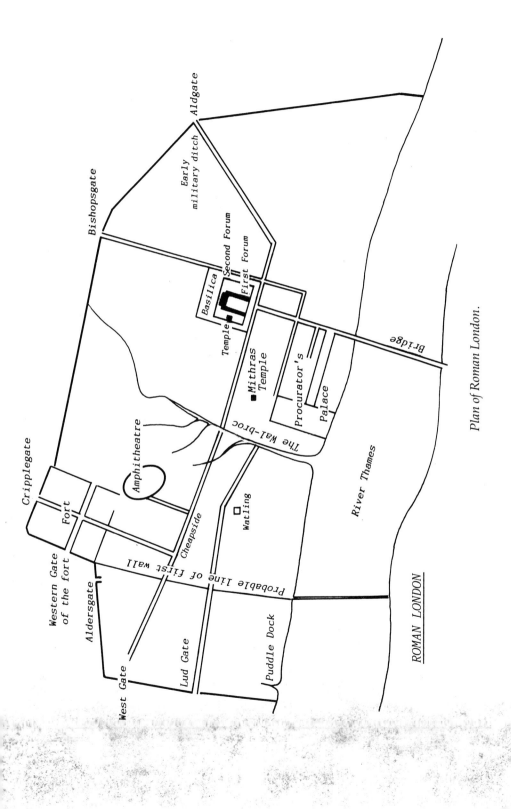

Plan of Roman London.

ROMAN LONDON

Aldgate

Bishopsgate

Early
military ditch

Basilica

Second Forum

First Forum

Temple

Mithras
Temple

Procurator's

Palace

Bridge

Cripplegate

Amphitheatre

The Wal-broc

River Thames

Fort

Western Gate
of the fort

Aldersgate

Cheapside

Watling

West Gate

Lud Gate

Probable line of first wall

Puddle Dock

straw pallet could be hired. Even though not licensed, they thrived in a society in which every official could be bribed.

Brothelry in Londinium is well attested: a freestone phallus has been found in Coleman Street; a sculpted architrave nearby depicts three whores, and there are a great number of small erotic figurines, brooches and lamps in lewd phallic forms. There is an extant letter from Rufus, son of Callisaunus: 'Greetings to Epillicus . . . look after everything carefully to squeeze the last penny out of that girl . . . turn her into cash at the best price. . . .'

The Roman attitude towards sodomy was elastic. In Julius Caesar's time the Republic had re-enacted the ancient *Lex Scantinia de nefanda venere* – the Scantinian Law against abominable sexual practices, '*stuprum con masculo*'. (In 226 BC Caius Lucius Scantinius Capitolinus, a senator and a tribune for the *plebeians* had made indecent overtures to the young son of Senator M. Claudius Maecellus. He was heavily fined and expelled from the senate, as also was Senator Lucius Quintus Flavinius in 184 BC for the same offence.) This 'eastern vice' was described in AD 90 by the Emperor Domitian as *stuprum* – filthiness. That did not stop the later Emperor Hadrian from openly practising sodomy. As a justification, Juvenal's *Satire VI* says:

> Isn't it better to sleep with a pretty boy?
> Boys don't quarrel all night
> Or nag you for little presents
> While they're on the job;
> Or demand more gasping passion . . .

and in *Satire II* goes on:

> . . . and queers stick together like glue:
> In the secrecy of their houses
> They put on ribbon'd *mitres*
> And many necklaces . . . while
> Another sips wine from
> A huge glass *phallus*. . . .

During the following centuries Londinium went from strength to strength, profiting from the great disturbances within the empire, as well as from alarums and excursions in the backlands of Britain and Scotland. About AD 300 Londinium was awarded the honorific title of *Augusta* – 'the Majestic' or 'Venerable' – and was worthy of receiving emperors and enjoying their 'Triumphs' and 'Ovations'. It was the custom on such occasions to inspan all 'the daughters of the City' from the most aristocratic to the plebeian harlot.

Even while the empire was crumbling under the attacks of the barbarians, the traders and financiers of Londinium did well – until that dread day in AD 410 when the Emperor Honorius withdrew the last legions, leaving the island's inhabitants to fend for themselves against the increasing attacks of the savage Saxon marauders. When the home-grown Romanized British legions were finally beaten in AD 457 in the battle at Crecganford (Crayford in Kent), 'fleeing in disarray over the bridge' into Londinium, the last vestige of Roman rule was over.

As tangible legacies of their long sojourn, the Romans left London with a bridge, a network of fine straight military roads, a red-light district and the remembrance of a set of laws that were later to be the basis of the unique laws of London.

2 Anglo-Saxon Attitudes: 'He cometh from the horhus'

On the northern fringes of the Roman Empire lived the Saxons, a group of peasant tribes inhabiting 'the pathless swamps' around the confluence of the mighty rivers Weser and Elbe; their kindred were the Jutes and Angles who inhabited the area today known as Denmark. Their main occupations included fishing and piracy, and they were a great thorn in the flesh of the Roman governors.

However, these tribes were themselves under immense threat from the incoming eastern tribes from the Steppes and being forced to find new homelands. As early as AD 200 the Romans had appointed a *Comes Littoria Saxonici per Britannia* – the Count of the Saxon Shores – to defend the eastern settlements 'from Portsmouth to the Wash' against these murderous raiders.

Saxon power really begins with the landing of the Jutish chief Hengest in Kent in AD 449, and in London when they defeated the Roman-British forces at Crayford in AD 457. They ransacked every dwelling before burning it to the ground, leaving a layer of ash 'several feet deep'. They massacred every man, woman and child

The Saxon assault upon Londinium, c. 460.

18

and for good measure broke down most of the walls. London was laid waste.

They had a deep distrust of towns and townsmen: their own *tuns* were stockade hamlets of small groups of kinsfolk, living in wattle-and-daub huts. Their war-leader, the *cyning* (king), would claim descent from Woden. They worshipped the phallic Fricge and his goddess-wife Freya, who equated with Venus in her attributes and lascivious behaviour. They tilled their small plots of land and herded their sheep, four to an acre, leaving all the hard toil to the aborigines whom they had reduced to slavery. Their lives were governed by the so-called 'Laws of the Visigoths', which were really a set of tribal customs of their ancient homelands.

Meanwhile other groups of Saxons were establishing themselves elsewhere. Those of particular importance to London were the South Saxons (in Sussex) and the East Saxons (in Essex). A group of South Saxons settled on the south bank of the Thames opposite Londinium; these were the *Suthrige*, men of the southern district, who secured themselves by forming a *burh* (a fortified enclosure) which guarded the southern entrance to the bridge. They were under the protection of their cousins, the Jutes of the kingdom of Kent. This *suthrige geweorc* (southern fortress) is today's Southwark.

Although the settlement on the northern shore of the Thames had been devastated, there would have been some hardy survivors around the riverside wharves and inlets – Saxon wharves have been excavated around Puddle Dock. The Thames was still a vital artery for galleys from Gaul. Lunden-wic, as these people called their city, began to grow important enough to spur Pope Gregory to try to have the pagan inhabitants proselytized. Accordingly in 597 he sent Bishop (later St) Augustine to Kent, whose king Aethelberht had married a Christian maiden and had formulated a set of laws based partly on contemporary Christian ethics. He now required his people to be Christians. His laws included some old Saxon customs, particularly establishing cash values for those guilty of sexual misbehaviour, the amounts varying according to the status of the miscreant: 'If a man lies with the king's *maegden-man* [maiden] he shall pay a *bote* [compensation] of 50 shillings'. For the king's 'grinding-slave' the *bote* was 25 shillings, but if she was only a female slave of the third class, the *bote* was reduced to 12 shillings. If the randy villain had seduced an earl's *birele* (female cup-bearer) it would cost him 12 shillings, but if she was only *birele* to a *ceorl* (a churl, then an upper-class servant), it would set him back only 6 shillings.

Figurine of the Saxon High God 'Frey with the phallus'.

However, a freeman who seduced another freeman's wife had not only to pay *wergeld* but also to '. . . provide another wife with his own money and bring her to the other man . . .'. If the aggrieved partner '. . . destroy another man's *eowende* [penis], let him pay 3 shillings *leudgeld*'. A man was entitled to kill *'erwige'* (without penalty) if he found another man in bed with his wife 'within closed doors'. Other punishments included mutilation – hands cut off, castration for rape – and drowning for witches. Lesser crimes such as murder and mayhem merited the payment of *wergeld* according to the status of the murderer and the murderee. However, sodomy was punished by drawing the offender through the streets on a hurdle before drowning him in a nearby cesspit.

By 520 the rulers of neighbouring Essex had established premises rather vaingloriously called 'a royal palace' in the neighbourhood of 'the Aeldormansburh' (Aldermanbury) with a *wic-gerefe* (town reeve) to oversee the king's interests, collect customs and other dues and taxes.

Pope Gregory had ordained a see in London, and by 602 his acolyte King Aethelberht of Kent had sufficient authority in Lundenwic to establish a church dedicated to St Paul. In 614 one Mellitus was appointed to be the first bishop of London, but he was never able to visit his see because of the intense hostility of the pagan inhabitants, who had no time for these new-fangled ethical restraints. They already had a simple form of democracy in their *folkmoots*, and they wanted no alien godheads to interfere.

There are tantalizing glimpses of Lundenwic's trading importance. Gold coins of Aethelberht of Kent have been found, as well as Frisian silver coins used in the slave-trade. By 670 the Kentish merchants had their own hall to which they could summon vendors 'to warrant their scales before the *wic-gerefe* [town reeve] in the King's residence': he was a royal appointee. The Venerable Bede (*c.* 700) says that Lundenwic was a large emporium, a trading-place, the capital of the East Saxons whose king levied tolls at the *hithes* (wharves) and 'a port where great ships tie up'. Nevertheless, the generality of the Saxon inhabitants were in effect only long-term squatters on sites, some very small and others very large, called *hagas* or *hawes* (fenced enclosures). These were to become the foundations of the later *sokes* and wards.

Within a few years the whole territory was to fall into the hands of the powerful and aggressive Mercians, under the famous King Offa, who established a mint producing golden *soldi* (pounds) and silver *sceattas* (shillings). Much international business was transacted with the Franks and Frisians despite the incursions of the Danes and Vikings, and the constant fighting between the Saxon kings for the leadership of the Heptarchy, their seven kingdoms, as a unity. The inhabitants of Lundenwic had frequently to gird up their swords and take up spears and axes to serve in their *fyrd* (local militia). As soon as the fighting stopped, they went back to their various occupations. Lundenwic was not yet a *burh* – its only defence was the remnant of the battered Roman wall.

The sexual diversions of the Saxon Londoners are undocumented. Beowolf's *Saga* is full of fighting, feasting and heavy wassailing without any hint of their sexual activities. However, the Venerable Bede castigates London's 'sinfulness', and such words as *horhus* and *forlicgerhus* in which *forlicgeres* (adulterers and fornicators) practised *unrihtlust* (lechery) demonstrate that human urges were catered for; moreover they were warned that attendance there might give them *ficges* – venereal sores. The *sceathingstole* (shitting stool), procuror of the sucking stool and ducking stool, recalls the report of Caius Cornelius Tacitus that '. . . cowards, sluggards, debauchees, prostitutes . . . useless members and pests of society . . . were suffocated in mires and bogs . . .', these 'useless members' being *flagitis abscondi*, sodomites.

The Londoners' social and sexual activities were governed by the so-called Laws of the Visigoths, which refer, *inter alia*, to adultery, rape and incest as well as the position in their society of women. The Saxons bought their wives, giving a bride-price, the *weotuma* to the father, then the couple lived in *trothplight* (pledge of fidelity) which permitted *haemed* (lawful sexual intercourse), and a wedding might take place later, when the *wed* (pledge, later a ring) registered the sale. The price depended on the status of the parties – women were bought or sold at the father's whim, although there was a caveat, 'Gif a man buy a mayden with cattle, let the bargain stand if it be without guile . . .' (that the girl was a virgin). There were some distinctions between those who were 'wedded' and those living as man and wife without a ceremony.

Then, if a man destroyed another's penis, he had to pay a threefold *bote*; if he only damaged it, it cost him six silver *sceattas*. A slave who raped a female slave was castrated.

With Christianity, conceptions of sin were now introduced. Copulation between a priest and a nun was 'a serious sin', the priest having to do penance for up to forty days in seclusion on bread and water. A freeman who committed adultery paid a sliding scale of *bote*: it depended upon whether the aggrieved husband was a 'five-*hynde* man or a twelve-*hynde* man'. A twelve-*hynde* (hides of land) men was a freeman who was a *gesithscundr* – a royal servant and thus a man of importance. He would get compensation of 120 silver *sceattas*. A five-*hynde* man could only get 100 *sceattas*, but if it were only a *ceorl* (a freeman), his *bote* was 40 *sceattas*. Rape of a churl's *theow*, his female slave, cost 5 *sceattas*, payable to the churl, not the victim; but if a male *theow* raped a female *theow*, he paid with his testicles. A female *theow* caught stealing could be whipped, burned or stoned to death or even just thrown over a nearby cliff. For a burning, eighty other female slaves each had to supply a log to lay on the pyre. A male *theow*-thief would be stoned to death, each of eighty other slaves having to supply a stone with which to stone him. *Theows* were chattels, bound to perform any duty, however menial or vile and could be bought or sold, mutilated or killed without any penalty.

Sodomy now became 'the unspeakable crime of unnatural lust', equated with bestiality: the penalty was to be buried or burned alive together with the animal concerned. Witches were drowned with their 'familiars' – a dog or cat or any other animal – and all their property was destroyed by fire.

There is a very curious ordinance by Archbishop Egberht, about 750, requiring that, 'Christians should not fraternize with Jews' – curious in that there were then no Jews in England with whom to fraternize. It indicates anti-semitism as a Christian principle at a very early date.

One of the very few reminders of the Saxon presence in London is the tiny church in Bishopsgate Street dedicated to St Ethelburga, daughter of King Annas of East Anglia and sister to the famous Eorkenwald, Bishop of London. He founded a great abbey at Barking in Essex, his sister being the first abbess, ruling over about a dozen high-born damsels. This chaste lady became famous for her heroic conduct during a pestilence, for which she was duly canonized as St Ethelburga the Virgin. Services are still held in this tiny church, which has been much altered since the thirteenth century.

The only remaining Saxon church in London: St Ethelburga's, Bishopsgate. Originally founded c. 680, rebuilt c. 1440, with shops obscuring the frontage, except for the entrance, for centuries.

The Saxons of Lundenwic left a number of legacies, not the least of which is the English language, wherein may be found today all the basic words for male and female genital apparatus as well as their functions. They also left us the names of the days of the week and, the greatest boon of all, the basic framework of democracy in their *folkmoots*, assemblies of free men.

With the advent of the West Saxon King Aelfred the Great, Lunden-wic entered upon its foundation as the greatest commercial centre in all England, albeit Winchester was still the nominal capital. This remarkable man, a younger son of the Christianized King Aethelwulf, ruler of the West Saxons and Kent, was taken at the age of four to be blessed in Rome by Pope Benedict III. Because of, or despite, this blessing, Walter de Hemingford asserted that '. . . in hys gyddye youthe the yonge Aelfrede . . . yeilded hys virile member to unriht uncleannesse . . . he strove to subdue manie virgines . . .'. However, he grew up to be a good Christian and an excellent soldier and ruler. In 886 he vanquished his great Danish rival, Guthrum, and by 'The Peace of Aelfred and Guthrum' became undisputed ruler of Lundenwic and 'all territories to the east of the River Lea in Essex'. Londenwic had hitherto been a much-fought-over waste borderland.

One of Aelfred's first acts was the rebuilding of the derelict Roman walls, leaving the city's *pomerium* spacious enough for training the *fyrd*, the local militia, and for market-gardening and pig- and sheep-grazing to supply food to the town's inhabitants. He ordered that all new houses should be of brick 'because of the danger of fire' and all the riverside wharves rebuilt – one of these, Aethelredeshithe, became the later Queenhithe. Although not so stated, he must have had the ancient wooden bridge strengthened or reconstructed, since no other, previous ruler would have had the time or manpower, and the bridge was a lifeline to his Kentish realm. 'All the lands outside the walls were in the King's hand from the Wal-broc [Walbrook] to the west': these lands were the '*sub urbs*'.

Within the walls he granted considerable blocks of land for development, thereby legitimizing many 'squatters' who over the centuries had occupied large or small *hagas* (fenced-in properties) or *burhs* (land which included one or more dwellings within a stockade). Some would have included small warehouses or craftworkshops and maybe a whorehouse.

From these divisions stem the privileges known as *sac and soc*, *sac* being the duties and *soc* the estate. As the rulers had no regular sources of income, this was a device compelling the new owners –

the *socmen* or *soke-men* – to develop these plots for dwellings or cultivation; some contained fields large enough to keep cattle and pigs. They were obliged to maintain law and order within their sokes, to be responsible for repairs to the wall nearest to them and provide, in time of war, soldiers recruited from their tenants and servants, to serve in Lunden-wic's *fyrd*.

It was stated that, 'In a man's own soke the preeste is his chaplain, his tenants will worship in his own church and contribute to its upkeep and repair.' Some larger sokes had their *court-leet* (a regular assembly of freemen or endenizened villeins) which had jurisdiction over all dwellers within the soke, and power to levy fines over 'myslyvers'. Some had the right to have a prison – even the privilege of sanctuary, an ancient Saxon custom which allowed that a villein who had managed to sojourn in a *burh* (borough) for a year and a day became endenizened and a free man. Sanctuary was a cause of great contention for centuries, and especially for the governors of London later on.

One of the earliest sokes was that of St Paul's, granted by King Aethelberht of Kent about 600 'from the west chepe down to the river': this is probably the so-called 'royal enclave' north-west of Cheapside including Aldermanbury on which a so-called 'king's hall' had been erected. About 660 King Saeberht of the East Saxons granted a charter as a liberty to the parish of St Martin-le-Grand in the Aldersgate area. In 790 the great King Offa of Mercia granted 'certain privileges to land in Londenwic', and in 857 his successor Burghred granted 'lands in Ceolmundeshaga to Bishop Alfhwine of Worcester' which were confirmed in 889 by 'Aelfred, King of the English and Saxons'. (This may be the present Coleman Street.) Indeed, in Aelfred's time 'the nucleus of resurgent London was 'a pride of *hagas* with their bundles of rights', laying the chaotic pattern for the city's later wards.

By now Londenwic was a borough *de facto*, if not yet *de jure*. It was the main centre of power as the principal commercial and financial entity. Each subsequent ruler had to heed the opinions of its *burgesses* – all freemen appointed by a *folkmoot*. The king's interests were safeguarded by his *portreeve*, originally the guardian of the gates. His *soke-reeves* collected money from customs, fines, tallages and rentals and saw that the king's laws were obeyed. However, London was already a miniature state, given that there was no concept yet of a national identity.

A superior sort of reeve was the *thegn*, originally a Danish *thane*, a lawman, whose qualification was the ownership of at least five hides of land; he was a nobleman with the status of an earl. Later

Plan of Saxon London.

thegns became *shire-reeves* (sheriffs) as overseers of large estates belonging to the king. Aelfred encouraged wealthy citizens to become *thegns* and to have military training.

Undoubtedly within many sokes there was permissible prostitution and whorehouses: St Martin-le-Grand, whose borders straddled the city wall, harboured many a house of ill-fame, and many were the disputes with the City authority when it tried to exercise its rights of *outfangthef*, the privilege of arresting citizens for felonies committed outside the City's walls, for trial in the City's own courts, but always blocked by the privilege of sanctuary. Similarly with the products of sokes, craftsmen competing with those in the City, free from the rules and restraints of the guilds.

Apart from the lucrative slave-trade, Londenwic was now an *entrepôt* for surplus agricultural products, particularly wool, and for the goods being manufactured in numerous small workshops. A wide range of goods was also imported and distributed, mainly luxuries from exotic places such as the Lebanon. Glassware from Italy was in great demand, and, of course, wines from France.

Aelfred now issued a set of laws, a curious mixture of old customs, some mitigated by early Christian principles, particularly those dealing with sexual offences. Fornication by a priest with a nun meant that the former would 'lose his honour'. Apart from the disgrace he would probably lose a well-paid job, which was a more potent punishment. However, fornication by a layman with 'a nun from a monastery without her leave' cost him a *bote* of 120 shillings, half going to the king and the other half to the *hlaford* (lord), the bishop 'who owns the nun'. If he raped an under-age girl, the *bote* was the same as if she were a fully grown woman. If he committed rape upon a churl's female slave, he had to give a *bote* of 5 shillings to the churl. However, if a male *theow* (slave) raped a female *theow*, it would still cost him his testicles.

The penalties for sexual assault were also based on class distinctions, and seemingly prostitution was recognized: 'If a man seize hold of the breast of a churlish woman, let him make *bote* to her with 5 shillings. If he throw her down but does not lie with her, the *bote* is 10 shillings. If he copulates with her, his *bote* is 60 shillings, but if another man had lain with her before, let the *bote* be half of that . . . but if this befall a woman more nobly born then let the *bote* increase according to her *wergild*. . . .' If a man deceived an 'unbetrothed woman' and copulated with her, he had to pay her father and take her as his wife, but if the father refused, the offender had to pay money 'according to her dowry'

The law regarding witches and enchanters was stark: 'Suffer them not to live.' They were usually tied up and drowned. The law reiterated the death penalty for buggery and bestiality.

Aelfred's son Edward the Elder also made a treaty with Guthrum who by now had turned Christian. This contained an interesting paragraph. Concerning incest with a sister or half-sister: 'If two brothers or near kinsmen commit fornication with the same woman, let them both make *bote* very strictly.' If the relationship was with the mother, it was 'a heinous crime' punishable by a most cruel death.

Edward's son Athelstan, 'King of the Anglo-Saxons', consolidated the kingdom, but on his death the Danes and Vikings recommenced their raids, burning monasteries, pillaging, raping and killing. They occupied London briefly but Edward's young son Edwy drove them off. This bright, courageous and passionate lad, although brought up under the stark tutelage of the bigoted Archbishop Dunstan, was a very profligate man. He was deeply in love with his lovely cousin Elgiva: '. . . after his sumptuous coronation feast . . . he jumped up and went to his chamber for wanton purposes . . . the *thegns* waited a long time . . . then Abbot Dunstan went into the chamber and found the King seated between Ethelgiva and her daughter [Elgiva], embracing both of them wantonly and shamelessly by turns . . . the Crown was on the floor. . . .' Dunstan's revenge was dreadful: the young girl was abducted, her face burned with hot irons, and then she was killed by his minions, who shortly afterwards killed the young king in turn.

Edwy was succeeded by Edgar, then aged sixteen, 'smal and littel of stature', brave and a man of violent sudden rages who, while professing Christianity, was utterly profligate sexually. John of Wallingford says: '. . . he abducted and raped the nun Eadgifu [Edith] and lived with hir in open concubinage for seven yeres. . . . this kynge hadde inordinate luff for hir . . . and tooke hys plesure of her, wherfore Seynt Dunstan caused the kynge to do penaunce. . . .'

No penances could stop Edgar's amorous escapades, his *spus-breaking* and *unriht* deeds, but his code of laws was the most progressive of his age, although as king he often flouted them. As regards sexual diversions, they show signs of Christian principle. For example, the man who deceived his betrothed was 'an adulterer', so forfeiting 'all Christian rights and a Christian burial'. If the adultery was with a married woman, she too forfeited all rights, '. . . unless she make immediate and severe correccion'. All

28

adulterers '. . . must fast for three days each week on bread and water'.

If a married man '. . . keeps a concubine, no priest must render him any Christian service: he must pay a fine and keep either wife or concubine, but not both'. If a married man copulates with another man's lawful wife, '. . . he must fast for three years on bread and water and for ever lament his crime'. If a married woman copulates with two brothers, 'one after the other', they must all 'make stringent penance all their lives'.

If a priest or monk or deacon committed fornication with a nun, the penalty was 'as for manslaughter', the nun having to fast for ten years and 'repent for ever'. He who persuades an unwilling nun to commit fornication, or likewise a married woman, must fast for a year on bread and water 'because he has injured them'.

If an ordained priest, monk or deacon 'being lawfully married and having deserted his wife' commits fornication with a concubine, he must fast for the same period as for manslaughter 'and earnestly repent'.

One curious penalty was for the man 'who tries to induce' another's wife to copulate with him 'against her will'. He had to fast for three quarters on bread and water, 'first in summer, next in autumn and thirdly in winter'. Another concerned the man who 'invites a married woman to copulate with him': '. . . must fast for forty days on bread and water'.

Edgar's most important contribution to London's government was his demand for regular procedures in the local *moots* and *leets* and fixed times of assembly. There is a curious reference in a Charter to Croyland Abbey confirming 'their possessions whatever whether bestowed originally by Christians or Jews . . .' – curious since there is still little or no evidence of Jews in Britain. (An old Jewish document says that, because of the great massacres of Jews in central Europe about 820, '. . . many fled to France and Italy and Britain', in which case there may have been a few in London, although hardly in a position to make grants to abbeys!)

The caste of *cnihts* had now grown in importance, and when thirteen of them asked '. . . to develop the desolate lands outside the gate east of the City [Aldgate] . . .', Edgar granted them a franchise for all the territory 'from Aldgate eastwards including east Smithfield from the *dodding-pond* into the Thames so far into the water that a horseman can ride at low water and throw his spear'. These *cnihts* then formed the *cnihtengild* with authority over the *port sokon* (sokes around the gate) which is one of today's wards; this charter was confirmed by every king up to the time of Henry I (1100–35).

Craftsmen now began to settle in particular districts: goldsmiths in West Chepe, with ironmongers and sopers nearby; candle and candlestick-makers in Candelwykstrete (now Cannon Street), food-producers in the Poultry, Milk Street, Bread Street and Wood Street; butchers in the Shambles (Newgate Street); but Coneyhope Lane – later called Conhop Lane – had nothing to do with rabbits, the 'coneys' being 'cunnies' more appropriate to the neighbouring Bordhawe next to the Gropecuntelane. Fishmongers were active in and near Fish Street by the bridge; and corn could originally be bought on the Cornhill. From these *congeries* grew the craftsmen's guilds or 'mysteries' which later became London's rulers.

In Edgar's reign the first mention of Old London Bridge occurs. In 975 a poor pagan widow, who could get no redress from Archbishop Dunstan's thieving father, who had swindled her and her son out of their little property, regressed to her pagan past and stuck pins into an effigy of the prelate. For this she was conveniently found guilty of witchcraft. She was 'bound with cords and thrown off London Bridge to drown'; her son was hanged.

Under Edgar's successor, Ethelred 'the Unrede' ('devoid of common sense'), who was a brave warrior but lacking the wit to control his over-violent rages, London was often in turmoil. But he was clever enough to ingratiate himself with London's rulers – the great guildsmen. He made laws for the regulation of the customs so that merchants had fixed guidelines for their conduct and their fees – of crucial importance because by then London was a very important port.

At Belinsgate (Billingsgate) a 'small vessel' paid a halfpenny when entering; a larger one 'with sailes', a penny; a 'large-keeled' capacious vessel paid 4 pence. A ship 'laden with wood' paid with 'one piece of the cargo'. Other vessels, depending on their cargos, paid between a halfpenny and 2 pence.

Ethelred's most dangerous enemies were the ever-increasing Danish and Viking raiders, who were pagan savages. The Norsemen (the Vikings) were perhaps the most dangerous: they killed and looted and raped without feeling or mercy. They proudly traced their descent from 'Thor with the Hammer' and 'Frey with the Great Phallus', wielding both weapons with unrestrained vigour. The contemporary historian Adam of Bremen gives a startling example:

Every Viking who could afford it had two or three wives – the rich and high-born set themselves no limit . . . their king had forty women in his harem and enjoyed them in public while his hired mercenaries were supplied with young girls . . . from the East. A man will copulate with a slave-girl while his companions look on . . . sometimes whole groups came together in this fashion. . . . A merchant comes to buy a slave-girl and must wait and look on . . . before the vendor concludes the sale. . . .'

The Vikings, together with a Danish host, returned in 994 under the command of King Olaf Tryggvasson of Norway. They gave Ethelred a bad time but the London *fyrd* repulsed them. However, in 1013, when the pagan Danes again invaded, Olaf, now con-verted to Christianity, came to Ethelred's aid, inflicting a famous defeat on his erstwhile allies. The great saga *Heimskringla* by Snorre Sturlasson describes. 'a great wooden bridge . . . with wooden parapets and turrets . . . so broad that two waggons could pass each other on it . . . crowded with Danish soldiers shouting defiance'. Olaf's ships pulled down some of the supporting piles, 'drowning hundreds of the Danish besiegers and slaughtering hundreds who had escaped drowning'. Olaf, he says, 'broke down the Bridge of London'. Olaf was later canonized, and the church of St Olave's still stands in Tooley Street on the south side of London Bridge. At one time the Danes were encamped hard by Newgate. They were not averse to lecherous pursuits, but they had some peculiar habits which caused great wonder to the burghers. Says Walter de Hemingburgh:

> . . . they were wont after the fashion of their country to comb their hair every day, bathe every Saturday and change their garments often . . . in this manner laying siege to the virtue of many women married and single and even persuaded the daughters of thegns to be their concubines . . . they paid dearly for these outlandish customs, for on a Saturday when they were naked the Saxons destroyed them . . . some English women had their breasts cut off or were buried alive and their children dashed to death against posts and stones . . .

– demonstrating that there was little difference between Christian and pagan savagery.

The Danes eventually won the kingship of England under their king, Sweyn 'Forkbeard', in 1016. A 'reluctant Christian', Sweyn was succeeded in the same year by his son Canute (Knut), who proved to be a civilized ruler anxious to treat his Danish and English peoples equally decently, although in order to do so he actually committed bigamy! To ensure his legitimacy to the English throne, he married Ethelred's widow, Emma, who ruled Christian Denmark in his name, what time he ruled England with his now 'half-wife' Aelgifu.

At a Great Moot held in 1019, Canute declared that he would govern 'by the laws of Edgar', although he regarded him as a 'leccherus tyraunt'. He leaned on the side of leniency, commanding that '. . . the Christian believers should not be condemned to death for too little reason . . .' and recommending that '. . . gentle punishments be decreed for the benefit of the people', although the punishment for sodomy and bestiality remained the same, as of old. 'Gentle punishments' were not actually described, but they certainly still included the pillory, the *thew* for women, and the stocks and cucking-stool.

Most sexual offences were still punishable by *botes* and *wergilds* or severe penances. An adulterous wife was to be shamed in public forfeiture of all her property to her husband, but 'forfeiture of her ears and nose' was abolished. Fornicating foreigners were 'to quit the realm and take their possessions and their sins with them'. Penances were levied on fornicators (*spus-brycges* – spouse-breakers) for their fornications (*ciefeshads*) and their *ciefes* (whores). The penalty for violating a woman was still 'the forfeiture of the virile member'.

For sodomy the penalty was still 'burning on a pyre', but for bestiality both man and beast were '. . . to be burnt or buried alive so as to remove all trace whatever of this heinous crime . . . their flesh, if any remained, to be fed to the dogs'.

Canute did not forget to appease the Londoners: the aldermen were promoted to be royal officials, *jarls* (earls), who were senators and nobles; from this time they are described as 'barons' because a principal function within their wards was the recruitment and training of soldiery. The title could now be passed on to their heirs.

There was also another very important movement under way. Steps had to be taken to create '. . . a language which all can understand . . . to bring to pass that all youths now in England born of free men may be devoted to learning (from books) until they can read well what is written in the English tongue'.

One means to ensure this was the compilation of *Glossaries*, the earliest extant being that of Archbishop Aelfric (*c*. 1000), which indicates the respectability of many of today's taboo words:

Mamilla	a tit
Capilla	tits-kycel [a nipple]

Virillis	a pintell [penis]
Anus	an arse-hole
Vulva	a cuntte
Coitus	gegandendo
hec anus	a nolde wyff [an old woman]
hec elena	a strumpytte
hec pronuba	a bawdstrott [a procuress]
hic leno	a baudstrott [a pimp or procurer]

After Canute's death the magnates of London selected the Norman-born Edward, Known as 'The Confessor', to be king. He was a deeply religious, retiring man aged about forty and accepted the job with some reluctance. He managed to placate his kinsmen the great earls Leofric of Mercia and Siward of Northumbria and the much more dangerous Godwin of Wessex whose vast estates included 'sixteen messuages on the Bank side in Suthwerke' which were brothels; on Godwin's death they became part of the estates of Edward the Confessor. In his reign too there is a reference to sinful behaviour in London itself. In 1058 Walter de Hemingford's *Chronica* noted with distaste '. . . a prostitute seated upon a jaded mule, her locks falling over her shoulders, holding a little gilt rod in her hand [who] by means of indiscreet clothing excited the travellers' attention in the high way at Corn Hill . . .' – the earliest description of an ambulant harlot openly soliciting in medieval London.

Edward the Confessor replaced many of his Anglo-Saxon courtiers with friends and acquaintances from Normandy. Amongst them were a number of Jewish financiers, on the basis that '. . . every Jew and his property belongs to the King and none must interfere with them . . .'; any interference would be punished. He needed them to help finance the huge increase in trade. Food and wine, gold and silver ornaments, exotic perfumes and rich textiles and a wide variety of other goods were imported. Despite all this, the burgesses remained obstinately Anglo-Saxon: the power of the craft and merchant associations began to be felt. Amongst the most influential were the goldsmiths, the haberdashers and the fishmongers.

On the death of Edward the Confessor in 1066, the Londoners supported the rightful heir, Harold. It was his ill-luck that in his hasty march down to Hastings he was unable to muster the London *fyrd* to help his exhausted troops, but the *fyrd* was standing ready when William of Normandy's army arrived before the gates, in 1066.

The only lasting memorial of Anglo-Saxondom is the ultimate

phallic symbol, the maypole – the old Norse *maegden* (maiden's) pole – around which in springtime youths and maidens frolicked and carnal copulation was unhindered even if not condoned. Maypoles lasted until 1642, when the Puritans cut them all down, but were eagerly revived 'in Good King Charles' Golden Days' after the restoration of the monarchy in 1660.

3 The Normans Have No Problem

By a very curious quirk of history, the Londoners, who had fought and bought off the Vikings for several centuries, accepted as their king the descendant of one of the most vicious of them, Rollo, who had compelled the French king Charles the Simple to grant him great lands which he then called Normandy – the land of the Northmen. William the Conqueror was a true Viking with a veneer of French polish, a 'cold-hearted cruel man of blood', to which qualities was added a cunning deviousness.

William, arriving before London, found the gates bolted and barred and the whole host of the London *fyrd* prepared to face him, headed by the stern port-reeve, Leofstane. The city therefore had to be propitiated before William could proceed to subjugate the land. The heads of the powerful guilds could foresee great benefits in co-operation, or useless blood-letting otherwise. They negotiated with William and secured a charter guaranteeing London all the rights and liberties they had enjoyed hitherto.

However, William realized that this staunch Anglo-Saxon city could still be a danger and proceeded to build the Tower of London, whose menace demonstrated to the citizens his real power. As a further precaution, he soon afterwards ordered: 'In every town and village throughout the land all people to put out their fire and candle after the bell for *couvre-feu* [curfew] had been rung at eight o'clock' – a precaution which was to remain in force until repealed by Henry I in 1115, although it is doubtful whether it much affected London.

William went ahead with the conquest with cold-blooded ferocity, burning and slaughtering systematically, especially for any killings of his knights – who were not of the 'parfait gentil' variety but mainly mercenary *knechts* (servants) to be recompensed by loot. All land now belonged absolutely to the king to dispose of as he thought fit.

A nominal Christian, although a Viking pagan at heart, William dominated the Church, imposing his own image of Christianity, which owed more to the Viking concepts of Odin's warlike bragging than to the principles of 'Love thy neighbour'. Simony, plurality and worldliness were now the norm. Priestly celibacy, which was *de rigueur* 'for all who served the altar' under the canon law of 1000, was now no longer obligatory. Pope Innocent I's injunction to married priests 'to be continent' was ignored. Those already married could stay married, and the single could either marry or keep a concubine. Vacant sees were filled by William's relations or Norman helots. Edgar's laws were kept as a loose framework. Some of the more barbarous Anglo-Saxon practices were abrogated, such as burning slaves for arson, ripping out their tongues for slander, nailing them to the door of the Mint for coining, and beating them to death for any whim. These punishments were altered not from any merciful principle but because they damaged valuable goods.

Serfs (*villeins* in Norman-French) were tied to the soil and were sold with it; they could not leave without their lord's consent, but they could not be sold as individuals. However, neither serfs nor slaves were 'moot-worthy' – only freemen could attend the moots. *Wergild*, as before, depended on the owner's status. Imprisonment and torture were now introduced as legal punishments. When castles were built at strategic points, all had *donjons* (keeps) with cold, dark, damp cells for recalcitrants.

Certain 'associations' – they were not yet guilds – grew immensely rich and powerful, particularly the goldsmiths and the fishmongers, who were to conduct a bitter savage rivalry; mercers and haberdashers were not far behind. However, all remained obstinately English and as such always potentially dangerous. It is the measure of London's power that Domesday Book, which in 1086 listed every pig and ox, every sheep and serf and every 'valuable' in the land, excluded London – although Southwark on the Thames' southern bank, and its sixteen brothel messuages on Bankside, is included.

In 1067 William granted 'an extra-mural *soke* of Cripplegate . . . extending from the Wall brook unto the *rivulus foncium*' ('the River of the Wells' – the Fleet) to a favourite. He also granted a *soke* to the King of Scotland, which had been created 'out of the lands of the King's Residence next unto Aldermanburie'. He also confirmed and expanded the ancient Charter of St Martin-le-Grand, ensuring its privileges as a liberty and a sanctuary; it helped, *inter alia*, to restrict some of London's powers.

When building the Tower of London, William took the opportunity to destroy part of the old Roman wall, thus moving the city boundary eastward. Somewhat later a part of the wall was pulled down to enlarge the monastery of the Black Friars and include it within the City, albeit as a 'liberty'. The circuit of the walls was then about 2½ miles.

A most important and far-reaching action was William's introduction of his Jewish financiers from Rouen, who were needed to facilitate many of his projected reforms. The ancient Rouen community undoubtedly helped to finance the invasion, since they were *servi camerae regis*, 'the king's Jews', under his protection and carrying out his commands. In Anglo-Saxon times trade was mainly by barter but with the coming of the Normans international commerce was to be the mainspring: a great deal of money was needed, and the expertise and means of international credit.

Much money was needed now for building, in the change from wood to brick and stone – even castles and monasteries were built with Jewish loans. The Jews were vilified as 'sleeping-partners in the King's usury', but in fact they were forbidden to practise any other trade or profession except medicine – even the most rabid anti-semites demanded the Jews' skill in that field. There was no ghetto, the first immigrants being settled around the Tower and a little later spreading around the West Chepe and Lothbury in the ward of St Mary de Colechurche hard by the Bordhawe and Gropecuntelane. It was common in those days to put Jewish settlements next to poor working-class districts and brothel quarters; the same thinking probably swayed the new conquerors. As the mob could always be assembled for anti-semitic riots, most Jewish houses were built of stone for safety against assault and destruction by fire.

The Jews' main business was with the nobility and gentry, the merchants and prelates, all of whom needed finance for the great spate of building going on, the more so since the Jews were the principal handlers of coinage. They even financed the building of monasteries and churches. They had little contact with *hoi polloi*, since they employed servants from their own ranks. Their greatest competitors were the Flemish Christian usurers, amongst whom William Cade of St-Omer was the leader, albeit usury was supposedly banned to Christians.

There were a number of whorehouses within the City's walls – apart from those in the Bordhawe and Gropecuntelane – in Sopers' Lane and Bread Street. The thronging thoroughfares of Cheapside and the Cornhill, with their maze of alleys, were full of potential customers at all times. Each ale-house and inn had its quota of women, and there was as yet no 'assigned place' to which these sinners could be exiled. A visit to one of the eighteen whorehouses on the Bankside required a special effort to cross the river or a long walk across the bridge. No interference was to be expected from the Conqueror, who owned at least three brothels in Rouen: his own henchmen would have needed them in their new inheritance. Their existence is attested in Domesday Book in 1084, which mentions a punishment, '*Cathedra in qua rixosas mulieres sedentes aquis demergebantur*', the stool in which loose women are seated and plunged into the water'; in another reference it is called '*cathedra stercoris*' 'a shitting-chair'. The Church's objections were to adultery, not to normal fornication; it was harder on married folk who were not allowed to '. . . make love on Sundays, Wednesdays and Fridays and then only five months in the year. They had to abstain forty days before Easter and the same before Christmas and three days before attending Communion.'

William died in 1087. He had achieved complete mastery over his new dominions, but with all his cruelties he was defeated in the most important thing – the English language survived him. The great mass of people never mastered the Norman-French tongue, although many words were anglicized and included in the common speech.

His second son, William, nicknamed 'Rufus' because of his fiery red hair, ascended the throne. A man of great personal courage but little diplomatic skill, he suffered vilification because of the exactions of his principal minister, Ranulf Flambard, 'an expert in ingenious and oppressive exactions' against which the London merchants inveighed. Rufus was by no means the evil creature known to history. His detractors were the churchmen who resented his off-hand attitude towards religion, and were shocked by his liberal attitude to the Jews; moreover, he had a bitter, mordant, anti-clerical sense of humour. He was clearly a man who meant to enjoy life without interference. His Court was described as foppish and effeminate: 'The courtiers wore long garments like women . . . with pointed shoes . . . the outward sign of the corruption within . . . spending their nights in revelry and dicing and loose talk, and their days in sleeping . . .' For this he was accused of practising 'the eastern vice of buggery', which view was reinforced because he had no known mistresses and begat no bastards. By his strong-handed governing, William Rufus had antagonized the baronage but had made himself popular with the Londoners. In 1100 he was murdered in the New Forest, most probably by minions of his younger brother Henry, who at the burial in Winchester Old Minster described his dead brother as 'an obscenity', so that there were no religious rites and he was buried 'as a sodomite'. Nonetheless, when in 1102 Henry convened the Council of Westminster, while it stigmatized sodomy, it reduced the hitherto savage penalties to 'severe penance under ecclesiastical ordinance'.

Henry I, who came to the throne in 1100, was described as a 'short, squat, avaricious man but smooth-spoken'. He was a sexual profligate of the first magnitude, having at least six mistresses, including an ancestress of the Tudors, Nest ap Tewdr. He had at least sixteen bastard children, 'nine of whom were girls and not one of them married any English man of consequence'. He was known as *'Beauclerk'* because he could read and write Latin, although it is doubtful if he knew much English. He proved to be a very able ruler. He established the first civil service and ordained a Charter for the Redress of Grievances – a step towards a limitation of the Crown's powers. As a sop to the Londoners he arrested

An early representation of a post-Roman hot-water 'stewes' – without sexual segregation, which encouraged carnal congress.

Flambard. Then, to establish his *bona fides*, he married Edith, Princess of Scotland, the niece of a former claimant to the throne, Edgar the Aetheling – albeit at the time she was a nun. She assumed the name of Matilda and proceeded to do a host of good works, including the establishment of many hospitals, and *leprosaria* at St James and St Giles, both of which were of great benefit to London.

About this time the citizens of London complained to the King about the cost of maintaining London Bridge: '. . . it is almost broken down . . .'. This was a matter of national importance, because not only was the bridge the hub of business in London but over it passed the vast bulk of the merchandise to and from the north and west. The bridge was repaired with elm wood, but doubts were now raised as to whether further repairs were needed or whether a new bridge should be built. However, at this period the royal revenues could not be stretched, and the citizens were left to make the best of it. London was still being governed by a portgrave, Hugh de Buche.

In certain towns and boroughs the King now allowed the burgesses to form voluntary merchant guilds to regulate their trades. London was the largest borough and the greatest provider of royal revenues, but the King had no revenues from Middlesex. In an astute move he granted 'the farm of Middlesex and London', allowing Londoners to appoint the sheriffs. This meant that London was now responsible for the collection of revenues in Middlesex too, saving the King time and expense; but it greatly increased London's power and influence.

Then Henry I died, in 1135, leaving an unexpected muddle in the royal succession, which led to a protracted civil war in which London was deeply implicated. London declared for his nephew Stephen in no uncertain terms, thus guaranteeing him his throne against the claim of Henry's daughter Matilda.

Stephen was that rarity amongst English monarchs – a mild, decent, civilized man. Faced with an implacable woman determined to seize power on behalf of her baby, he was forced to retreat and Matilda, styling herself 'The Lady of England', entered London, quickly arousing distrust and apprehension by her arrogance but also by the heavy taxes she levied. The resentment festered until a day when '. . . the citizens seized weapons and poured onto the streets like a thronging swarm of bees from a beehive . . . she, over-confident and bold, was just reclining at a well-cooked feast . . . hearing the noise of the tumult outside . . . she and her retinue . . . mounted swift horses . . . they had hardly reached the suburbs when the citizens, exasperated beyond all endurance . . . plundered everything that had been left behind. . . .'

Stephen was back on the throne by 1147 and kept the allegiance of the Londoners until he died in 1154, when Matilda's son, now aged twenty-one, became Henry II and the first to style himself Plantagenet.

He was a dominating personality with a keen legal intelligence and a very orderly mind, coupled with restless energy and driving force. He selected able men to run affairs, one of whom was Thomas à Becket. In 1140 young Thomas was employed as a clerk by Osbert Eightpence (*Huitdeniers*) before leaving to join the court of the Archbishop of Canterbury and start his great career.

Perhaps the most important of Henry's reforms was the appointment of a justiciar to construct a code of laws from the chaotic mass of ancient codes and ordinances – a task that has never finished to this day. In 1173 he added 'King, by the Grace of God' to his titles and in the following year abolished the curfew, because '. . . by reason of wars within the realm many men gave themselves over to robbery and murders in the night, banding themselves together to rob the houses of wealthy citizens and murdering anyone found in the streets at night . . .'. The policing fell upon the local authority, but the felons were sentenced in the king's courts. In London a portreeve oversaw twenty 'wards', with their 'earls' (aldermen) obliged to hire bellmen and beadles of the watch.

They also had to deal with the many small brothels, mainly in unmarked houses in the alleys by the side of churches; their existence was well known, but the general attitude was 'live and let live' unless some fracas or large disturbance occurred. There are mentions of the *goging-stole* (dung-chair) in 1159, and in 1166 a note about *fellatio* (*'qui in os semen effuderit'*), which was punishable with seven years fasting as penance. Very many sexual crimes, formerly thought heinous, were now punishable under ecclesiastical law by light or heavy penances.

First-hand descriptions of actual life in London in the early medieval period are rare, but fortunately two almost contemporary accounts survive. Most often quoted is that of William fitz Stephen, written about 1170, which is almost a panegyric. It dilates upon the lovely gardens and houses 'in the suburbs', the delightful meadowlands and flowing streams and busy mills, the abundant crop, the excellent clear springs of sweet clear water, and the youth of the city going out to take the air in the summer evenings. The city was 'ennobled by her men, graced by her arms'. 'The citizens . . . are respected . . . above all others for the elegance of their manners, dress, table and discourse . . . the matrons of the city are perfect Sabines.'

He describes the establishments on the riverside bank: the wine shops, the public eating-houses in which every day 'according to season' would be found '. . . viands of all kinds, roast, fried and boiled, fish, large and small, coarse meat for the poor, the more delicate such as venison, fowls and small birds for the rich . . . canisters of bread are heaped on high . . . by the riverside every thing is instantly procured . . . however great the number of soldiers or strangers . . . at any hour of the day or night . . .'

Every Friday in the smooth field (Smithfield), 'Earls, barons, knights . . . as well as citizens . . . flock to look or buy' horses for every conceivable use, from riding and racing to humble ploughing and pulling of drays. Further descriptions deal with sporting activities: schoolboys with fighting-cocks, the older youth rushing outside in summer 'with lances and shields and pikes' for sham fights, and tournaments.

In summer there was 'leaping, archery, wrestling, stone-throwing, javelin-slinging and fighting with bucklers [shields]'. In winter, 'foaming bears and huge-tusked hogs . . . fat bulls or immense boars' fought for their lives, being baited with dogs; and on the great marsh north of the city (now Moorfields), 'crowds diverting themselves upon the ice'. Other citizens amuse themselves 'sporting with merlins, hawks and other birds . . . and dogs . . . hunting in the woods' – the citizens then having the right to hunt in all the surrounding counties 'in Kent as far as the river Cray'. There is no hint of any crime or misdemeanour or dishonest trading.

The other side of the picture is given by the monk Richard of Devizes, *c.* 1177, resident in Winchester. Of London, he says:

I do not like the city at all. All sorts of men crowd there from every country . . . each brings its own vices and customs. None lives in it without falling into some sort of crime. Every quarter abounds in grave obscenities. The greater the rascal, the better man he is accounted . . . whatever evil or malicious thing . . . you will find in that city. Do not associate with the crowds of pimps: do not mingle with the throngs in eating-houses: avoid dice and gambling, the theatre and tavern . . . the number of parasites is infinite. Actors, jesters, smooth-skinned lads, moors, flatterers, pretty-boys, effeminates, paederasts, singing and dancing girls, quacks, belly-dancers, sorceresses, extortioners, night-wanderers, magicians, mimes, beggars and buffoons . . . if you do not want to dwell with evil-livers, do not live in London. I speak not against learned or religious men or Jews . . . [although] they are less perfect there than elsewhere. . . .

It is also clear from Richard of Devizes' report that all the common human frailties, including sexual aberrations, were an integral part of London's life. The reference to theatres is curious, however, and must refer to the itinerant entertainments in tavern yards by mummers, or groups of mountebanks, since he could not mean the quasi-religious performances of itinerant players. He also mentions, '. . . there is a whole collection of men who have been abandoned . . . who now through lack of bread and work, die in the open daylight in the streets . . .'

Under Henry II's energetic direction a great spate of construction was going on. We hear of *ingeniators*, who were actually architects as well as practical men, *ordinanters*, controllers of building works, and master masons who moved from site to site, introducing themselves to local fellow-craftsmen 'by a particular form of salutation' – a handshake, one of the earliest forms of craft association known in England.

The other building crafts were graded. Tilers, thatchers and carpenters were collectively known as *helyers*. Lower down the pecking-order were plumbers, glaziers, smiths, plasterers and painters, who were helped by *hottarii* – hod-men. The clerk of works was the *dealbator*, in charge of the men who built the huts. However, both *ingeniators* and master masons were often also merchants or dealers in building-materials – very necessary in those days, because they would be called to sites all over the country and have to secure materials from all sources 'from north to south, from east to west'.

In 1161, with Becket's assent, the King promulgated the 'ordinaunce for the Government of the Stewes upon Bankside' which legitimized the eighteen 'brothel-howses' there, which had been controlled 'from tyme oute of mynde' by the bishops of Winchester. In the following year Becket was appointed Archbishop of Canterbury. In 1166 the Assize of Clarendon opened a new period of criminal jurisdiction, which was a move towards uniformity and centralization, although one of its side-effects was to legalize 'tryall by water' in cases of murder and robbery; but at least from this time all criminal cases had to be tried in the king's court before justices appointed by the king, instead of any local sokeman's courts.

Richard of Devizes' remarks demonstrate the measure of the friendly relationship which existed between Jews and non-Jews. It was apparently so close that some orthodox Jews asked their great sage, Rabbi Ephraim of Bonn, how they should behave when Christians sought greater conviviality, especially when they were invited to drink with them. The Rabbi replied: They should be

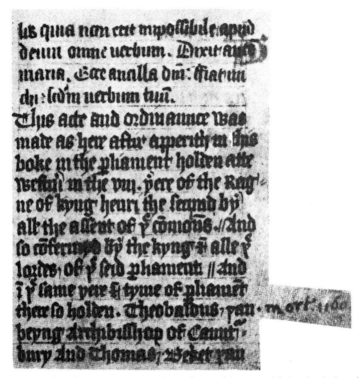

This acte and ordinaunce was made as here aftir apperith in the boke of the parliament holden atte Westminster in the VIII yere of the reygne of Kyng henri the second by alle the assent of the comons And so confermed by the kyng and alle the lordes of the seid parliament And yn ye same yere and tyme of parliament there so holden. Theobaldus then mort 1160 beynge archibisshop of Caunterbury And Thomas Beket then

First page of the Ordinance for the Government of the Stewes in the Bishop of Winchester's Liberty of the Clink on the Bankside in Southwark. AD 1161.

lenient in the matter of drinking strong drink in the manner of the Gentiles in the *Land of the Isle* [Britain]: perhaps there would be ill-feeling if they were to refrain. . . .'

The King's friendliness occasioned a rebuke from William of Newbury that, 'He favoured more than was right . . . Jewish usurers because of the great advantage the King had from their usuries', alleging – correctly – that the King was a sleeping-partner in usury. Although the effects of the Second Crusade, with its rampant anti-semitism brought back by returning soldiers now began to be felt, the King stood steadfastly behind 'his Jews' and allowed an extension of the Jewry in London, granting them a burial-ground 'next to a fair pool by the churchyard of St Giles in Cripplegate Without'. This 'Jews' Garden' was the only place in England appointed for Jewish burials. The community was then large enough to have an 'Arch Presbyter' – a chief rabbi.

Roger de Howden, *c.* 1170, relates that, 'Sons of influential citizens used to gather in large gangs at night making the streets unsafe for law-abiding citizens.' Bakers were still selling bad bread, butchers selling bad meat, ale-wives selling adulterated beer, and traders cheating unwary shoppers by passing off inferior-quality goods. And, of course, amid this plethora of goods and services there were the great mass of those 'who lacked a penny' to buy food or raiment and who lacked a roof over their heads or even a straw pallet to sleep upon. Not many years later these unregarded elements were to stir, helping to secure London's future liberties – although their own liberties were not to be granted for centuries to come.

In 1163 it was again reported that, because London Bridge was falling down, 'a new bridge made of elm wood' had been constructed, but it was clear that something more substantial was needed, because the volume of traffic far exceeded its strength. The traffic jams were horrendous. Whereas formerly only humans and horses passed over, there were now great iron-shod dray carts, galloping knights in heavy armour, potentates with their vast retinues, troops marching with their ordnance, and burden-carrying villeins. There was much talk of a stone bridge, but the revenues from the tolls were never enough for proper maintenance, let alone build a new bridge – it was a royal responsibility.

This stirred Peter de Colechurche, chaplain of St Lawrence-by-the-Jewry (in which Thomas à Becket had been baptized in 1118), to drum up support for a new bridge like that marvellous one at Avignon built by the famous Isambard – indeed, he asked for Isambard's services. His Jewish neighbours, who appreciated the benefits from a new wide bridge at the hub of the nation's commerce, promised financial support, but there was no money forthcoming from Henry II. Peter managed to scrape together enough to start building in 1179, but by 1192 only one span had been completed.

It was useless to expect any financial help from King Henry's successor, Richard I, *Cœur de Lion* (1189–99). He was spending the national finances on his adventures abroad and then on the Crusades. In addition a year's revenue had to be collected to pay Richard's ransom in 1194, which was met by savage taxation, especially onerous on the London burgesses as the richest commercial group, and there were murderous exactions from the Jews, who were almost completely ruined thereby. The burgesses were, however, able to force Richard to renew the 'farm' of London and Middlesex, which helped them recover their disbursements.

It is perhaps rather apposite that Henry II's energetic reign should close, in 1189, with the first indication of modern civilization being installed in London's new houses. In that year the portreeve issued an ordinance, 'of neccessary-chambers in Houses': 'It is enacted and ordained that if the pit made in such a chamber be lined in stone the mouth [thereof] shall be distant 2½ feet from the land of the neighbour even if they have a common stone wall between them: but if it be not so lined then it ought to be distant 3½ feet . . . the Assize is granted to every one that shall demand it . . .' In case of dispute, a jury of twelve men were, by a majority verdict, to decide whether '. . . the pit was reasonably made or not . . . and to any kind of pits made for receiving water whether clean or foul'. Contemporary illustrations show some of such 'previes' on the first storey overhanging a garden.

At the same time it was ordained that all the lanes '. . . leading towards the Thames . . . from Castle Baynard unto the Tower of London shall be cleansed so that persons on horseback may without hindrance ride to the Thames . . .'; if any impeded them, they would be 'heavily amerced' (fined).

From this time the City's governors began to make regular annual enactments regarding sanitation, which, however, were equally regularly to be disregarded by the citizenry.

4 Of Politics and Princes: of Pedlars and Plutocrats

Early in the twelfth century a great movement towards municipal liberation was sweeping throughout Europe, provoked by the colossal dislocation caused by the Crusades. It started in Italy as early as 1080 and caused much anxiety amongst the rulers and the papacy, especially when in 1143 a great Commune was established in Rome. However, as early as 1141 the citizens of London had formed a *conjuratio* (Commune), taking advantage of the power-vacuum after the death of Henry I, but this embryo civic organization – about which nothing but the name is known – disappeared without trace.

The Crown's difficulties were the Londoners' opportunity, and when in 1189 King Richard *Coeur de Lion* went overseas, another opportunity presented itself. He had appointed 'a low-born Norman', William Longchamp, his justiciar, to be his representative, but the King's brother John disputed this and claimed to be the surrogate during his absence. Longchamp was an unpopular tyrant, and there was great unrest. Realizing that they held the scales, the Londoners bargained for a Commune as the price of their support. John at once agreed, was received 'by great crowds with lanterns, torches and rejoicings' and the following day, 8 October 1191, '. . . in St Paul's Cathedral took an oath to the Commune'. For the first time London had its own free municipality. Richard of Devizes observed that, '. . . neither Henry II nor Richard I would have allowed the Londoners to have a Commune, even for a million marks!'. John received about £2,000, '. . . to ensure confirmation of London's rights and liberties'.

Who these Londoners were and how they were selected is unknown, but in fact they were leaders of the most powerful guilds or important soke-men and aldermen. They appointed the immensely rich Henry fitz Allwyn fitz Leofstane as a 'malore', and two other *probi homines* (honest, worthy and rich men), Henri de Cornehylle and Richard fitz Reiner, to be 'shire-reeves' or 'bayliffes'. They also appointed twenty-four *echevins* (probably sheriffs or aldermen). They recorded an oath (a) to administer justice fairly; (b) to make special provision against bribery and (c) to expel any member convicted of taking a bribe. Their actual activities thencefrom are unknown, because from this time no more is heard about the Commune. In 1199, when John became king, he repaid these Londoners by renewing the grant of the sheriffwicks of London and Middlesex for £300 a year, with authority 'to choose and appoint the sheriffs at their pleasure'.

As a further measure of ingratiation, on Good Friday 1203 he paid 'for the feeding of a thousand needy persons' and in the following year gave 'a farthing loaf and a dish of gruel daily to 300 London paupers'. He also had a curious habit which did not endear him to most people: he had a hot bath every three weeks – a manifest sign of depravity! However, John was 'King of England', not just 'King of the English', a very important distinction.

Another important innovation in 1189 was the 'Charter of Privileges' whereby many new boroughs were being created, naturally against an appropriate fee.

It was a bourgeois revolution but not free from opposition and disturbances. It had been the practice for the wealthier oligarchs to pass much of the heavy burden of taxations and tallages onto the shoulders of their poorer brethren, which naturally aroused great resentment, which became organized by a returned Crusader, William fitz Osbert. He had prospered and become wealthy but had made his name by championing the underdogs, thus arousing the hatred of the *probi homines*. In 1196 they persuaded the King's justiciar, Hubert fitz Walter, to send a constable to arrest him, but he killed the constable and took sanctuary in St Mary-le-Bow Church. The church was set on fire to flush him out with his nine accomplices, and all of them were hanged at Smithfield, fitz Osbert being described as 'a supremely wicked man who had betrayed his class'. The place of his execution became for many years a shrine and a place of pilgrimage – to honour the first English revolutionary!

On 6 June 1215 King John was forced to grant the Magna Carta which, *inter alia*, assured all citizens of London of all their ancient liberties and free customs: moreover, the King could not proceed against any free subject except by legal process.

John was an unlucky man. He opened the splendid new stone-arched bridge in 1209, but on St Benet's Day 1212 'Londonbrigge and the mooste parte of London was brent'. The fire started in Southwark, and a huge crowd thronged the bridge to see the spectacle. The wind changed and swept the fire over the bridge: three arches collapsed, and many of those who jumped into the river were drowned when the small rescue-boats capsized in the millrace pouring through the narrow arches. Three thousand people perished.

This Commune is undoubtedly the parent of today's Lord Mayor and Common Council; and the groups who sent their representatives were already by 1180 quite powerful, even though legally unrecognized. Henry fitz Ailwyn, a draper, was to be appointed the first mayor and held that office from 1189 for twenty-four years, dying in office in 1211, having in the meantime become a goldsmith – an equally prestigious guild. These tradesmen's associations were undoubtedly the rock upon which London's affluence and glory were founded.

A thirteenth-century 'beautician' stocking mirrors and combs as well as perfumes and unguents. The customer is a prostitute, the caption stating that she is preening herself in the mirror, being 'ffoule of synne . . . and to hyde her ffylthy' cult.

As early as Edward the Confessor's time there is mention of groups of tradesmen and artificers, such as butchers and bakers, brewers of ale, goldsmiths, grocers, fishmongers and drapers – not to forget barbers and dung-rakers and, most ancient of them all, masons. In the earliest days they were known as 'fraternities' – quasi-religious organizations: the skinners are the oldest example. Craftsmen's organizations were known as 'mysteries', keeping the secret of their crafts to themselves. In essence they were 'closed-shops', since masters were succeeded by their apprentices, who, when they became journeymen, could set up on their own. They sold their own manufactures directly to the public; 'forestalling' – retailing through third parties – was not allowed.

From about 1170 they were licensed; about 1180 legalized as guilds of trades and crafts, and later they could seek a royal charter, which enabled the masters to wear a 'livery' – a special garb by which they could be recognized and, even more important, esteemed.

From their ranks were chosen the mayor and aldermen and sheriffs, all 'discreet and wealthy men' reliable in the eyes of King and Church, and eventually from their ranks were chosen two burgesses to sit in Parliament.

The basis of their power was the *folkmoot* which in Anglo-Saxon times met three times a year: it was an assembly of all freemen and their endenizened servants. The focal point was the Guild Hall, and it was often complained that they were '. . . attended by a vast multitude . . . tumultuous affairs', time-wasting and, all too often, riotous. By the time of William the Conqueror, the maze of liberties, *hagas* and *sokes* had been simplified into some twenty 'wards', each governed by an elected alderman – then known as an 'earl', who gave his name to his ward. The alderman was elected by a *ward-mote* of all 'householders and their hired servants', all being freemen. The *ward-mote* appointed the 'scavagers' (originally inspectors of imported goods – only much later, when they were responsible for seeing the streets were clean, were they called 'scavengers'), the 'bedels' (beadles) and the 'ale-conners' (inspectors of ale).

The ward-motes were likewise noisy and riotous, especially if eligible freemen had not received their summons – failure to attend meant a fine of 4 pence, a considerable sum; but 'non-attendance' usually meant that the elections were being rigged, a not unusual occurrence. The alderman had to be 'honest, rich and circumspect', and this fiddle was resented by the mass of 'proletarian' (i.e. less rich) freemen, although '. . . if wardsmen from malevolence or pride refuse the nomination [some other person must be chosen] . . . taking into consideration the advantage and honour of the City'. In practice this meant another 'patrician', equally 'wise, discreet and wealthy'. The promise of the Commune of 1189 about bribery was by now a mockery – bribery was a matter of course.

For the choice of mayor, 'to avoyde the vaste tumultes as of yore', the current mayor and aldermen '. . . weren wont to meet a few dayes beforehand to nominate the more discreet and sufficient Citizens in each Warde and them summons thereto on October 13th. but it often happened that those who had not been summoned rushed to the Guildhall . . . in anger and frustration . . .'. Each side then gathered 'at either end of the Guildhall and after much cogitation' (and not a little mayhem) nominated 'after the Roman tradition of Senators for Patricians and Plebs' two ex-sheriffs, one from the rich and powerful guilds and the other from the 'plebeian' guilds, and the new mayor and his successor were then elected 'by the plurality of votes'. Before 1332 a mayor could stay in office for several years, but Edward II agreed that the tenure should be one year, as it is to this day. When, in June 1354, the mayor was granted a 'sergeant-at-mace' and a 'sword-bearer' to precede him – the privilege of an earl – he might be called 'My Lord Mayor', although the first reference to this title is on 12 July 1414, when Henry V addressed him as 'The Worshipful, the Lorde Maire'.

Among the alderman's duties were the mustering of the citizens in his ward as soldiers in time of war (they usually had to supply their own arms) and the maintenance and repair of that portion of the City wall adjacent.

Over the centuries the number of wards also increased. By the time of Henry III's accession, in 1216, there were twenty-four. In 1393 Farringdon (the only ward to retain an alderman's title) was extended over the wall as 'Farringdon Without'. In 1550, when Edward VI sold Southwark to the City, it became 'Bridge Ward Without'. No alderman was elected from Southwark – the Common Council appointed one. The City's oligarchs had bitter memories of Southwark's intransigence, its contempt for laws and the unacceptable 'liberalism' of its inhabitants. Moreover, it had been a borough long before the City had been established.

The centre of all this civic activity was the Guildhall, situated in the small street still called Aldermanbury. The *gild-halle* was originally the place where money – *gild* or *geld* in Old English – was collected from taxes and customs. 'Aldermanburistrete' is recorded as early as 1128 – the 'bury' or 'burh' indicating a substantial house or mansion. Nearby was the Court Hall of the aldermen.

It was in the Gild-halle that the first mayor of London, Henry fitz Alwaine, a scion of the family of the portreeve Leofstane, was appointed in 1189, the first of a long line of citizens, many worthy but quite a few rascals and chancers or royal toadies. It was also the seat of a host of officials, the sheriffs, the common councillors and the treasurer, called the city chamberlain. Many were poor lads who had worked their way up to the top by hard work, or various stratagems, or marriage to an alderman's daughter or widow. Many were dedicated men who loved their City and helped to embellish it by great benefactions, such as bringing in clean water or setting up orphanages and old-age homes – even public latrines. Yet others were dubious financiers or tricksters, even whorehouse-owners. Some were staunch in upholding the City's rights, even standing up to a king; others were royal toadies who sold their fellow citizens for a royal approval or high office. Some were true to their wives; others were 'wont to go to the horhus a-nights'. In short, they were ordinary human beings elevated for a short time to the highest positions.

The famous Dick Whittington was an exception to the general rule, since he came of good family, his father being Sir William Whittington of Pauntley in Gloucestershire. Hence the legend of a poor boy with a cat is rather far-fetched. Moreover, he married the fair Alice, daughter of the magnate Sir Ivo Fitzwaren, 'who possessed much land and great wealth' – his ancestors came over with William the Conqueror. Dick proved to be one of the most caring men for his fellow citizens who were poor and indigent as well as for his beloved City – a true paragon amongst philanthropists.

The high ideals of the Commune were often not realized, particularly regarding bribery. In the *Liber Albus* there is the paragraph:

> The King and His Justiciars to be Conciliated.
> SEEING THAT IT IS quite impossible for the barons and citizens of London to do otherwise . . . than go through the hands of the king and his justiciars, it is a matter of necessity that . . . all citizens court their favour and goodwill by making ample presents to them . . . [and] their clerks . . . to the end that the citizens may not be molested or disturbed . . . on the contrary their liberties . . . peacefully maintained. . . .

In excuse they stated that, 'The ancestors of this City, strenuous in defending its liberties . . . were wont to do the same . . . it is no dishonour for us to follow in their footsteps who showed such tact . . . it can only be to our advantage to do the same as they did.'

The Guildhall was also a court of justice, settling disputes between the often sparring guilds, ever-growing in importance and arrogance, as well as from time to time dealing with national matters, such as the trial of the unlucky Lady Jane Grey, the condemnation of Archbishop Cranmer and the prosecution of the Jesuit Henry Garnett for his part in the 'Gunpowder Plot'.

An alderman was a person of considerable status and could sometimes act as a judge. In 1387 a royal official, William Hulett, '. . . had his hand struck off in the Guildhall for an assault upon Alderman John Rote, ex-Sheriff'. An alderman '. . . always took his seat with the more opulent men of his ward' and could summon to the Common Council 'between four and sixteen of the wisest and most wealthy citizens . . . all freemen'. Much also depended on which was the most powerful guild at the time: their jostlings frequently manifested themselves in bloody struggles between gangs of their apprentices, leading to larger disturbances in which *hoi polloi* gleefully joined in.

Nevertheless, despite its importance, the original Guildhall seems not to have been so grand, for in 1410 the mayor, the rich grocer Thomas Knoles, '. . . began to rebuylde itte as newe . . . instedde of an olde lytel cotage . . . made a fayre and goodlie howse more neere unto Sint Laurence Churche in the Jurie [Jewry] . . .'. It took eleven years to complete, and this fine structure was to last with occasional repairs until burnt down in the Great Fire of 1666.

The principal guilds, in order of their importance, were the mercers (originally *merciers*, dealers in small wares, wool, linens and silks), grocers (orginally pepperers, then *grossiers* – wholesalers of bulk goods), drapers (originally importers and exporters of wool-cloth), fishmongers, goldsmiths (originally a 'fraternitie' controlling all gold and silver activities), merchant taylors (who originally made tents and padding for knights' clothes under their armour and had control of the 'staple' the authorized measure of cloth) and skinners, stemming from two ancient religious brotherhoods, originally known as 'pelterers'. There was also the haberdashers, originally pedlars of small wares, including 'hurrers' (cap-makers) and 'milliners' (importers of fashion goods from Milan in Italy).

The choice of mayor did not always satisfy some patricians, who often tried to dispute the method of selection: in 1366 the fishmongers succeeded in having the mayor appointed 'by the respective *mysteries* and not the wards': '. . . there were grete tumultes and the sadde and discreete Greate Men weren helde in contempt by the smal . . . consequently there were grete disputes . . . after whiche the original usage hadde to be restored. . . .'

The oligarchs' rule was upset at times by arbitrary interference by the king, particularly Henry III, who nullified the City's charter in 1254 by imposing his own creature as mayor and in 1278 appointing a *custos* (warden) with all the mayor's powers. Then followed a series of appointed mayors alternated by a *custos* until the day in 1285 when the elected mayor, Gregory de Rokesley, resigned, on the grounds that he had not been given the guaranteed forty days notice to attend an inquest at the Tower of London. He and eighty other prominent citizens were taken to the Tower and held for four days, then dismissed from their offices, and the City was 'taken into the King's hand'. The king, now Edward I, appointed two sheriffs and a *custos*, ensuring that, '. . . they must be trusty towards Us, discreet and firm for Our Government'.

The citizenry were outraged, and there was constant turmoil until 1298, when after violent riots in the streets '. . . and manie serious citizens broke open the Tun on Cornhyll releasing the prisoners', the King restored London's liberties, 'the mayoralty excepted'; hand-picked mayors lasted another five years. Only after the accession of Edward II in 1307 did the City recover all its liberties, rights and privileges.

What is noteworthy is that throughout all this early period the City Fathers concentrated all their efforts on the sanitary aspects of their realm – exhortations to keep the streets clean, the 'kennels' (gutters) unblocked, the air kept pure by the banning of 'sea coal', and strict inspection of the quality of foodstuffs and drinks. Concern over sexual delinquencies appears to start with the accession of Edward I in 1272. Clearly the City's rulers did not regard fornication and brothelry as matters of municipal concern – it was the business of the spiritual power.

Their pride in the City created a host of really 'goodlie' men who during their lives and in their wills created great benefactions, some equalling those of the famous 'Dick Whittington'. Robert Chichele, grocer and lord mayor in 1421, apart from many other munificent bequests willed, 'On hys Mynde Daye eache yere 400 poore menne be given a competent Dinner and Two Pence in Monie.' In 1436 William Eastfeilde, mercer and lord mayor, gave money 'to convey sweete water from Tyburne unto the newe buylt Conduit in Aldermanberie . . . also to Crepelgate'. In 1404 Alderman Stephen Spilman, grocer (then sheriff) willed all his goods to make and repair bridges. In 1446 Simon Eyre, draper and lord mayor, '. . . buylte the Ledenhalle as a granary for the City' and gave 5,000 marks for charitable uses. In 1458 Mayor Geoffrey Bulleyn gave liberally to those in prisons, hospitals and lazar-houses, and in 1477 Sheriff Richard Rawson did the same. In 1415 Thomas Falconer, mercer and lord mayor, breached the city wall at Moorgate by building a postern for easier access to the fields outside, giving money to have the city's ditches all round cleansed – he later lent King Henry VI '10,000 marks against his jewels etc'.

In 1471 the lord mayor, John Stockton, and eleven aldermen 'were knighted in the feilde' for their good service to Edward IV.

Nevertheless, the city over which these worthies ruled was, despite their annual exhortations and regulations, a crowded, dirty mixture of broad thoroughfares and narrow, noisome alleys, mainly unpaved and ill-lit, choking in dust in summer and knee-deep in glue-like mire in winter. Only Cripplegate today shows the old Roman road-pattern. Frequent fires and rebuildings have destroyed almost every old building. The haphazard pattern of *sokes* and *hagas* made town planning almost impossible – not until the Great Fire of 1666, when most houses perished and boundaries were obliterated, could a planned reconstruction be possible.

There was an immense diversity of dwellings cheek-by-jowl: wattle-and-daub hovels juxtaposed with the slightly better houses of tradesmen and skilled artisans, a great many consisting of four walls and a roof, with an opening in one wall as an entrance and some holes in the walls for windows. He was thought rich who had a real door, and oiled linen in the window openings – even richer if he had lattice windows with panes of thin horn, or just shutters against bad weather. Most roofs were of thatch, although tilers had been known from the Conqueror's time, roofing the dwellings of the high and mighty. Some few stone houses still existed – mainly in the 'old Jewry', where they had been for protection against pogroms. Wall tiles were imported from Italy; bricks were of poor quality. The plastered walls might be just whitewashed or painted with vivid primary colours. The floors were of earth, covered with straw or rushes, not often changed, so that lice, fleas, cockroaches, mice and rats were constant companions.

Normally there was only one sleeping-chamber: the family and guests would all sleep happily together in the nude, although a head-covering was essential; only a really wealthy woman would have a sleeping-smock. For beds, the better-off might cover the straw mattress with a blanket and a coverlet of some coarse material; the poor and the servants bedded in straw or bracken on the floor, with sacking as a cover and a log for head-rest. The Normans introduced boards with pegs to raise them off the ground, on which mattresses filled with flock made for comfort, with a sack of chaff as a pillow. Pillows were unmanly – 'meet onlie for women in child-bed'. By about 1400 the more comfortable would have mattresses stuffed with feathers, with linen sheets under a blanket for warmth – and by then a servant was thought pampered if he had a straw pallet.

Public concern with filth and dung in the streets is found in numerous ordinances, and some small concern for hygiene – about which in those days nothing much was known. However, there were a surprising number of latrines and even 'previes'. The very first 'previes' recorded were both royal: in 1141 for King Stephen in his palace at Woodstock, and in 1152 'a glazed prevy chambre' at Clipstone.

There was a public latrine, with two entrances, on the new London Bridge in 1207, and some holed planks alongside some of the brooks. In 1290 the aldermen '. . . made a judgement for the removal of a *jakes* . . . whiche were a nuisance', and in the following year the unfortunate '. . . John de Abyngdone, coming out of the comon prevy in London Wall in Crepelgate Lane at the hedde of Philipslane was sett uppon by Roogues and Killed . . .'.

The bridges over the Fleet and the Walbrook had privies which were flushed by the rivers' tides, although in 1275 '. . . the Monkes of White friars protested to the King that the putrid exhalations therefrom overcame even the frankincense used in their Services and had caused the death of manie Brethren'.

The first illustration of a private 'prevy' shows it was a projecting penthouse with the ordure free-falling into a cesspit in the garden. This was not without its dangers, and about 1300 there was a report of '. . . an ingenious Woman who constructed her own *prevy* and connected it with the outflow by a wooden pipe into the rainwater gutter, which became blocked and the neighbours' complaints brought her a heavy summons. . . .'

When houses were built on London Bridge, all had a small chamber overhanging the bridge, with 'chutes' which often turned out to be a hazard to waterborne passengers but kept the inhabitants free of plague because both the houses and the air were free of pollution. In 1321 it was complained that the public privy at Ebbgate was leaking, and '. . . the excreta fell on the heads of passers-by'.

There were 'four-holers' at the bottom of Fleet Street and Queenhithe, 'both roofed-in', and one of Dick Whittington's greatest boons was his 'House of Easement', called 'Ye Long House', in Langbourne ward, which had '. . . two rows of sixty-four seats, parallel, one side for men and the other for women: the seats overhung a gully which discharged into the Thames and was flushed at each tide . . .'. He also built others in the Vintry over some almshouses, although these were considered 'unhygienic'. On the other hand, some houses in Bassishaw ward in 1422 were considered 'defective' since they had no 'previes' but only seats over chutes into the cesspit twelve feet below!

There is no mention at all of another important requirement. Toilet-paper did not exist. In the home one could use a sponge soaked in salt water, or a bunch of herbs or even a wad of grass; goose-feathers were also used in wealthy households, although scraping with a mussel-shell was recommended 'as used in Holland'.

The task of cleaning out the public and private 'laystalls' was done by the very ancient guild of gong-farmers (probably originally dung-farmers), whose charges changed with the client or the job. In 1372 Queen Philippa's two employees were Nicholas Richeandgoode and William Mockynge. There were dunghills at strategic places: Dunghill Lane near Puddle Dock, another at Brooke's Wharf in Queenhithe, and another which was later cleared and cleaned to make way for the famous Three Cranes Inn in the Vintry which was sometimes still known as 'Dunghill Stairs'; and yet another adjoining Whitefriars, which must have added more olfactory discomfort to the friars. The last word must lie with Sir John Harington, Queen Elizabeth's 'lovynge cozen', describing in his *Metamorphosis of Ajax* the daily procession: '. . . the greate Wickednesse daily and hourlie wroughte . . . with his Carte full-laden and no Man envyinge his full Measure but hasteninge from this soure stynking carriage to the other syde of the streete . . .'.

What it was like to be in London without money is graphically described by the poet John Lydgate in *London Lackpenny* (c. 1450). He came up from Kent to make a complaint 'to a Judge at ye Kynges benche' who had 'a greate rout of clarkes writing away with spede'. John could not even understand the clerks' speech, but it didn't matter, because without money they would not heed him. He found the same response at the Court of Commons, where 'some satte with sylkene hoodes', and at the Court of Rolls, where the 'Clarkes of Chancery' were all earning 'muche pense' – they liked his case but passed it up when he had no money. At Westminster Hall 'he kneeled before one in a longe gowne', pleading 'for Mary's sake', and was refused nonetheless, although 'I shulde dye!'.

On the way into London he was importuned by 'Flemmynges . . . to buy fine felt hattes or Spectacles', but he went on, being importuned by cooks who offered him 'breade with ale and Wyne, Rybbes of Befe both fatte and fyne', but when they began to spread a cloth, he walked away. The hustle and bustle bewildered him:

> 'Hotte peascoddes one began to crye:
> Strawberrie rype and cherries on the ryse
> Pepper and Sayferne . . .

but he had to go hungry. Then he came to Chepe, 'where muche people I sawe', standing with a bewildering choice,

> One offered Velvet, Sylke and Lawne –
> Here is Parris thredde, the finest in the Lande,

and he remarks that, 'I never was used to such thynges.' In Candelwykestrete he was offered 'much clothe by Drapers', all the while being pestered by hot food hawkers offering 'hotte shepes feete' and 'makerells', and sellers of 'green rushes' and even 'a hoode to cover my hedde'.

He went on to East Chepe, where the hucksters were still offering 'ribbes of befe' and all sorts of meat pies, as well as assorted kitchenware, such as pewter-plates and jugs 'in heapes'; he heard the Welsh pedlars 'playing harps and pipes and singing', and coarse Londoners swearing 'Yea! by Cock! Nay! by Cock!'. But the cacophony tired him and he walked down Cornhill, 'where there was muche stolen geare' – he saw his own hood which had been stolen but he had no money to buy it back. With his last penny he drank a 'pint of wine' and then had to walk back home to Kent because a barge-man told him that in London 'he would not get any alms'. When he got home, he prayed that God would send some honest lawyers, 'so that they who lacked money' could get help – a vain thought, as history demonstrated.

After 1350 some notions of luxury became available to the wealthy. They put tapestry or embroidered silk hangings on their walls; lattice windows now contained glass panes; wooden floors were now laid – although they were still covered with rushes, these might be changed more frequently. Trestles were for eating upon (tables came much later); there were settles, perhaps even a chair for the master of the house; and a chest of drawers – possibly one of the new-fangled dressers favoured by the Welsh barbarians. There would be a wooden wash-handstand with a metal basin and jug – medieval etiquette required that the hands, face and teeth be cleaned once a day, usually in the morning. Bathing was not highly regarded. Soap made from wood ashes was obtainable – the very wealthy might use real soap from Castile by 1400, but it was fearfully expensive. About 1350 there was an invaluable utensil for

Two fashionably dressed gentlemen gambling with dice in a brothel, with two courtesans anxiously watching the play. The young man appears to be losing and looking worried.

the very wealthy – 'the schyttynge-panne', inserted under the seat of the master's arm-chair; it was deemed suitable as an heirloom to be inherited.

The trestle might be covered by a cloth, with knives and spoons laid out with wooden trenchers or thick slices of bread; forks were then unknown. Vessels were of wood or crude pottery – pewter was just coming in. The principal drink was home-brewed ale or bought from itinerant ale-wives, but by the end of the fourteenth century the Dutch had introduced a malt liquor laced with hops which, as beer, had by 1500 become the national beverage.

Shops were usually the ground-floor rooms of a house, opened up to the street by a shutter which was used as a counter. The master's wife and daughters would help as salespeople (the sons would be apprentices or at the wars), and they would add to the hubbub by calling their wares in competition with the innumerable hucksters roaming the lanes. If the 'counter' were permanent, it

The earliest representation of a medieval 'stewes', a huge wooden tub filled with hot water. There was no sexual segregation, which led to such establishments becoming brothels. All are enjoying a good time, with ministrels entertaining them and amorous gropings in the shrubbery. However the papal representative in the top right-hand corner observes the scene. c. 1250.

needed a licence and was known as a 'bulk'; at night these might be resting-places for poor whores.

A huge number of men were carriers: what could not be loaded on pack-horses or donkeys had to be handled by men – and not a few women.

In pre-plague periods slaves competed with villeins and freemen for whatever jobs were going – which kept wages low and led to many bloody encounters. Men were needed as stable-hands, as messengers for any menial task – except dung-removal which was the preserve of 'gong-farmers', though they could be 'rakers' for dirty rushes and other rubbish, and they were needed to carry ladies' litters through the muddy or dusty streets, or as ostlers. Yet still there were thousands of unemployed and unemployables to swell the ranks of thieves and pickpockets and hooligans.

Public baths, forgotten since the times of the Romans, had made some sort of come-back when the returning Crusaders remembered the Turkish *hummums*. A 'Company of Bath Men' had come into being, their premises usually being known as the Turk's Head. The 'stovers' (stokers) were then members of the barbers' guild, and the 'stewes' were immense wooden tubs constantly filled with hot water – small boys were sent running through the streets announcing when the water was hot. Even then there was no sexual discrimination: contemporary prints show men and women disporting themselves and being diverted with minstrels in garden-like surroundings. In 1399 Henry IV inaugurated at his coronation the Order of Knights of the Bath Tub, the initiate '. . . being led to a Bath hung within and without with Linen, he being shaved and his hair cut; then undressed and immersed and while lying there instructed touching upon the order and chivalry, taken out and put in a dry plain Bed . . . then finely apparrelled . . .'.

Knighthood and chivalry – homage paid to ladies – were artificial creations: they did not always go together. The original Norman knights were very ungentlemanly, and the ladies were froward and outspoken. Chivalry did not extend to women below that rank. Tournaments were part of the 'bread and circuses' for the public, and touts, pickpockets, bookies and whores were great beneficiaries, as also were the undertakers.

5 Queene Eleanor is Foule Reproved

The long reign of Henry III (1216–72) despite his many family and foreign vicissitudes and extortions, brought great prosperity and expansion to London – if not all Londoners. He regarded the kingdom as his personal property, and spent its revenues as he pleased. The City taxpayers who had to foot a large part of his extravagances much resented his constant irresponsible demands. He lacked foresight and judgement – only his family life was irreproachable, his piety being due to utter subservience to the Pope. His vice was avarice. This, matched with the extravagances of his queen, Eleanor *la Belle* (daughter of the mighty Count Raymond of Provence), whom he married in 1236, caused even greater resentment.

London's first taste of this lady was when she rode through the City to be crowned Queen of England: '. . . the City was adorned with Silkes and in the Nyghte lit up with Lampes and Cressets withoute number. The Citizens rode to meet her in long garments broidered with Gold and Silver and Silkes of divers coloures: three hundred and sixty Men on horsebacke each holding a Gold or Silver Cupp in his Hand with the Royal Trumpetters leading. . . . Wine was served to all. . . .' Thousands of 'Daughters of the Citie' were mustered, from the high-born ladies down to the humblest – but prettiest – prostitute. Rich gifts were proffered by City worthies – they were to regret it. Further to commemorate this grand spree, the King ordered his treasurer – at the City's expense – 'To feed six thousand people at West Minster . . . the weake and the aged to be placed in the Great Hall . . . the healthy in the King's Chamber . . . the children in the Queen's Chamber . . . when the King knoweth the Charge he will allow it in the Accomptes. . . .'

One of Henry's first acts had been to grant the City the right to '. . . disaforest the Great Forest of Middlesex . . . since when the

Suburbs hath been mightily encreased with Buyldings'. The next move was to confirm, in 1226, the City's Charter: 'KNOW YE THAT we have granted and confirmed to our Barons of the City of London that they may select amongst themselves their Mayor each year . . . to be trusty towards US, discreet and fit for the Government of the City . . . the Sheriffs shall have two Clerkes and two Serjeants. . . .' Thereby he had flattered the aldermen by calling them barons and giving them a noble's attendants, but the operative words were that their duty was to him first and the City second. In this way he would have constant and ready access to huge sums of money.

It gave the King the excuse that any trumpery reason would be good enough to ensure the City oligarchs would have to do as he bade – as John Stow observed: '. . . to speak the plain truth the Princes have taken hold of small matters and coined good sums of Coin . . .' Indeed, Stow went on that the whole reign of Henry III '. . . was a continuall warfare conceived against his Citie . . . whiche nowe and then had manie a Snubb at the King's hands . . . in the end . . . he both seized their Liberties and suck'd them drye . . .'.

On one occasion, in 1254, Henry seized the liberties and arrested the mayor because he had allegedly 'not examined the Assize of Bread' – which was nothing to do with the king at all. The next year he dismissed the mayor, sheriffs and aldermen from office. He got away with it because the guilds were split between those who supported him and those bitterly opposed to him because of his incessant demands for money and his constant interference with the City's liberties and laws. The situation became so fraught that in 1265 the citizens barred the streets against his officers with iron chains.

The most important event of this reign, however, was the convening in the same year of a 'Great Council' – a parliament at which for the first time two burgesses from each borough were summoned to attend to sit with the barons: the first admission of a middle class into state affairs. The King had so bled the barons that they were compelled to widen the scope to include those who actually had to find the money. Henry had before then described London as 'an inexhaustible well of riches', but this time their terms were so harsh that he showed his appreciation by calling them 'sons of whores'.

Some years earlier, in 1253, the King had '. . . tampered with the coinage in suche manner as to cause dismaie' when raising money to pay his brother, Duke Richard of Cornwall, whom he owed the immense sum of £20,000. He had to sell all his gold and silver plate to the City moneylenders and give his brother the 'farm' of the Mint. Between 1243 and 1250 he had squeezed out of the London Jews '3,000 silver marks . . . in the Queen's gold'. The community was almost ruined. He seized a 'large stone house built in AD 1231 which had been a synagogue' and in 1260 sold it to the Fraternity of St Anthony de Vienne 'to be an hospital'.

In 1257, when Henry had abrogated London's liberties, it was reported that London Bridge was in a bad state of repair. He had already passed over to his rapacious Queen 'all its revenues', which she had dissipated on her own extravagances. By 1270 the bridge had 'fallen so into disrepaire to the anger of the citizens' that one day, 'Elianore ye quene was foule reproved and almoste sclayne uppon London bregge . . . [the mob shouting] drowne the bitch, drowne the bitch . . . throwinge offal, refuse and dung atte her as shee passed under in her boate. . . .'

To soften the blow, Henry re-enforced an ordinance of Henry II that the citizens should be free of pontage: they would not have to pay the *brudtol* for crossing the bridge; but as against this he made a levy for the repairs to the bridge which rightly should have been paid by the 'foule reproved' Queen: he only furthered the citizens' anger.

Because of the constant turmoil, in 1253 Henry commanded that 'watches' were to be recruited in London for 'the better observing of peace and quietness among the people'. Each year thereafter there was a great pageant, the 'Marching Watch' around the city's boundaries from St Paul's and back. On one occasion, '. . . the streets were lit by seven hundred cressets, while five hundred splendidly attired Liverymen paraded with two hundred Magnates of the City . . . two hundred and forty Watchmen had each a cresset, one half of them marching in the parade and the other half standing watch in every street and lane. . . .' These Marching Watches were to be a feature of London's life until Queen Elizabeth's day, but every year the Common Council grumbled at the expense.

During all these turmoils, as might be expected, 'unriht lust' was flourishing. There was a host of little brothels in and around the precincts of St Paul's, occasioning brawls and robbery. There was the notorious 'Powles bruehowse', established in 1162 (*vide* Hoccleve, by whose time it had become the Powleshedde Tavern):

Of Venus' female lusty childeren deere
at Seynte Poules Hedd me maden ofte appere.

In 1282 the City tried to maintain the Law of London against the Dean and Chapter of St Paul's regarding 'certayne shoppes buylded abowte the walles of the greate church yarde', asserting, '. . . that wee shal nott permite butchers, poticaris, gouldsmythes, cookes, or comon women to dwell in these same shoppes by whose noyse or tumultes or dishonesties the quietnesse . . . shalbe trobled . . .'. Furthermore, they would not be permitted to use 'sea-coles or suche other thynges thatte doe styncke', because that was the Law of London 'from tyme immemorial' which could not be changed. Many of the nuisances, mayhems and murders were committed during the regular brawls by apprentices when their guilds were jostling for power: one ploy was to pull down brothels and beat-up the inmates.

The feudal *jus cunni* – the lord's right to deflower a bride before her marriage – was still in force in rural areas. Many girls fled to the city to escape it, only to fall into the hands of bawds who put them to prostitution. Moreover, there was still the *leyrwite*, a fine exacted from girls who had lost their virginity or even from unmarried women who had become pregnant. Incest was quite frequent, especially in rural areas where a daughter was expected to replace a dead or sick mother. In excuse, they might refer to the biblical example (in Genesis 38) of Judah and Tamar – in the unlikely event that they had ever seen a Bible or could even read.

Rape was quite frequent. On 11 October 1226 Emma de Goggeshall accused Gregory, 'son of Master Gregory', of ravishing her by force while his friend Richard, 'son of Thomas the Image-maker', aided and abetted the deed. She was represented at court by two bakers, brothers Richard and John de Keningstone, but because Emma did not appear when called, both men were fined and she was arrested. It then transpired that the bakers had conspired with Emma to make a false accusation – an attempt to blackmail the son of an important liveryman. However, Gregory was still fined half a mark, '. . . because he was aware of the illegal compromise'.

There was a wide range of crimes which were subject to the Great Law of London, which actually meant they were heard before a 'jury' of freemen, the size of which depended on the nature of the offence and whether it was at a 'hustings' or a folkmoot. At times it could be turned into a court of inquest into more serious or unusual occurrences. For example, when a boy was dragged into the river while holding a horse, the owner of the horse was acquitted of responsibility, and a verdict of misadventure was given. Murder, however, was frequent.

Laurence Duckett, a goldsmith and a scion of a long line of

goldsmith oligarchs, having wounded a miscreant, Ralph Crepin, fled for sanctuary into nearby Bow church. During the night a gang of Crepin's 'evill' friends burst into the church, 'slew hym and hangyd hym upp as if he hadde hangyd hymselfe', and thus, as a suicide, he was 'drawne by the feete on an hurdle' and buried outside the city. It then transpired that he was a homosexual and that the catamite, Crepin, had been supplied by one Alice. Laurence was exhumed and 'honestlie buried' but Alice, 'the cheif causer of the sayd myschiefe', was burned at the stake. Four men, one of whom was Ralph's brother, were indicted and, together with a dozen other sodomites, 'weren drawne and hangyd' but others '. . . beyinge richer, after long imprisonment weren hangyd by the pursse'.

There was John de London Stone who killed his wife Agnes with his sword on Easter Day 1238, for which he was outlawed and all his chattels 'worth four shillings and eightpence' were seized. Then it was disclosed that he had stayed in the house five days after the murder and that 'two members of his household', John Clarke le Dubber (refurbisher of old clothes) and Thomas de Berkynge Marshe had witnessed the crime but had not raised the 'hue and cry' as required by the law. They were committed to prison, but the murderer, 'being a freeman', was allowed bail to go before a folkmoot. (The outcome is not known.)

About the same time William FitzHerbert and his servant Richard went to the Jewry and killed Josce (Joseph) the Jew and Hannah his wife, stealing a silver cup. William was hanged, but Richard and an accomplice, Milo le Epicier (pepperer) fled to St Saviour's, Southwark, for sanctuary, where Richard 'died of his wounds' (who inflicted them is unknown). Milo, being a freeman, pleaded that, as the murder had occurred in the Jewry, then under the jurisdiction of the king's constable of the Tower, the sheriff had no jurisdiction in this case.

The vexed question of 'sanctuary' was a constant cause of concern to the City's government. Every church had the right of sanctuary, and many of the liberties, such as St Martin-le-Grand and Southwark, had rights extending beyond their borders – particularly St Martin's, whose borders extended into parts ('within the wall') around Aldersgate Street. Escapees could live there and even carry on a trade. There were also many brothels, run by 'Froes of Flanders' and the like.

These liberties then included Blackfriars, Whitefriars, the Tower, the Temple and Duke's Place in the Portsoken of Aldgate. Over the centuries their privileges became greatly abused and a serious threat to the peace and safety of the City's inhabitants, because of incursions of gangs of hooligans causing murder and mayhem. They were abolished only in 1697, by 'Dutch William'.

Sanctuary was limited by some important restrictions. There was a blockade which meant that no food was allowed in – effectively starvation, meaning death or surrender, but the criminal could send for a coroner and swear to 'abjure the realm' and never return. He was assigned a port and given a large wooden cross to carry along a route from which he could not deflect, to take the first ship. If no ship was immediately available, he 'must walk each day up to his knees in the sea'. If he turned aside from the direct road, he became at once an outlaw and could be 'slain like a wolf or other vermin' by anyone who met him. However, there were some sanctuaries, such as the bishop of Winchester's 'Liberty of the Clink', where the malefactor could stay for a year and a day – against a fee and good behaviour, thus defeating the City's privilege of *outfangtheof*.

The City also claimed some rights of sanctuary under William I's charter, but in 1236 this was tested. One Ludowic, a goldsmith of Cheapside, killed his wife and fled for sanctuary to St Mary Staining Church in Aldersgate ward. The King's treasurer, with the permission of the mayor (who was then a justiciar), allowed Ludowic 'to abjure the realm'. Then there was a bitter argument as to whether Ludowic's sureties should be fined, according to the Law of London. The City's claim was disallowed, '. . . because the King's official had given the permission'.

However, the City's population was now growing apace. There were consequently growing demands for more food and a wider variety of goods, which in turn demanded more artisans and workshops and more buildings. It became necessary to expand 'outside the walls' but still ensure the City's jurisdiction. Hence the ancient *pomerium* outside Bishopsgate became 'Bishopsgate Without', and the area of Cripplegate was extended to Everardeswell-streete (now Chiswell Street) and included Grobbestreet (to become notorious as Grub Street).

There was a *murage* – a wall-tax at the gates, and a collector who collected rents, tolls and customs. The latter were very considerable. Every cart bringing in corn paid a halfpenny – but if it came over the Fleet bridge, it paid a penny. Fish and poultry paid 2 pence – a halfpenny more over the Fleet; and 'for every dead Jew to be buried in London' 3 halfpence for the *Presbyter omnium Judaiorum*, the Chief Rabbi, who at that time was the famous Elias *le Mire* (the physician), whose services were in demand by the highest in the land, including the most rabid anti-semites. The Jewish cemetery was just outside St Giles, Cripplegate Without.

The wealthier citizens were already building fine houses and gardens leading down to the fast-flowing Fleet river or to the lovely village at Isledon (Islington). Their wealth had not always been gathered by strictly honourable means, though many had risen from poverty, '. . . from hawkers to pack-men; from pack-men to carriers; from carriers to waggonmasters; from hucksters to trades-men . . . and with growth of trade grew the Love of Money!'. 'Forestallers' now became retailers, and a contemporary wrote:

> Swindlers, some buyers and brokers buy corn from country folks and give, on the bargain being made, a penny or halfpenny as earnest, then tell the peasant to take the corn to their house for payment, only to be told that the wife is out or the key cannot be found so that he cannot get at his money; or the peasant must come again and the buyer is not to be found or feigns something else so that the peasant cannot be paid ever. Or even [the buyer] goes to the length of making the corn wet for brewing, telling the seller that it is spoilt and give him a lower price. . . .

There were all sorts of ruses and devices to buy cheaply or avoid payment, even surreptitiously stealing goods during negotiations with simple peasantry.

In 1270 the famous Franciscan preacher Barthold of Regensburg, who was quite familiar with London, castigated tradesmen:

> YE THAT WORK in clothing, silkes, or wool, or Fur, or shoes or Gloves or Girdles . . . men must needs have Clothing therefore ye shoulde doe your worke truly; not to steale half the cloth nor mixe haire with your wool or stretch it oute longer whereby a man thinketh he hath good cloth . . . yet thou hast made it useless stuffe.
>
> NO MAN can finde a good hat . . . the raine will pour through the brim to soak his bosom. A man sells old skins for newe . . . yet thou swearest loudlye how good thy wares are . . . but what doth it profitt the buyer?
>
> MANY TIMES THOU TAKEST THE NAME OF GOD and all Saints for wares that are worthless. That which is worth five shillings thou sellest a sixpence higher . . . YE KNOW WHAT LIES AND FRAUDES ARE BUSY IN THY TRADE!

In Soperslane, the ancient street of the soap-boilers, which was of old a 'street of whoredom', it was complained in 1259 that, '. . . their gray-soape made in London is dearer than that bought from Bristol!'. This 'gray-soape' was speckled with white soap and sold for a penny a pound, whereas 'black soap' was only a halfpenny a pound, but even so early John Lane, master soaper of Grace-church Street, was selling 'hard cake of white from beyond the seas called *Castell'* (Castile) which only the wealthy and most sophisticated could afford.

The fur trade was flourishing mightily, there being an incessant demand for such luxury furs as ermine and sable and beaver – most of them coming, courtesy of the Viking traders, from Russia. It had some unlikely aspects: in 1138 Cardinal Alberic was sent to England as a papal legate, and in the course of his visit he saw fit to issue a statement 'on papal authority': 'WE FORBID that nuns wear furs of *vair gris*, sable, marten, ermine or beaver, or put on gold rings or make-up their hair . . . on pain of excommunication. . . .' They were permitted only goat or sheep skins. ('*Vair-gris*' was grey squirrel skin.) There was another hazard. The type of fur worn denoted – indeed, conferred – status. Ermine and sable were reserved for the highest nobility, including royalty. Richard I once paid £13 for one ermine skin and four sables, and he ordered that, '. . . all squirrel skins taken from his enemies must be kept for him.' An alderman of the City of London was amerced (fined) because he had the wrong fur collar on his gown. There was, however, much breeding of squirrels, both red and grey, for the ladies of the nascent middle class.

The breeding of sheep and cattle for their skins brings to mind the origin of one of today's favourite expletives. In 1276 mention is made of one John le Fukker – John the breeder (from the Dutch word *vokken*), breeding animals. This then had nothing to do with 'unriht lust', although the word '*forlicgerhus*' where one could pick up a 'ficg' (a venereal ulcer), was still in current use in the language.

King Henry III died in 1272, after he had dedicated his abbey at Westminster. The anomaly is that, despite half a century of mis-rule, local and foreign wars and tremendous extortions of money, the City of London had grown immensely richer and had built up a very powerful political machine which enabled it to weather the oppressions of the new king, Edward I. Sadly, however, the great increase in wealth was matched by a great decline in business and political morality, although sexual morality remained much about the same.

6 Of Common Bawds, Whores and Scouldes

The reign of Edward I (1272–1307) marks an important turning-point in London's history, particularly in the great increase in its financial power and its effect on the nation.

Edward was a clever and courageous man with a dreadfully cruel streak in his make-up, worsened by sudden rages which resulted in great suffering to many remote and innocent citizens. (He once threw down his crown in a rage and trampled on it – the bill for the repair is still extant!) He was determined to rule autocratically – in contrast to his father's idiosyncratic reign, and his participation in the Crusades had made him a religious bigot and a relentless anti-semite.

Because he needed money, in 1274 he convened a 'parliament' to which he summoned representatives of the boroughs and the lesser clergy; London's two 'burgesses' attended. This assembly established three royal courts of justice which exist to this day: the King's Bench, the Court of Common Pleas and the Exchequer. All were to administer the 'common' law, a *mélange* of ancient customs and precedents then in process of being codified, while safeguarding the rights of the feudal lords. All this was vital to the burgeoning London financiers and merchantmen. During his reign the City was governed in turn by subservient mayors or an imposed *custos* (a warden), and equally subservient sheriffs.

When Edward had organized the City according to his lights, he turned his attention to the correction of sin within its walls, which he often linked with physical cleanliness in his ordinances issued through the mayor. Almost the first is in 1272: 'Of the Cleansing of Streetes and Lanes . . . and that no courtezan or comon brothel-keeper shalbe residing within the walls of the Citie under pain of imprisonment.' This is linked with the ordinance, 'Concerning

70

Persons wandering by Night. IT IS FORBIDDEN that any person shall be so daring as to wander about the streets after Curfew has been rung at St Martins-le-Grand, St Laurence Jewry or All Hallows Barking, with sword or buckler or other arm for doing mischief . . . unless it be some Great Lord or other Substantial Person of good repute . . . he shall be taken by the Keepers of the Peace and put into the Tun . . . and on the morrow shall be brought before the Mayor and Aldermen . . . and punished. . . .' Any taverner who 'allowed bad characters or transgressors' into his premises was held liable and could be severely punished if any offences had been committed.

Ordinarily any man seeking fornication would take a wherry over to the legalized brothels on the Bankside or take a walk over the bridge, where prostitutes lurked in the alcoves in the parapets. To discourage sin in the City, the wherrymen were ordered 'at nightfall to moor their boats on the City side'. This ensured '. . . that thieves and other misdoers shall not be carried [but] . . . only

A conversation scene in a medieval brothel: one gentleman has made his choice, the other has to decide between four other beauties.

Men or Women, Denizens or Strangers caried unto the Stewes in the day time . . .'. In this way fornication in the daytime was an allowable recreation at the stewes – still, despite all minatory injunctions, there were many brothels operating within the city.

In 1284 the exasperated monarch issued a decree 'Of Thieves and Courtezans': 'WHEREAS thieves and other persons of light and bad repute are often . . . harboured in the houses of Women of Evil life within the City . . . through whose evil deeds . . . murders do often happen . . . from henceforth no common woman shall dwell within the walls . . . if any such be here after found . . . [they] shall be imprisoned forty days. The Wardens to search . . . where they are received, who they are and when found let their limits be assigned to them. . . .' This seems to be the first mention of the 'assigned place' as such.

Further painful punishment was in store: 'AND LET NO such person henceforth wear *Miniver* or *Cendal* on her dress or hood. If she do so let her lose both *miniver* and *cendal* . . . the same to be forfeited to the Serjeant who shall have found her in such guise. . . .' (Miniver was 'a costly fur', and cendal 'a rich thin silk'.) Such forfeits were found in the Conqueror's time in Rouen and in the Stewes ordinance of 1161. The wearing of such costly garments was the prerogative of high-born ladies – a mark of status not to be usurped.

Fornication 'within the walls' had undoubtedly been recognized in previous centuries, as witness the existence, even then, of Gropecuntelane and the Bordhawe (Brothel-area), both leased from St Paul's Cathedral 'in the parrishe of Ste Marie Colechirche'. In the vicinity of the Guildhall were Love Lane and Maid Lane, 'so-called of wantons there', and another Love Lane 'where yonge couples were wont to sport'. In 1276 Gropecuntelane belonged to the wealthy Henri de Edelmonton. From 1217 to 1277 there was a Grope Street in Cripplegate – today known as Grub Street! The Bordhawe (literally an enclosure in which brothels were found) can be traced back to 1125, when it also included the 'broces-gang' (the path alongside the arm of the Walbrook at that point).

In 1405 it had its true name, Burdellane (Brothel Lane) and is last recorded in 1557 as Brodhawelane! Gropecuntelane was still in existence in 1349. Cock Lane off Smithfield is first mentioned about 1200, and an 'assigned' (i.e. legalized) place of fornication in 1241.

Nightwalkers were to be 'emprysoned in ye tonne [Tun] on cornhyll', then carted and whipped and 'put outsyde ye newe gate'. Nevertheless, there were many joyful goings-on, Fabyan recording '. . . dysynge and cardynge til past midnyghte . . . ther

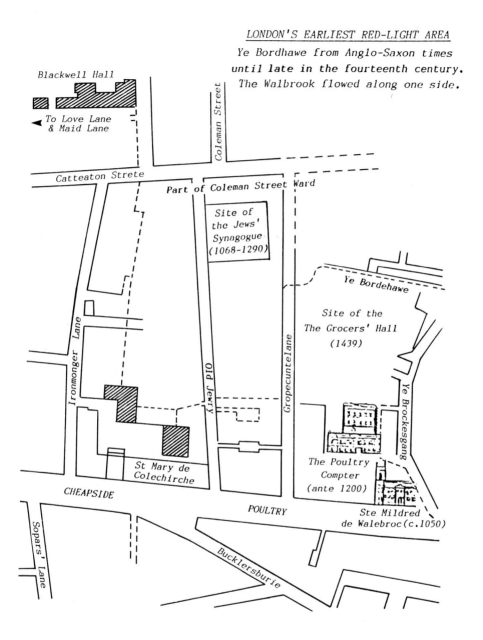

Ye Bordhawe from Anglo-Saxon times **until late in the fourteenth century.** *The Walbrook flowed along one side.*

Blackwell Hall

To Love Lane
& Maid Lane

Coleman Street

Catteaton Strete

Part of Coleman Street Ward

Site of
the Jews'
Synagogue
(1068-1290)

Ye Bordehawe

Site of the
The Grocers' Hall
(1439)

Ironmonger Lane

Old Jewry

Gropecuntelane

Ye Brockesgang

St Mary de
Colechirche

CHEAPSIDE

The Poultry
Compter
(ante 1200)

POULTRY

Ste Mildred
de Walebroc (c.1050)

Sopars' Lane

Bucklersburie

The Bordhawe in St Mildred's parish and Gropecuntelane which extended into the neighbouring parish of St Mary Colechirche and (later) Coleman Street ward. The Walbrook can be seen on the right with the Brocesgang alongside. Sopers Lane was also a brothel-street; and on the other side of the Cateaton Street (now Gresham Street) were Love Lane and Maid Lane, both haunts of 'wantons'.

one pyckes anotheres pursse . . . felons doth resorte theym [whores and clients] in ande owte atte a backe dore . . .'.

In 1290 the King thought up the brilliant idea of raising money by compelling rich citizens to accept knighthoods. A royal writ of 30 June was served on the sheriffs, 'Enforcing knighthood': 'WE DO STRICTLY COMMAND you that in the City wherever it shall seem expedient to make Public Proclamation that all such as hold Forty pounds in Land or in Rents *per annum* and for three whole years have held the same, and are not Knights shall receive the Order of Knighthood before the Feast of St Laurence next August 10th . . . under Peril that thereunto pertains.' The sheriffs were commanded to make 'diligent enquiry and in no wise omit' any likely recipient but in their reply stated that they could not be certain they had found everyone, because '. . . there were tenements sometimes let for more . . . or less oftentimes stand empty yet require divers outlays and frequent repairs . . . also destruction by fire and other perils [so that] there was no certainty as to true value . . .'. Moreover, many citizens held land and property 'outside our bailiwicke', where they knew nothing and were unable to make inquisition.

In fact, many rich burgesses did not want to be knights. They did not want the true extent of their wealth to be known, because of further exactions; they did not want to be bothered with the 'obligations' of knighthood, including military service – they were moneymakers, not warriors. The King repeated the demand in 1302 and received exactly the same reply from his sheriffs.

The futility of all the anti-sin ordinances is demonstrated by the need in Edward's last year, 1307, to issue the warning *Pro Meretrabes et Pronubes* (Concerning Whores and Procuresses) whereby all such would be 'removed immediately . . . taken to the Compter in Wood Street' and kept there before being expelled. This was the sheriff's mansion-cum-prison, standing on the east side of Wood Street since 1185. The ordinance had as much effect as all the previous ones.

One of Edward's first edicts had been about 'cleansing the streets': '. . . the places and lanes of the City shall be kept clear of all manner of annoyance such as dung rubbish pigsties', and food-vendors in the Chepe and Cornhill had to stand in the middle of the streets 'between the kennels' (gutters), so as not to be a hindrance or a nuisance, especially on market days; the penalty was forfeiture of both stall and goods. Dogs were also forbidden – except pets of the wealthy.

The citizens' personal habits were also nasty: the streets and lanes were still used as latrines – indeed it was quite common for people to excrete out of upper windows into the street below – although as early as 1237 Queen Matilda's 'necessary House' (originally built in 1140) had been enlarged 'for the comon use of citizens'. Hence in 1263 Pyssyngelane (known from Saxon days as Mihindelane, from the word *micgan*, to piss), between St Paul's and Paternoster Row, did not belie its name. There was many a Stynkyngelane in London, especially in areas such as the Shambles and Poultry, where livestock were slaughtered and the blood and guts stayed scattered around.

There was a large public lavatory on London Bridge, known to history only because in September 1306 one William de Prestone failed to pay a debt to John le Spenser, who ordered his servant to follow him, '. . . the whyche hee dyd thorough diver stretes untill they came to London Brydge where he [William] told the servaunt to waite for hym while hee went unto the *privie* ther . . . and then hee left the prevye by an other entrance . . . .'.

There were rules to prevent swindling of both suppliers and customers. A city serjeant always stood nearby to make a 'hue and cry' and apprehend any malefactor. The usual on-the-spot penalty was 'double the payment to customer or supplier' but there were many ways of making a dishonest penny.

Bakers and ale-wives were the most constant offenders. When customers brought their own dough to the baker's, they put it on the counter; a small boy hidden under the counter would open 'a litel trapdore' and take a quantity of dough 'before the customer's very eyes' – before the baker took up the dough to his oven.

As far as possible, the punishment was made to fit the crime. The seller of bad wine was put in the stocks, and it was poured down his throat. The seller of bad meat was stood in the pillory, and his bad meat burned in his face, so that he was forced to inhale the smell. Fraudulent bakers were stood in the pillory with their loaves 'braced round theyre neckes', or put on hurdles with their light-weight loaves slung round their necks and drawn by a horse through the streets – in a really bad case, head down, bumping against the cobbles.

Brewing was usually done at home by ale-wives, and the brew was to be adjudged and passed by the City's 'ale-conner', but much was sold unproven. In that case the ale-wife would find herself in the 'thew' and made to drink her own product. Most taverns also brewed their own ale but when it was ready had to put an 'ale-stake' (like a barber's pole) outside after each brewing.

One particularly apposite punishment was meted out to a man

A group of whores being 'carted' to exile outside the City to one of the two 'assigned places' – the Bankside or Cock-lane, Smithfield. c. 1240.

'who tapp'd the public supply of water': he was led through the streets with a rope round his neck with a constantly filled but leaking bucket over his head.

Other tricks included using false weights and shoddy material, or selling shoddy goods 'in a poor light of flickering candles'.

The punishment of the pillory for a host of minor offences is indicative of a certain humanity at a period when mutilation and other savage penalties were being inflicted outside the City. The variety of offences for which the pillory, as well as its female equivalent the 'thew' was used covers lies, deceits, falsehoods and slanders but also some unusual misdemeanours.

The greatest number of cases were for selling unwholesome foodstuffs: 'putrid fish, putrid poultry, putrid meat' and substandard bread and ale. These included such curiosities as selling 'a peck of stinking eels', two 'stinking capons', 'raw stinking meat', 'a stinking pig' and 'rotten conger eels' and for 'selling oats where outside was good but inside was bad'.

One man was pilloried for 'enhancing the price of corn' above the City's regulated price, another for a 'deficiency of coal in sacks', and yet another for 'forestalling of poultry' – bringing to market unlicensed goods; and full many for 'false assize of ale', quite apart from those who brewed weak or adulterated ale outside the City and brought it in, the main offenders being 'brewsters' and 'ale-wives'.

Others were punished for 'lies against the mayor', 'against the city recorder', 'against an alderman'. Indeed, men were committed after the pillory to prison for crimes including 'divers opprobrious things said against a serjeant in the mayor's presence' and the like against Alderman William Wotton of Dowgate – this was akin to insulting a judge, as also was 'rebelliousness against the constable of Bread Street Ward' and 'against the alderman of Walbrook'.

Several were punished for false pretences: pretending to be a sheriff's serjeant, going to Stratford-atte-Bow and arresting some bakers 'until they paid a fine' (this cost him a gaol sentence and a whipping in addition); pretending to be a physician: and pretending to be an archbishop's summoner; one 'claimed to be an Holy Hermit' but was a beggar from Bedlam hospital.

There were many instances of counterfeiting, mainly for selling gilded brass as gold, and rings and bracelets plated with silver. There was a big trade in shoe buckles – gold or gilt shoe buckles were a mark of a gentleman and were an essential part of a confidence-trickster's clothes. There were scribes who executed false deeds and bonds, as well as letters – the latter being a very frequent offence, and because ninety per cent of the clients could neither read nor write, this was a serious breach of confidence. Forging a deed or a bond usually meant a heavy fine or imprisonment or both.

An unusual offence was the manufacture of 'false dice', and the con man who used them, 'playing and deceiving people' was also pilloried. Perhaps the most curious was 'practising the art of magic' or 'soothsaying', in the latter case pretending to recover a stolen 'mazer' (a drinking-cup) by necromancy. And of course the common offences of pickpocketing, stealing and begging. Contempt of court merited committal to the Tun.

The *thew* was less often in evidence. It was a device especially meant to chastise women, being a stout wooden whipping-post with a *healsfanger* (neck-holder) on a short chain. The earliest reference is in 1287 which states that 'communs tenseresses' (common whores) must be chastised 'by the judgement which is called 'the thew' (which is Old English, to chastise). It was then fixed on a *tumbrell* so that the miscreant could be trundled through the neighbourhood, being shamed before the public. The same item mentions '*sac* and *soc* . . . (and) borughpeny and thewpenny . . .'; which must infer that a *socman* or a borough official was entitled to make this charge for its use.

An illustration of an early thew for the punishment of women, first mentioned in 1287.

The scope was widened to include 'common procuresses', 'common scolds' and 'women oute at nyghte after laeful houres' and also for those 'selling putrid fish or flesh', or swindling 'by givinge a false quart of ale, pitch beynge put in the bottom of the utensil'. It was uncomfortable and shame-making rather than a torture but as time went on women were more often put on the pillory and the thew fell into disuse.

The pillory was also used for such oddments as 'exposing for sale divers papal bulls' or for a chaplain who was a 'nyghtewalker' or three men who 'counterfeited the Seals of the Pope & certayne greate Lordes of Englande'. For deceivers and liars there was 'imprisonment for a year and a day' and to stand 'each quarter in the pillory for three hours with a whetstone tied around the neck, for lies that were disproved'. The whetstone was reserved for 'great Liars' who were then said 'to be lying for the whetstone'.

The general indifference of the citizenry to the cleaning ordinances, as well as the incompetence of the street-cleaners, meant not only that the thoroughfares were choked with human and animal excrements but that nearby rivers, such as the Fleet and the Walbrook, were also used as lavatories and dustbins. In 1290 the King was informed that, 'the sweet waters of the Flete are taynted by impurities'; a few years' later Henry Lacy, Earl of Lincoln, complained 'In former tymes the waters runnynge under Hole-bourne brydge had been of suche depth and breadth that ten or twelve large shipps were wont to come up . . . yett by the filthe of tanners and others impedimenta the course is nowe decaied and shipps cannot enter. . . .'

Although the King ordered 'the creek to be cleansed to make it useable', it was never restored to its former condition and was in popular speech demoted to 'the Turnmill [or Trimill] brook'. However, it was occasionally dredged, and in 1502 it was reported to Henry VII that 'ships laden with stone for the repair of St Paul's' had got as far as the bridge.

Personal ablutions were still primitive, partly because water – other than the river water – was not readily available: it had to be bought from itinerant water-sellers. However, in 1256 King Henry III '. . . would repair to the Wardrobe . . . where he was wont to wash his head'; the public was not informed how often His Majesty performed this strange and possibly dangerously unhealthy function.

On 7 July 1307 Edward I, 'that formidable man', fell back dead on his bed after a terrific quarrel with his son over the latter's homosexual liaison with Piers de Gaveston. Edward II was then twenty-three years old – 'a strong, handsome lad . . . much given to frivolous pursuits . . . and the company of base-born people such as carters, diggers and blacksmiths . . .'. He was also 'very fond of the company of harlots', evidencing that he was not averse to 'straight sex' also. In 1311 the barons got rid of Gaveston, and there is no more mention of homosexual behaviour.

Edward was popular with the Londoners because when he

restored their charter in 1307 he added '. . . that the Bridge shall be entrusted to two reputable men of the city other than aldermen', although this was a good device to shift the intolerable upkeep onto other shoulders. He also commanded the mayor to 'extend the Wall from Ludgate down to the Thames', giving citizens free access to the river there.

He was unlucky in many respects through no fault of his own, apart from the disastrous defeat at Bannockburn in 1314. In the following year the harvests failed and there was a terrible famine. The storehouse on London Bridge, 'for storage of corn agaynste tyme of dearth', was unable to cope: 'The poore people eate from hunger cattes and horses and houndes . . . they stole children and ate them . . . a great dearth of corn and all other Vittals . . . a Bushell of Wheate was five shillings & that made Bakers Lordes . . . the Quicke were unable to burie the Deade . . . Dogges-flesshe was goode Meate. . . .' The bakers complained, however, that '. . . they were compelled to buy mouldy corn from the Bridge-house . . . which was a great hazard because of the City's stern Bread Laws against bad bread . . . but the Bridge House payde no attencion to their complaints'. Next year the harvest was good but '. . . there was a Murrain of Kine . . . that dogges and ravens feeding on them were poysoned'.

At this time there is news about the bridge. There were now many shops and tenements: an ordinance of 1320 forbade *inter alia*, 'retailers of ale to continue to sell', which indicates that there must have been quite a big illegal business beforehand.

There was a great deal of political manœuvring going on, and at times the Londoners were exasperated by the King, preferring his wife's lover, Mortimer. When eventually, in 1320, Mortimer was captured, the mayor, John de Gisors, '. . . and a large number of influential citizens were forced to flee'; '. . . citizens rose up and wonne the Tower . . . delyvered alle the prysoners'. They affirmed that they were '. . . for Quene Isabella and her sonne' (the future Edward III). They had already proved their loyalty to her by beheading her enemy Walter de Stapledon, Bishop of Exeter. For good measure, Mortimer's enemies the Despensers, father and son, both chamberlains to the King, were barbarously done to death in 1326. The younger Hugh Despenser having already been castrated, '. . . feeling the Executioner's knife rummaging about his kidneys, spoke his last words "Jesus! yett more trouble!"', after which he was hanged, drawn and quartered.

In the midst of all this carnage, the Londoners' leaders still harped on cleanliness! Dogs, swine and cows were not allowed in the streets, and indeed none was to be 'reared within the howse' under pain of forfeiture. Places were now ordained for all rubbish and filth to be deposited, where rakers would take it up and put away in other authorized dumps: 'The *Rakers* to have sufficient rakes: the Constables and Beadles shall help them to collect their salaries from the folk in their ward.'

The City's great prosperity was now leading to breaches of its own laws governing wages and control of workers: they were paying well over the odds for artisans' services. It was then decreed: 'No one is to hire masons, carpenters, daubers [plasterers] tilers or any other labourers otherwise than at the wages laid down by the Assize of the Common Council, on penalty of double payment of any such excess . . .', but this, like other demands, was ignored – property was booming and the developers (many of them the City's own *magnificos*) were not going to stop making money. There was another facet now discovered: bailiffs were also 'on the make' – 'WHEREAS MERCHANTS have been molested by bayliffs of the City sometimes eight days or more so that they could not unload their Goods . . . no-one shall be put in such manner that he cannot freely unload his goods. . . .' Clearly these minions of the City's laws were waiting for the *douceur* 'for the job'. In a 'free' society with low-paid custodians, fiddling had to be expected. The constables sometimes turned a blind eye even to serious offences: 'IF ANY MISDOER escape into a Church [for sanctuary] those who ought to have kept watch shall be answerable to the King for One Hundred Shillings.'

In 1327 Edward II was forced to abdicate, and a few months later he was atrociously murdered in Berkeley Castle, '. . . being smothered, and with a hotte broche putte thro the secret place posterialle . . .' – in plain English, a red-hot poker thrust up his anus, a piece of deliberate savagery against his homosexual behaviour, for which he has been much traduced. But he must be remembered with much gratitude for his compassion in opening two Lock Hospitals, one in Southwark for the treatment of women suffering from the *'morbis indecens ae cunniensis'*, otherwise the 'perilous disease of the brennynge' – syphilis, and the other, in Kingsland, for men suffering from the *'morbis turpis'* – gonorrhoea. Soon afterwards another women's hospital was opened in Knightsbridge.

His son, Edward III, clever, politically astute and realistic, his strong Plantagenet will modified by his great charm and *bonhomie*, held the respect of the baronage, the oligarchs and *hoi polloi*, particularly in London. His first act was to withdraw his father's *diktat* over London and not only to restore all its ancient privileges but to add a vital proviso, 'THAT THE LIBERTIES of the City of London shall not be taken into the hands of his Lordship the King for any personal Trespass or personal Judgement of any Officer of the City and no *Custos* [Warden] shall in the same such context be appointed.' From this time forth no whim of the ruler could override the City's rights, liberties and privileges. Moreover, no citizen could be compelled 'to go or be sent to war beyond the City'. It was also a tremendous blow against feudalism and feudalistic thinking which had always thwarted every attempt at public improvement.

Sexual freedom was the prerogative of royal and aristocratic circles, whose members could indulge their carnal wishes without much challenge, but still the less important were harassed, and women at the lowest end of the social scale, the poorest prostitutes, were hounded unmercifully. The situation was then summed up by the phrase

> Those who were riche were hangid by the Pursse:
> Those that were poore were hangid by the Necke!

The rolls of the City of London from 1338 onward give very many examples. In June William de Dalton, a member of the spicers' guild, was charged with 'keeping a house of ill fame in which married women and their paramours were wont to resort'. These would have been the sexually deprived wives of City worthies too busy with their trading to spare time to attend to their womenfolk's sexual needs; such establishments have a long history. However, William, being a person of consequence and a liveryman to boot, was sentenced to only two months.

Next month it was the turn of a cordwainer, Robert de Stratford, charged with 'harbouring Alice Donbelly and Alice Tredewedowe and other prostitutes'. He claimed his right to be tried by a jury according to the Law of London, was found guilty but only fined 6s. 8d.: the normal punishment should have been a carting, shorn hair and an hour in the pillory. The prostitutes' *noms de plume* are interesting: one 'gave her belly' and the other was a 'trade-widow' – whereas usually their surname was their town or village of origin.

During the Christmas junketings in 1339 Ellen de Evesham '. . . living in Flete Street was charged with keeping a Disorderly House harbouring theeves and prostitutes . . .'; in this case the offence was more serious because 'some foreigners' (strangers) went out of the house and attacked a passer-by, beat him up and took him back into the house, 'shee lighting their way with a candle in her hand', proving that she was an accomplice.

A fortnight later Gilbert le Strengmaker, living in the Hospital Rents in Flete Street, was charged with keeping 'a Disorderly House harbouring prostitutes and sodomites'. With him were charged Margery de Wantynge and Isabella de Actone, both living in the Chauncelereslane (Chancery Lane), and Joseph Sewy and his concubine, both living in 'Fayterslane [Fetter Lane] in the Rents of the Prior of Saint Marie Overy Southwarke'. St Mary's prior was clearly not worried about these venal sins committed on his property.

At the same sessions two prostitutes, the sisters Agnes and Juliana of Holborne, were charged with harbouring 'men of ill-fame' – sodomites; and Agnes, the widow of Robert-atte-Hale, was fined for 'lettynge her house in Sholane [Shoe Lane] to a woman of bad character'. Juliana-atte-Celere (Juliana in-the-cellar) and Alice de Lincolne, both of Cokkeslane, were charged with keeping a disorderly house in Hosier Lane. There were many Flemish, German and French whores in London, besides the many native ones who adopted foreign names – Juliana or Petronella or Clarice; Piers Plowman mentions 'Purnell [Petronella] of Cokkeslane' and 'Pernel the Flemish whore' and also 'Ionette [Janet] of the Stewes' on Bankside.

The City Fathers were now very worried about the increase of crime; taverns and brothels harboured and encouraged criminals of all descriptions. Ordinances were passed forbidding anyone of any condition, 'except the varlets of great lords carrying their master's swords or the serjeants-at-arms of the King, the Queen or their children', to go armed by day or night about the City. Hostellers and 'harbergeours' (inn-keepers and lodging-house-keepers) were to ensure that any guests 'leave their armes' before they left the premises. Powers were given to make 'citizen's arrests' of felons and wrongdoers. Even drawing a sword or a knife in public meant a fine of half a mark, or fifteen days in Newgate; if 'he draw blood', the fine was 20 shillings or forty days in Newgate. If anyone hit another with his fist, the fine was 3 shillings or eight days in prison; if blood was drawn, it was 40 pence or twelve days in prison. This was designed to stop hooliganism and assault.

A great round-up in all the wards was carried out in June 1340 against 'Evildoers and Disturbers of the King's Peace', and hundreds were caught in the net: '. . . as regards Cripplegate Ward Without . . . John Mazerer, Walter Kyng, Thomas *consanguinis* Litelwatte, Thomas *fitz* Simon, Nicholas de Westsmythfielde,

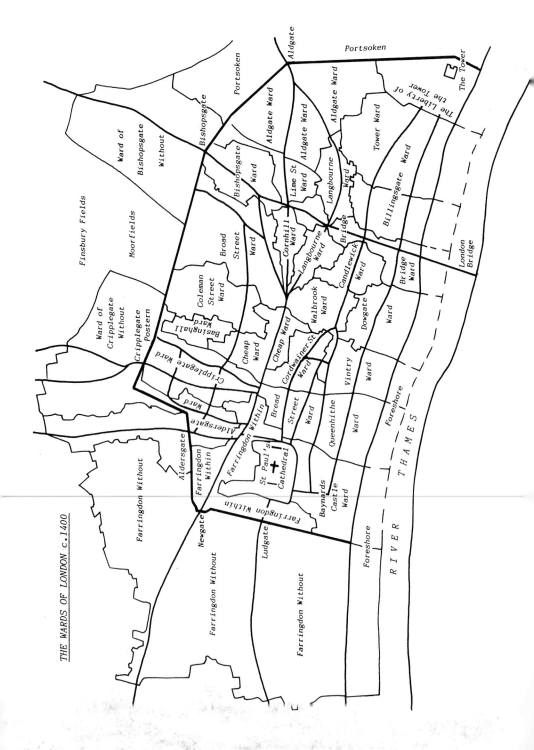

THE WARDS OF LONDON c.1400

Walter le Tyretener & John de Wantynge, are evildoers and nightwalkers and disturbers of the peace . . . John de Catton keepes a comon bawdy-house and John le Clerke is a receiver of Bawdes . . .'.

Margery de Wantynge's husband had been trapped far away from Fleet Street, and now a clergyman was involved with bawds. Then the jurymen in other wards considered local problems. Henri de Pountoys (Pontoise in France) and a brewer, Nicholas de Kent, were found to be receivers of 'men-of-ill-fame' in Aldersgate ward. Then the jurors considered the wards of the Tower, the Bridge and Billingsgate. Hugh de Staunton is exposed as visiting Alice de Stanewell's bawdyhouse, as also does Alice la Jueler (a player); Andrew and Beatrice Wrenne had wounded Alice le Shepster in the street outside their house of ill-fame. There is also a robber, Henry, 'late Keeper of Henry Combemartin's Wharf', who has stolen '22 pieces of Brass worth forty shillings' from William de Satnes, a potter. There is a French nobleman Sayer (Sieur) de Valoins (Valence), 'who prefers bad companie to goode' – although to a Frenchman visits to a whorehouse were normal avocations; he is dismissed with a caution, since he has committed no known offence under the City's laws.

Pick of the bunch are Agnes de Chedyngefielde and Clarice la Claterballock, both 'common whores' in Bridge ward: Clarice's speciality must excite some speculation as to her *modus operandi*. She was found guilty, but the jury 'made no presentment' against her.

Next come the malefactors in Broad Street ward. Jone la Tapstere (ale-housekeeper) and William atte Pond of a house of ill-fame called 'Atte the Pye on the Hope' in Abchurch Lane, which was also a brewhouse, are found guilty of keeping it as a brothel. John le Leche and Jon Albon (St Albans) are violent thieves, but their friend Thomas le Keu is a 'herberger' (lodging-house keeper) whose house is also a brothel 'in the Rents of the Abbot of St Albans'. Sarra le Mareshal's disorderly house was in the rents of the Archdeacon of Colchester. One of le Keu's gang was Master Gerard le Armourer, distinguished leader of an honourable guild, who supplied the gang with their swords and other weapons. One of these 'armed nightwalkers' was John le Keu: he and his servants had threatened the beadle of Aldgate ward because he had refused to open the gate at midnight. The jury noted the existence of some brothels, singling out 'Le Breggehouse' 'to which prostitutes re-sorted', and also the houses of Hugh le Peleter and John le Hosteler, the latter an innkeeper.

London: The Synfulle Citie

Simultaneously, at a meeting of the wardmote of Farringdon, Thomas de Hundesmor, 'living in the Rents of the Church of St John, Clerkenwell', was indicted as 'an armed Bully' and manager of a group of prostitutes. It was disclosed that, '. . . the male and female inhabitants of these disorderly houses committed assaults in consequence of whiche the Neighbours did not dare to come oute-of-doores at nyghte'.

In the whole tally there are men and women from country places far from London – Lincoln, Staunton, Houndsmoor, St Albans and many villages today unidentified, demonstrating that London was the magnet where sin was most profitable, for the distances were great and the journey was incredibly difficult and dangerous, yet thousands of women came to join the ranks of prostitutes, albeit many would have been innocents cozened into brothelry or concubinage by panders waiting at the termini.

Some of these London 'houses' must have been of considerable luxury, for those days, especially those visited by courtiers or London *magnificos*, by which term the aldermen and sheriffs were known. With their international connections they would have been foremost in discovering the latest female fashions in clothing and millinery to be immediately demanded by respectable ladies and damsels. *The Brut* (1345) inveighs against 'ladies . . . waerynge Foxetayles sewed wythynne to hide their arses'. Knighton's *Chronicle* talks of the knights and courtiers and their ladies at the tournaments, which by then had degenerated into circuses and booze-ups and occasions for picking up tarts and catamites: '. . . they dressed in a lascivious scurrilous and lubricious fashion with their breasts and bellies exposed down to the umbilicus . . .', adding, '. . . they were ladies from the more handsome and more beautiful class but not the better one . . .'.

In the midst of these junketings came the dreadful scourge of the Black Death, which lasted from 1348 to 1350. It was a form of bubonic plague imported by troops and camp-followers returning from abroad. The population of the country was reduced by a third, and the consequent great shortage of labour led to a new economic situation, where for the first time the labourer's services were being sought and the existence of villeinage, the basis of feudalism, was threatened. To meet this, the infamous statutes of Labourers was enacted in 1351 to restrain the upsurge of wages and to maintain the servitude of villeins. The Keepers of the Peace, an organization founded by Edward I, used the harshest measures to damp down the consequent unrest and violent crimes committed by the mass of returning soldiers. In London there had now grown

86

up a class of independent and semi-independent journeymen, who were wage-earners, and a growing class of small master-craftsmen, who were in fact paid employees of the wealthier guild masters. Parliament, which was still controlled by the major land-owners, strongly resisted any change, but the pressure of the great wrongs and unfairness was boiling up.

A host of prostitutes had also grown up, fed by thousands of indigent widows and girls. Things had so much deteriorated that in 1352 the mayor, Adam Francis, procured an Act of Parliament, again seeking control over City prostitution and repeating the ancient proscription, '. . . that no known Whore shoulde be so bold as to wear any Hood or Attire on her Head except ray [striped red cloth of diverse colours] . . .'. This proved just as ineffective as all previous injunctions.

As against this, in 1347 the King ordered that all leprous people be 'voided out' of the City into the fields, where he had built several extra Lock Hospitals, following his father's compassion, one at Stratford-atte-Bow and the other at Knightsbridge, 'west from Charringcross'. (Cnihtesbrigge has been known from 1042.)

In 1362 the *Eulagium* of the monks of Malmesbury contained a chapter headed 'MEN, LYONS in the Hal, HARES in the ffeildes . . . in this yere . . . Englishe Menne have gone starke madde over fashyons in Dresse . . . when their Backes are turned you thinke they are Women . . . they weare smal hoodes fastened at the Chinne . . . with a Latchet in their Jackets called *a harlotte* . . .'.

However, that year, 1362, was momentous for quite another reason: parliament was for the first time opened by a speech in English, the historian Massingham writing

> Lerid and lewed [the learned and ignorant]
> Olde and yonge
> Al understanden
> Englisshe Tongue.

Thenceforth all court pleadings and judgments were to be in that tongue.

Despite all injunctions, threats and cajolings, sin thrived in the City. In November 1364 Joan atte Grene, having been found guilty, 'gave an oath' that henceforth she would not keep her house as a brothel. In March 1366 Zenobius Martyn was charged as a 'comon bawd' and associate of prostitutes, but he pleaded that he was a 'Flemynge' and he had a 'lodgyng-howse for aliens' to which whores were admitted; nor was he a freeman of the City. It transpired that there were quite a number of such refuges, usually run by one of their own nationals.

In the higher sphere the King had become a senile widower, besotted with his young mistress, Alice Perrers, who '. . . interfered muche in publick affaires and was profligate with power and money, acting in every way as if she were a Queene'. She aroused great resentment, especially when, in 1375, 'Dame Alice Perrers the Kings concubine, as *Lady of the Sunne* rode from the Tower through Chepe accompanied by manie Lordes and Ladyes, every Lady leading a Lorde by his horses bridle until they came to Smithfeilde and then began a Greate Jouste which endured seven Dayes . . .'. As the King lay dying, in 1377, she stripped the rings off his fingers and seized whatever money and valuables were available, but she had made so many enemies that she was banned from Court, stripped of her title as Lady Windsor and all her property and was lucky to escape with her life.

7 Wo was Than the Gentilman?

The accession of the boy Richard II in 1377 played into the hands of Parliament, the great lords (by then known as 'peers of the realm') and the oligarchs of the City, the latter quick to demand full powers over their ancient *bête-noire* the borough of Southwark. Their reason was purely commercial: tradesmen and artificers on the south bank were able to undercut prices because they were free of guild restrictions. The poor and the dispossessed were, as usual, disregarded by all the major players, who were, however, fearful of the effect of John Wycliffe's teachings and the revolutionary exhortations of the defrocked priest John Ball, calling for equality under the slogan 'Whan Adam dalf and Eve span, Wo was thanne the gentilman?'

The King's accession was greeted by a marvellous pageant and tournament on London Bridge. The bridge was cleared for 'the son of the Black Prince'. 'One hundred and thirty Citizens with innumerable Trumpetts, Sackbuts, Cornetts and Wax lights, rode from Newgate thorough Chepe over the bridge to Suthwarke to meet the yonge Prince with several Earls and forty-eight Esquires, and forty-eight Knights, and one arrayed as an Emperour richly arrayed . . . they gave a Bowl and Cup and a Ring of Gold to his Mother and to the Lordes each a Gold Ring. . . .'

Richard's advisors were his uncles, Thomas, Duke of Gloucester, and John, Duke of Lancaster – better known as 'John of Gaunt', the richest and most powerful man in the kingdom, the first of whose actions was the institution of a poll tax of one groat (4 pence), the first tax on persons as against taxes on property, and a flat rate, manifestly unfair considering the immense gulf between the landless peasant and the greatest lords. It was quickly dropped and in the following year replaced by a graduated tax from a groat for the poorest up to vast sums for the wealthy. This was impossible to put into operation against the opposition of the City guilds-

England's first revolutionary, John Ball preaching before 1380 that all men were equal, and calling upon them to organize against their oppressors. The result was Wat Tyler's rebellion.

men and the great lords, so that in 1381 it was fixed at a rate of 3 groats a head, leaving it to each village to charge the poor less than the rich. Where everyone was poor, all had to pay the full rate! There was widespread evasion: females 'disappeared' from the lists.

By March 1381 the government, aghast at 'the shameless negligence and corruption of the collectors', sent special officials round. The harsh actions of these new 'collectors' fomented the famous rebellion headed by Wat Tyler of Kent and Jack Straw of Essex. On the evening of 12 June no fewer than 60,000 'Men of Essex' were outside the City gate at Mile End, what time some 50,000 Kentish men were encamped on the Black Heath.

Long before then the Londoners had hated John of Gaunt – not the least of whose possessions were eighteen whorehouses on Bankside – and as early as 1376 (*vide* Stow), 'The Citizens of London minded to destroy John of Gaunt . . . they sought him upp and downe . . . without the Gate there were infinite numbers swearing this day might be his last . . . he was at meat . . . but leapt so hastily he hurt his leg and would not drincke Wine for haste . . . he fled oute of a back-gate . . . never stayed rowing till they came to a howse near Kennington when he went to make complaint to King Richard. . . .' The most graphic account of the current situation is in *Piers Plowman*:

> The neediest are our neighbours . . .
> Prisoners in the dungeons
> The poore in their cottage
> With a crewe of children
> With a Landlords rent.
> What they will win with their spinning
> To satisfy their babies
> They must spend on the Rent
> And themselves suffer hunger . . .
>
> Pittiful it is to read the cottage woman's woe,
> Ashamed to begg, ashamed to let the Neighbours know!

London was caught in this great rebellion. After killing the tax collector in Maidstone, this motley collection of villeins, cottars, dispossessed peasants, small tradesmen, out-of-work archers and soldiers marched on London, on the way releasing the preacher John Ball from Rochester Castle, 'despoylinge the brothels on Bankside', looting Winchester House and releasing the prisoners in the Clink. They were welcomed 'with open arms by the comons of Suthwerke', and the gate of London Bridge was opened to them by Alderman John Sybyle, fishmonger, and Alderman John Horne, draper. One of the brothels they had destroyed was 'The Rose', owned by William Walworth, lord mayor of London. The rest is history: Wat Tyler was killed at Smithfield, and his followers were hunted down and destroyed like vermin – there were so many severed heads that they had to be distributed around because the spikes on the Bridge Gate were overfull.

The next mayor was Sir John de Northampton, master of the guild of drapers, one of whose first acts was to order the constables and beadles 'to roam the streets and arrest Nyghtwalkyng women'. There was a certain venality about this because, as a contemporary recorded, '. . . such women as were neither handsome nor rich enough to bribe his officers, were carted through the streets in great pomp with their hair shorn, and trumpets and

Wat Tyler's rebels burning the Priory of St John in Clerkenwell in 1381. The prior, Robert atte Hale, was deemed to be a particular enemy.

pipes playing . . . although this was contrary to the Bishop's command . . .'.

In the round-up John Kempe and Isabella Smythe were taken in adultery, their heads shaven, and they were publicly paraded 'with pipers and trumpetts and papers on their heads 'and put into the Tun on Cornhill. But by this action Sir John had 'sett at naught the prerogative' of the bishop of London over 'breaches of chastity'. Worse still, he had incurred the bitter enmity of the fishmongers, having persuaded the King to abrogate their monopoly to fix the price of fish. This had made him popular with the poor, but in 1382, when the fishmongers' Alderman Nicholas Brembre had him arraigned 'for treason' (he had been a supporter of Wat Tyler), he was sentenced to 'perpetual imprisonment and confiscation of his goods and chattels'. Three years later the political wheel had changed: Brembre was indicted for 'fomenting a great riot in the Guildhall' and hanged. Sir John was completely rehabilitated and later elected MP to the 'Merciless Parliament' of 1388 (which almost deposed the King). He was back again on his old 'purity' tack.

From 1384 a series of wardmotes had indicted '. . . certain men and women as Common Whoremongers and Common Adulterers, Common Bawds and Common Courtezans and Common Scoldes . . . all to be removed from the City TO THE PLEASING OF GOD and the Cleanness and Honesty of the City. . . . Henceforth any Person of such evil and wicked life . . . shall be taken to prison until cleared . . .'.

An ordinance regarding male whoremongers instructed that, 'Let all his head and beard be shaved except for a fringe on his head two inches in breadth . . . taken to the pillory with minstrels and set thereon . . . at the discretion of the mayor. . . .' For a second offence there was an extra ten days imprisonment; for a third, 'multiple punishment and expulsion through one of the Gates'. Similarly with a female, except that the 'thew' was substituted for the pillory. Her hair would be 'cut about her head' and she would be taken to Aldgate, '. . . wearing a hood of ray, holding a peeled white Rod . . . with minstrels proclaiming cause . . . marched through the Chepe and through Newgate to Cokkeslane there to take up her abode'.

'Common brawlers' were to be taken with a 'dystaff with Towen' (a distaff dressed with a wad of flax) held in the hand, and led 'with minstrels to the *thew*'. The minstrelsy was the means to attract a large crowd who could be guaranteed to pelt the offenders with dirt, dung and stones all the way, to express their disgust – or rather to enjoy some other poor wight's misfortune.

Then there were a series of complicated proscriptions aimed at the carnal copulations of priests with married and single women and nuns – all described as 'adulteresses', the penalties being harsher than for plain fornication. All these had to be indicted at the Guildhall and then put in one of the sheriffs' compters after a parade with minstrels through the Chepe.

This obsession with carnal copulation resulted in the re-enactment of an Ordinance of Edward II, 'As to the Sale of Fish and the Dress of Common Women':

> WHEREAS the common lewd Women dwelling in the City have of late . . . assumed the fashion of being clad and attired in the manner . . . of good and noble Dames and Damsels of the Realm . . . IT IS ORDERED . . . that no such woman shall be attired by Day or Night in any kind of Vesture trimmed with *Miniver*, Badger, Squirrel . . . or lined with Cendal, Bokerames, Samytes or any other Noble lining, NOR YET be clothed . . . in Coates Surcoates or Hood relieved with such fur or lining, ON PAIN OF FORFEITING the said Vestments . . . to the end that all folks shall know what rank they are.

This was hard lines on the wives and daughters of the rich London merchants 'on the way up' aping the dress and manners of the nobility. Prostitutes anyway had to wear striped materials. Like all previous ordinances, this was ignored by the women: for centuries the fashions of the unchaste had been the forerunners of the chaste.

In this connection there is the case of Elizabeth Moring, who in July 1385, under the guise of 'the Craft of Broiderie', was inciting her 'apprentice's to consort 'with friars and chaplains and all such men as desired their company', for sums agreed on in advance. It all came to light when she sent 'little Johanna' to a customer to stay all night: when the child returned empty-handed, 'she used words of reproof' and told her to go back next night 'and see what she could acquire' in addition to the fee. Next morning Johanna '. . . arose from the chaplain's bed and beynge afrayde to go back withoute carrynge somethynge to hir' stole a breviary, which Elizabeth sold for 8 pence 'to a man unknown'. 'And manie other tymes . . . this Elizabeth received the like base gaynes from the sayde Johanna and her other sewynge women . . . she beynge herselfe a comon harlot and procuress . . . lyvynge abominably and damnably.' She was sent to prison, but the chaplain's name is never mentioned. If she had not incited the girl to thievery, she could have carried on indefinitely, for no 'man of God' was going to split on her.

Again the mayor returned to this plague of lust, with 'Regulations as to Street-walkers by Nyghte & Women of Ill-repute'. Only lawful citizens of good repute carrying a light could go 'abroad' after 9 p.m.; no 'alien' (non-resident) could be out after 8 p.m.; all because of 'broyles and affrays and murders caused by . . . those consorting with comon harlots at taverns and other places of ill repute and more especially through Flemish women who profess and follow such shameless and dolourful life'. Additional precautions against assault and battery included a strong warning to 'hostellers' about any man or woman of bad repute. One Henry de Palyngetone was set upon by a gang of hooligans and 'beaten, wounded, imprisoned and maltreated' in a house in Fleet Street, and goods worth £100 were stolen. Fleet Street was then 'in the suburbs', and it transpired that it was within the liberty of St Martin-le-Grand, so that the City had no jurisdiction *de jure*; it took two years to persuade the King's marshal to surrender his rights and allow the City to proceed with the prosecution of the assailants.

Any prostitute found wandering would be liable to forfeit her 'upper garment and her hood . . . every officer and serjeant shall have power to take such garments . . . to the Guildhall and shall be given the lower half for their trouble'. It would thus seem that the woman would have to walk away naked, which would have been yet another offence! However, it was then admitted that all these regulations had been disregarded for years – 'No correccion hath hitherto been made', a sure sign that the constables, beadles and serjeants had all had their palms greased.

But even the scions of the nobility were castigated, because, '. . . they displayed their legs in tight hosen radiant in colours coats of rich materials with sleeves slod upon ye earth [scraping the ground] and long pointed shoes, *harlottys*, with golden chaines to the waist . . . and costly jewelry . . .'.

There were other troubles. The Black Death and Wat Tyler's rebellion had wrought great changes amongst peasants and working men. Despite the repressions, artisans and journeymen had even 'struck' to secure higher wages and better conditions. John Wycliffe commented that, 'Men of sutel [skilled] craft as Free Masons and others conspire together that . . . none other than their own shall work at the craft', and moreover they would do nothing to prejudice their workmates even by doing other types of work, '. . . even though he might make his master gain twenty pounds!'

Working people also had more time on their hands, as witness

Parliament's moan in 1389 that, 'Artificers and labourers and grooms and servants keep greyhounds & other dogs & when good Christian folk be at church on Sundays and Holy Days these others disport themselves hunting in parks, warrens and coneyries of their Lords. . . .'

The endless wars had created rich wool-cloth merchants, army contractors and financiers. Huge imports of luxury goods, mainly for the wives and daughters of the burgeoning middle class, were creating other difficulties. Great guild masters were now employing small masters, selling the products at large profits. This was causing rifts within the guilds, the governing still being conducted by the 'wealthy, sadde and discreet men' to the disadvantage of the small men. This manifested itself by increasing unrest amongst the apprentices, who could see their eventual masterships and independence disappearing; street rioting became frequent. Commercial morality also plunged to ever lower depths.

Langland, in his *Piers Plowman*, bemoans this development. He commenced:

> First I learnt to lie and page or two of lies,
> then to weigh false was my second lesson.

A draper taught him

> How to draw the edges out of Flannel
> so that it might seem longer.

He describes how he bought barley to be brewed into 'penny ale' to sell to ignorant labourers, although it was displayed as 'Best Ale', and short-measure was given in the cups. He learnt how to 'mix merchandise to make a fine array' with the inferior items displayed inside the shop in 'poor light'. Finally he learnt how to clip coins, 'paring the heaviest'; the clippings, when melted down, were sold 'under the counter' to goldsmiths. In all, says Langland,

> They that bake and brew, butchers and cooks
> They are the people that harm the poor
> who can but buy in pennyworths.

> And privily and oft they poison them,
> They grow rich by retailing what the poor must eat,
> They buy houses, they become landlords –
> If sold honestly they could not build so high
> Nor buy their tenements.

Mayors and their Officers, the King's go-betweens
Charged, between King and Commons, to keep the Law –
These they should punish in Pillories and Stocks!

In Lothburie, the braziers (brassfounders) made 'good gold out of brass candelsticks making themselves richer than the Goldsmiths of Cheapside', and indeed, 'There were reputable Goldsmiths not averse to selling lower-grade gold.' Also, by its proximity to the Bordhawe, 'Lothburie was a sanctuary for Wenches and Souldiers' – a dangerous place for attacks and affrays. In 1340, after a bloody affray between skinners and fish-mongers, two men were hanged 'at the Standard in the Chepe'.

Pressure on space compelled the Common Council in 1394 to create an extension to Farringdon ward outside the City wall, this henceforth to be called 'Farringdon *Extra*'. 'Farringdon *Infra*', the only ward to be named after an individual, was so-called after Alderman William Farringdon, goldsmith, immensely wealthy and influential – and, incidentally, a grandson of Thomas Farring-don who had supported Wat Tyler's original manifesto. The new ward covered a huge area, stretching down to the Thames, along Grays Inn Road and Chancery Lane to the Temple, and including the ancient soke of Clerkenwell and Turnmill Street. For the next 200 years it was 'all that lordship of Lecherie, its length and breadth!'.

Richard's closing years were full of trouble. He antagonized the Londoners by brutally suppressing the Lollards; his crowning folly came, after the death of uncle John of Gaunt in 1399 ('of putrefac-tion of the genitalls due to overmuch carnal copulation' – 'a euphemism for third-degree syphilis), seizing his vast estates, thereby earning the hatred of his cousin Henry, Earl of Hereford and now Duke of Lancaster, who brought him down, imprisoned him in the Tower, forced him to abdicate and had him 'done to death' in Pontefract Castle soon afterwards.

Richard's successor was his cousin Henry (Henry IV), whose reign initiated almost a century of alarums and excursions, before the Plantagenet dynasty met its end, but in the main London and the Londoners were able to get on with their lives without too much hindrance. One of the new King's first actions was to give an immense banquet 'with Mummers' to which he invited not only the mayor and the aldermen but their wives 'and their sons' – it was reported to have been 'an uneasy occasion' because of the manner in which the previous King had been disposed of.

One of the first improvements was in the water supply:

drinking-water had first been brought into London in 1285 in wooden pipes all the way from St James' to the Great Standard in the Chepe; in 1401 the ancient prison, the Tun on Cornhill, was converted into a 'conduit' (a water tower) where it was 'encisterned'. The water was then sold by water-carriers from large jugs carried on a pole; some years later this was modernized into two men carrying a large wooden barrel with a tap so that the water could be measured out accurately.

Five years later one Richard Whittington was elected mayor, but the great rejoicings were ruined by the onset of a 'dreadful pestilence' – probably smallpox, which was endemic and cost the lives of some 30,000 inhabitants.

The inhabitants' quiet life was interrupted one morning in 1410 when

> The king's sons, Thomas and Henry caused a riot at three o'clock in the morning of the Feast of St John the Baptist in the East Chepe. Their armed retainers fought drunkenly with the retinues of other courtiers. It took the Mayor and the Sheriffs and their Constables more than a hour to break it up . . . which made the Malefactors highly moved against the City. . . . They were summoned before Lord Chief Justice William Gascoyne, they asserting 'that it was not all their fault because they had maintained the Peace under the Law' . . . whereupon the King remitted all his ire.

This did little to create confidence in the King's justice, especially when soon afterwards these sons rose against their father, when the Londoners were called upon to come to his aid. In 1413 the elder came to the throne on his father's death as Henry V, 'a lawless and disreputable youth' and warlike man whose exploits abroad are enshrined in England's history; but he managed to find time the following year to put down a Lollard revolt in London, mercilessly hunting down the 'rebels' to extinction. That year, 1414, was also marked by the King's writing for the first time to 'Oure Worshipful the Lorde Maire', officially establishing this usage from that time forward.

He also found time in 1417 to promulgate 'before an immense multitude of Commoners' an 'ORDINANCE FOR THE ABOLITION OF STEWES WITHIN THE CITY . . . against the manie Grievance, Abhominations, Damages Disturbances, Murders, Homicides, Larcenies and other common Nuisances . . .', which certainly demonstrates that there had been a serious breakdown in law and order within the City. Forty years of war and civil unrest had caused a great upsurge, '. . . wherein lewd Men and Women of Evill life . . . as well Wives, Sons, Daughters, Apprentices and

Servants of reputable City Men . . . were oftentimes resorting to the Stewes . . . all such . . . except honest hot baths are banned . . .'.

Things came to a head in 1420, when Sir Robert Wattes, chaplain to the mighty fishmongers' guild '. . . was taken in adultery with Alice Soureby . . . in the stewes neare St Magnus' church at the Bridge entrance . . .'. Simultaneously many other reverend gentlemen were taken in stewehouses in Billingsgate and Queenhithe; it was reported that none of these stewes had been run by 'Froes of Flaundres'. These latter ladies were acknowledged as the best in the profession, running efficient and luxurious 'bordels' as in their homeland, where brothelry had long been recognized and tolerated as a way of life. Contemporary literature often says of husbands that, '. . . they were wont to go to the whorehouse in the evening' – a sort of club with trimmings. These houses were also deemed to be more hygienic and less likely to spread the 'French Pox' or the lesser 'pox'. Continental Catholicism regarded this as an acceptable way of life, so that it is curious that the English co-religionists thought it abhorrent.

However, the ordinance of 1417 sheds a fresh light on this 'menace' – these brothels were meeting-houses for the growing number of political dissenters bred by the breakdown in law and order due to the everlasting wars causing starvation and misery amongst the poor. Another factor was the great preponderance of women after the carnage amongst menfolk in the Crusades and the dynastic struggles. Prostitution was the only way out for thousands of widows and daughters.

In 1420 it was decided to take vigorous measures to ensure physical cleanliness in the City: inspectors made a sweep through every ward. The reports were depressing: no ward got a clean bill.

In the Vintry, Master Skinner John Welles threw filth and pushed it under the house of Master Skinner John Mildenhall.

In Dowgate, Ebbgate Lane was stopped with filth, and the public highway Ermenterslane also and the stairway to the Thames was broken, so that none could go down to get water. Wolsey Lane was stopped with filth from the privies on either side, '. . . so that none could avoid stepping into it'. (Ebbgate had been stopped up since 1306.)

In Hayswharflane fullers washed their cloth, so that none could draw water or do their easements, 'to the great nuisance of the commonalty'.

In Bread Street ward the dunghills on both sides of the common privy door were 'defective'.

Farringdon received the most censure:

The comon prevy at Ludgate is defective and perilous and the ordure thereof rotteth the stone wall and maketh an orrible stench and a foul sight . . . it is a disgrace to the City that so foul a nuisance should be . . . though often [complained about] no remedy hath yet been ordeyned . . . the Dungyll within the Temple Gate encumbers the high waie.
   They made stricture upon William Emery for laying Dung in the high waie all through the year and for casting out hot pisse that had stoode under his horse a month so that no man can pass there for the styngle [pungent stink].

Further investigation then uncovered moral filth in addition. At Temple Gate they indicted John White the carpenter and his wife, '. . . for being as Common Bawds as any in all London and being receivers of Strumpettes: although they have twice been indicted . . . yett no execution hath been levelled . . .'. The reason was not far to seek: John White was a liveryman and common councillor.
   In Queenhithe, '*The Pye* [tavern] was a privy place for theeves . . . where many bargains were struck . . . many Strumpettes and Pimps have covert there.'
   Strong criticism is levelled against Crepelgate ward, where they indicted '. . . Gerard Clayson and his wife of *Le Stewehouse* in Grubbe Street, as evill-doers and receivers and maintainers of harlotrie and bawderies . . . of horrible life . . . keeping Strumpettes and other malefactors . . .'. [These latter probably sodomites.] 'Adam Remy and Richard Kere are not only usurers but their wives are common Bawds, keeping a stewehouse there.'
   Then they presented, in Wood Street ward, '. . . John Sherman, Cooper, for kepynge Duckes to the nuisance of his neighbours; and also John Rich, the Carter and Brewer, because the wheeles of his cart have iron strakes which destroy the pavement and make a great noise when the cart is loaded with barrels . . . and the Wood Street *Stewehouse* is a nuisance because it is a common house of Harlotry, a great resort of theeves and Preestes and their Concubines . . . likewise the privy is a nuisance because of great corruption . . .'.
   They went on to condemn more and more 'previes' which dammed the common watercourse into the City ditch near the Moor – 'on the back of which the privies of John Brynkele the Goldsmith and Thomas Lucas, the Grocer rested' and stopped the flow, 'causing an overflow when there was a flood of rainwater'. Clearly the gong-farmers, although highly paid, never did a

thorough job. Pyssynge Alley (later Chick Lane) and Shitebourn Lane (later gentrified to Sherborne Lane) also received due mention.

It was confirmed that, '. . . manie of these houses belong . . . to Aldermen and substantial Commoners', who were now urged not to keep such places, 'because of the horrible damage and scandal to the reputation of the City . . . for the trifling Gains made by letting these houses . . .'. Parliament wanted to know how it came about '. . . that divers personnes of ryghte greate povertie and dissolute . . . have come suddenlie to gete richesse [buying large properties such as taverns and hostelries] . . . recettynge Theves commune Women and other Misdoers and [reaching positions of authority] . . . able to sway the course of Justice . . . manie are ffrensshemen, Piccardes and Flemynges . . .'.

It is about this time too that a very ancient centre of sin comes into the news. Shortly after the Norman Conquest three windmills for the grinding of corn were erected alongside 'the River of the Wells' (the Fleet), and the track on the river bank from Cow Lane to Clerkenwell Green became known as Trimillelane. It was a thoroughfare serving the splendid houses of rich London merchants whose gardens ran down to the river – a very salubrious address, just outside the wall but within easy reach of the businesses in the City.

However, by 1290 they had succeeded in damming the river 'with the filth and ordure and rubbage heedlesslie into the streame' so that there was 'a noysome stynke and other inconveniences', so it was now demoted to 'Turnmill brook'. In 1399 Henry IV ordered that it '. . . be cleansed anew and called uppon certayne Persons . . . to repayre a stone brydge over the Flete neare unto Trymylstreate'. This was the forerunner of the Holeburne Bridge which was later to link the two halves of Farringdon ward.

Since the City authorities were pressing hard on prostitution inside the walls, there had been an exodus of 'unseemlie' characters into Trillmillestreete area. *The Chronicle of London* for October 1415 recorded that, 'William the Parchmentmaker . . . harboured in his house Syr John Oldcastle (the Goode Lorde Cobham) . . . and was drawen and hangid and hys hedde smytten off and sette vpon London brygge for tretory [treason]. . . .'

The ordinance of 1417 'Against Harbouring Vicious Persons' was followed in 1422 by one for 'The Abolition of Stewes within the City'. It transpired that Trimillstreet was actually within the soke of the King of Scotland, so there was no bar to this new industry – it became the centre of crime and prostitution for centuries to come.

About the only endearing aspect of the street is the inability of its chroniclers over the centuries to decide how to spell its name – in fact, Three Mill Street became Turnmill Street, even Turnbull Street! Its activities were in full swing in 1519, when Cardinal Wolsey, '. . . raided houses in Tyrmyl strete . . . [including] *Ye Cocke in ye Tyrmill* in Cock Alley', which was already ancient and still in existence in 1651.

What was more worrying was the dramatic increase in crime. There were reported 'gangs of hooligans who demand money with menaces from the poore washerwomen who tyme oute of mynde have fetched and taken their water and wasshed clothes and done other thynges for theyre owne needes'.

Two of the worst areas were Love Lane, near the Guildhall and the Poultry, brothel areas from time immemorial, where there were constant disturbances. An Italian visitor remarked: 'It hath often been seen in England that three or four theeves, for poverty, have sett upon six or seven true men and have robbed them all . . . there be more men hanged in England for robbery and manslaughter than in all Fraunce . . . the English man is of another courage for if he be poore and seeth an other man have riches which might be taken from him by might, he will not spare to do so.'

Suddenly in August 1422 Henry V died and once more a child, Henry VI, was the heir, under the tutelage of his uncle Humphrey, the 'Good Duke' of Gloucester, as 'Protector of the Realm'. Gloucester was well known and popular with the Londoners, not the least because in his own liberty of Baynards Castle near Ludgate was the row of tolerated brothels known as 'Duke Humphrey's Rents'. The youngster was not crowned until November 1429. He turned out to be a feeble, vacillating ruler in a long reign disturbed by unceasing wars and dissensions.

As regards sin, the justices of the peace were directed to make a sweep of 'untrewe lyvers' in the City. The following year '. . . in harvest tyme weren two bawdes sett upon ye pillorie and three Strumpettes held in New Gate . . . [there must be] noo moor comyn wythynne ye walles . . .'. On the other hand, Magdalen Johnson of Queenhithe '. . . swore that her stewes was respectable and shee would nott allow anie prostitution, adulterie or fornication to take place there', in proof whereof '. . . an eminent Skinner stood suretie for Ten Poundes', a very considerable sum.

A month later, in the Bordhawe, 'One Margaret procured a younge girl, Isobel Lane . . . for a certayne Lombard and other unknowne men, who deflowered her agaynste her wille. She then sent Margaret over to the Stewes for immoral purposes . . . she

The Guildhall as it appeared about 1420, after rebuilding by Lord Mayor Thomas Knoles in 1414.

tooke Joan Makelyn to a house in Colemanstreete where a certayne Lombard gave her twelve Pence for her wycked and unlawfull behaviour. [She gave Margaret 4 pence out of that and in turn Joan sent Margaret] . . . to a verie prodigall Venetian. . . .' It was also disclosed that 'manie protestitutes and comon procureurs' were operating in the Tower ward.

Homosexuality, although rife, was very seldom reported. One of the earliest references to it was in February 1445, when 'George Fynes, Esquier was put into Newgate because for more than four years he had encouraged open fornication and detestable lyffe with men . . . in his howse. . . .' Mr Fynes, being a gentleman and thus a person of repute, refused to plead or seek bail and was remanded to the sheriff's custody. His silence was clearly because he would not implicate City worthies who availed themselves of his services.

The King now showing signs of the mental instability which was to dog him for the rest of his life, political matters began to get out of hand. In London the fishmongers and drapers wrestled for power, hoping to gain influence by deeds of charity, after Dick Whittington's example. Of the most meritorious were those of the mayor, John Reinwell, fishmonger, who built fifteen tenements for the poor, and Ralph Holland, a sheriff and mercer, who gave £120 for the relief of 'poore impotent persons', £80 to 'prisoners in neede' and a further £20 to hospitals. In 1431 John Welles, mayor and grocer, 'erected the Standard in the West Chepe' which was later to be a place of execution, and in 1438, 'a tyme of greate Famine', the mayor, Stephen Brown, grocer, bought from his own pocket '. . . large quantities of rye from Prussia and sold it cheapley to the populace . . . which did great relief'.

One of the greatest philanthropists was Alderman Philip Malpass, sheriff in 1439. In 1448 he was deposed by the Common Council '. . . because he had been appointed by the King and not by the Council'. Earlier, in 1440, he had forced his way '. . . into the sanctuary of St Martin-le-Grand and seized five men whom he had led fettered to the Compter, thence chained by the Neckes to Newgate'. Complaint being made to the King, these men were released into sanctuary, but Malpass was unrepentant.

In 1449 came Jack Cade's 'rebellion' which was supported by many of the gentry and City grandees – even mayors and constables in the counties. Cade, a young Irishman living then in Maidstone, marched on London as 'Capteyn' of an army of disgruntled peasants, dispossessed yeomen and ex-soldiers from Henry's wars, unpaid and unpensioned. They had no manifesto but wanted 'the removal of certayne traytors having too much influence'. It was a time of great social unrest throughout the country. On their march they looted Winchester House, released the prisoners in the Clink, burned down all the Bankside whore-houses and 'reviled the women'. On 2 July the mayor convoked the Common Council to stop the rebels, but sentiment was with the rebels, and the Bridge Gate was opened. However, after a few days in London the rebels' discipline began to crack and they began to lose public support through drinking and looting and bad behaviour. Cade 'invited himself' into Philip Malpass' great mansion

'The Green Gates', dined well and then 'spoyled his host of muche goods to great value'.

The mayor, with Matthew Gough, keeper of the Tower, organized a citizen force but it was defeated on the bridge, 'many citizens slain or drowned' and Gough losing his life. They later regrouped, and after an all-night fight the Kentish men had to give way. William Waynflete, Bishop of Winchester, arranged 'a General Pardon', and the rebels marched away. Then the King offered a reward of 1,000 marks for Cade, 'dead or alive'. Cade was captured alive and conveyed to London '. . . in a cart, but died on the way. His naked body was exposed all day, then beheaded, quartered and the remains put on a hurdle, paraded around Southwark and the City. Then the head was stuck on London Bridge and the four quarters sent to Blackheath, Gloucester, Norwich and Salisbury for public exhibition. His followers were mercilessly hunted down. . . .' If anything, it demonstrated how wide had been these rebels' support.

As to Malpass, on his decease he gave '. . . £125 to the poor prisoners in the jails: and every year for five years 403 shirts and smocks, 40 pairs of sheets and 150 gowns of frieze, to the poor. 100 marks to poor maydes' marriages, 100 marks to making highways and to 500 poor people in London every one six shillings and eightpence . . .'.

In August 1453 King Henry 'fell into a state of imbecility', and the long trauma of the Wars of the Roses began. In March 1461 the 'Yorkist' Edward, Earl of March, entered London and was acclaimed by the citizens as Edward IV, but Henry was 're-invested with his crown' in late 1470. In May the following year Edward's forces overcame all resistance, seized Queen Margaret and imprisoned Henry in the Tower. But the Londoners could not yet rejoice.

Thomas Neville, bastard son of the mighty Earl of Kent and popularly known as 'the Bastard Fauconbridge', 'came up the river with a great navie' to rescue Henry VI. Landing at Southwark, he was refused permission to cross the bridge, the mayor stating that '. . . hee wulde holde London onlie for King Edward'. He ordered 'the bankes to be strengthened . . . payles and water and bowles for threwynge on anie fyres the Rebells myghte starte'. The rebels set fire to the gate, the flames 'spread like wildfire over the bridge'. Fauconbridge and his 5,000 men were repulsed 'with great slaughter by the trained bands of London', and in due course, 'Thomas Fauconbridge hys hedde was yesterdaye sett upon London brydge lookynge into Kentward.'

Thomas Neville, the 'Bastard Fauconbridge' being repulsed at the Great Gate of London Bridge in 1471. His head was later spiked over the gate.

King Henry was murdered on 21 May in the Tower. Edward knighted 'a whole host of citizens for their support'.

From time to time the Common Council tried to improve the gaol arrangement dealing with malefactors in the City. The very earliest were the sheriffs 'compters in Bread Street, the Poultry and Wood Street, and the sheriffs' own mansions, to which debtors and minor offenders went to pay their amercements. The earliest on record is that in Bread Street from about 1180, but at times it seems that the Wood Street compter was the most important. By City ordinance they were to be 'farmed out' to porters (keepers) or other sheriff's officials, but later the sheriff had to bear the charges for rent and candles.

Prisoners in a 'compter' in Edward I's time '. . . were to pay nothing . . . for one night except only one Penny for the first night . . . [but if they preferred to stay rather than go to Newgate] then for their comfort pay to the Sheriff Fourpence, sixpence, eightpence or twelvepence per week towards the rent of such House and no more . . . [he can] have his own bed there if he has one . . . if not the Porter to find him a bed, taking each Night one Penny as in a Lodging-house . . .'. Any victuals, bread, ale, charcoal, firewood could be supplied 'only by due measure and a reasonable price' – the offending official being liable to a fine or imprisonment. The differences for accommodation referred to 'the Masters' Side' and 'the Knights' Side' down to the ghastly 'hole' for the penniless. There was no distinction as to sex, although as a rule women were sent to the Tun on Cornhyll, later to Newgate. Disputes between tradesmen were also held in one of the compters in the earliest times.

About 1450 new regulations were made for Newgate and Ludgate, following 'greate wrongs and *misprisions* done by Jailers . . . to the grievous impoverishment of the poor lieges of the King'. Henceforth it was ordained that, '. . . no Prisoner . . . shall pay any money for the lamps or for any bed . . . all Prisoners shall pay the Gaolers fourpence and no more for his fee, except treason or felony . . . No person . . . to be chastised and punished shall pay anything [except] as aforesaid and if any Gaolers, Officers or Servants shall take money contrary to this ordinance . . . he shall lose office without restitution and pay Ten times and much as he has taken, one half to the Chamber [and] the other half to him at whose suit he shall be attainted [charged]'. However, gaolers were entitled '. . . to take sureties from prisoners . . . for 100 shillings . . . they can charge for removing *Irons* [handcuffs] Leg-irons [fetters] . . .', which latter were known as 'the Widows Alms' in the Bread Street compter.

Edward IV, having secured his kingdom through rivers of blood, now set out to popularize himself with the rulers of London, masking his cruelty and treachery with an outward *bonhomie* which particularly endeared him to womenfolk. He was 'a masterful voluptuary' and boasted that he had three concubines, 'one the merieste, another the wilieste and the thirde the holieste harlotte in the realme'. The merriest, Jane Shore, is the only one who figures in history, and although she was hounded and vilified, she out-lasted all her enemies, dying at a very great age.

Edward protected and encouraged the English merchants and leaned heavily on the middle-class London entrepreneurs, causing the growth of a new class of guilds of yeomen – embryo trades unions of craftsmen, in the process undermining the honesty of City officials. In 1468, 'BY JUDGEMENT OF THE MAYOR, divers people, being Common Jurors forsworn for taking Rewards or giving Favours to Parties at the Assizes, were rode from Newgate to the Pillory with Mitres of Paper upon their Heads, and thence to Newgate.' They had been guilty of partiality and of allowing interference in the methods of measuring (assizing) upon which the whole basis of the City's honesty and repute depended. Not that this fiddling was anything new, but the scope and incidence had grown to dangerous proportions.

There was also plenty of carnal sin going on: in 1472 the lord mayor, Sir William Hampton, issued a prescription *'de Correccio Meretricium'* ('For the Punishment of Whores'), calling for 'diligent and sharp correction' . . . upon Venus' servaunts, causing them to be Garnished and attired with Ray Hoodes and shewed about the City with their Minstrells before them . . . [He] spared none for *meed* or *favour*, albeit that some of them offered large sums of Money to have them prised from that open Shame'. He also set up stocks in every ward 'to punish these Vacabunds'. However, the main purpose of these deep raids was to root out the hundreds of fugitives from Bastard Fauconbridge's failed revolt, many of whom were being hidden in brothels.

A rare vignette about regal cleanliness discloses that, 'The Barber shall have every Saturday Nyghte, if it please the Kynge, to cleanse his Heade, Leggs or Feete, and for his Shavynge . . . he shall get . . . Two Loaves and One Pitcher of Wine.' It is from this time that there is the earliest sketch of a medieval 'overhanging prevy' in an enclosed garden; the excrements appear to free-fall into a laystall below, to the surprised gaze of some bystanding ladies.

Suddenly, in April 1483, Edward IV died, and his son Edward, a lad of twelve, became Edward V under the regency of his uncle Richard 'Crookback', Duke of Gloucester. A few days later, in the boy King's name the lord mayor issued the famous ordinance 'For to Eschewe the Stynkynge and Horrible Synne of Lecherie, '. . . the which dayly groweth and is used more than in dayes past by the means of Strumpettes, mysguyded and idyll Women dayly vag-raunt and walkynge abowte the streetes and Lanes . . . repairinge to Tavernes . . . provokynge manie other Persons to the sayd

Edward the Fifth's famous ordinance in 1483 'For to Eschewe the Stynkynge and Horrible Synne of Lecherie'.

Synne to the grete displesure of ALMYGHTIE GOD and the brekynge of the Kynge's . . . Peace . . .'.

The boy king was murdered in June and his uncle became Richard III. The Londoners had no love or time for him. He was killed at Bosworth Field in 1485, calling for his horse. The victor, Henry ap Tudor, became the land's new ruler.

8 Henry VIII Acts Against Sin

Henry Tudor was the right man at the right time. He was a cool, careful, calculating and brave man, not given to sexual profligacy. His victory broke the power of the feudal lords, and with it came the breakdown of the feudal system. It created the conditions for a great commercial expansion in which London was to be a prime beneficiary. It was remarked that he had '. . . started the country as a nation of shopkeepers', but the fact is that his strong rule and peace brought not only great prosperity but also the creation of a new factor – a strong middle-class interested not in an archaic notion of chivalry but in down-to-earth moneymaking.

The break-up of the feudal system, however, created great problems, not the least of which was the flood of labourers and their womenfolk into the urban area seeking work which did not then exist. Although there was a great spurt in building activity which created jobs for men, the opportunities for women were few, so that many fell into prostitution merely to keep alive. The result was an immense increase in 'vagabondage', whereby men, women and children were shunted away from urban areas to roam and beg on the highways, with a consequent rise in crime. A contemporary Italian visitor remarked, 'There is no country in the world where there are so many thieves and robbers . . . few venture to go out in the middle of the day, least of all in London!'

The King was also aware of the dangers of venereal disease. In 1487, mindful of the epidemic of syphilis ('the French Pox') sweeping Europe, he ordered '. . . that no whores should follow his armies', although there is no record of any such decree to control the many small brothels that still existed within the City and the liberties. In 1490 St Martin-le-Grand came under fire because 'unthrift and riot run unchecked' – 'Yea! and rich men run thither with poor men's goods. There they build, there they spend and bid their Creditors go whistle! Men's Wives run thither with their

Old London Bridge about 1480.

Husband's Plate, saying 'They cannot abide their Husbands for beating.' Thieves bring thither their stolen goods and live thereon. They devise new robberies; nightly they steal out to rob: they reave and kill and come in again as though these places give them not only a Safeguard for the harm they have done, but a Licence to do more again.'

In that year John de Norfolke and John White were 'punnyshyd uppon ye pillory in Chepe' and a couple of years later Thomas Toogood, a well-known and wealthy whoremonger/brothel-owner on the Bankside, was put in the pillory, '. . . by cause that he entysed two women dwelling in Queenhithe to have men coming to his howse'.

In 1501 the Lord Mayor Sir John Shaa '. . . caused a Cage to be set in every ward for punishment of vacabunds'. In that same year he also '. . . caused the Aldermen to ryde from ye Guildhall to ye watersyde and took hys Barge to Westminster to be sworn in by the Kings Privy Council' – this was the first of the magnificent gilded barges used thenceforward until the practice was substituted by a great procession, still known today as 'The Lord Mayor's Show'

By 1503 the syphilis epidemic had reached England, and in the following year the King ordered the closure of the Bankside whorehouses; ten were re-opened a year later, and some months later all were working again. However, his original decree had caused the procuresses and their girls to scatter, as Wynkyn de Woorde, Caxton's successor, recorded in *Hickescorner*:

> Some at St Katherines strake a-grounde
> and manie in Hole bourne were founde:
> Some at Saynte Giles, I trow
> also in Ave Maria Alley . . .
> and some in Shoreditch drew there
> in grete lamentacion . . .
> and by cause they have lost that fayre Place
> they will buylde at Colman Hedge a space
> an other Noble Mansion. . . .

(Ave Maria Alley is next to St Paul's Cathedral; St Leonard's in Shoreditch had been a whores'-nest for generations; St Katherine's was by the Tower of London, and – most surprising – Colman Hedge was a far-out suburb where today's National Gallery stands.)

Hickescorner also gives details of a small City brothel with four resident whores, Kate, Bess, Sybil and Jane all '. . . full pretty and wanton (they) will make you weary!' naming them as *The Bell* and *The Hartshorne*: and refers to a character Imagination '. . . of the stewes I am made Controller of all the houses of lecherie: no man shall play doxy there or elsewhere without they have leave of me!'

In another work Wynkyn de Woorde remarks

> 'Now-a-days in England
> Bawds be destroyers of many yonge women
> and ful lewde councill they give unto them . . .
> Mayors on Sin doeth no correccion . . .
> Courtiers go gay . . . many with harlots
> At the taverns haunt . . .

ending that they 'had liever be by the nose in a wench's arse (than go to Heaven)'. In *The Worlde and the Childe* he remarks 'Lecherie is the seventh Kynge' and in the same work describes the City's protective ditch at Houndsditch: '. . . in olden tyme so deep that divers horses and their riders were drowned while watering . . . since cleaned of filth, dead dogs and waste products . . .'. Nearby, also in Bishopsgate Without, was a narrow, winding footpath already called Wentworth Lane, better known today as Petticoat Lane. All these suburbs were known for their violent activities, and an explanation was given: 'Do wee nott commonlie see at the ende of Warres more Robbynges, more Beggynges, more Murderynges than before? . . . There are those who stande in the Waie to aske Almes, whom ye are affrayde to say Nay! lest they take away from you violently . . .', and a great many unemployed sit at home idle, 'affrayde they will never be let to work agayne'. To cope with this spread of violence, in 1509 the lord mayor, Sir William Capell, ordered 'that smal howses [cages] be sett up in every parish'.

In 1506 Henry VII '. . . caused to be released from the Sheriffs *Compters* . . . many Debtors who owed Forty Shillings and even some that had owed up to Ten Pounds', further to ingratiate himself with the citizenry, and in his Will he gave money to those in the City 'amongst the blynde and lame, the bedridden and most needy folke who would nott aske for alms . . . and miserable prisoners condemned for debt . . . who could not pay the fees . . .'. His son, Henry VIII, carried out his father's wishes immediately.

A merry fiddler in the stocks. In 1533 Henry VIII legislated against ballad-singers and fiddlers as subversive elements. This was not well received by the populace as witness the tankard of ale being brought to him by a sympathizer.

Henry VIII (1509–47) made himself popular with an endless succession of magnificent pageants and processions, balls, banquets, and masques. Most spectacular were the annual 'Marches of the Watch' which grew more sumptuous with every passing year, until even the mayor and aldermen complained at the cost. He could also unbend: on one walkabout in the City he was manhandled and stripped of his rings and ornaments in a drunken spree but took it in good part. On another occasion, on St John's Night 1510, he went down to Cheapside dressed as a Yeoman of the Guard, with 'an Halberd on his shoulder', and was merrily carousing in a tavern when 'seeing the Watch, he departed privily'.

An early action of Henry VIII was his proclamation 'Forbidding Brothel-keeping in the Host', all whores having to be dismissed, and a further proviso that they would be 'branded with hotte yrons' on the face for fornication with soldiers.

In 1515 an outbreak of plague struck the City, killing all the nuns in the abbey in the Minories, hard by the Tower. 1517 saw 'Evill May Day', when the apprentices rioted against 'John Mutes a Piccard in his house *The Green Gates* [because] he calendered Wool in defiance of the rights of the Citizens and harboured Frensshemen therein'. It almost turned into an insurrection when they were prevented by the constables from beheading these 'misdoers'. 'The Green Gates' it may be recalled, was Malpass' old mansion – not a very lucky house.

In 1518 there was a magnificent spectacle when the great Cardinal Pietro Campeggio came as legate from Pope Leo X to obtain a large subsidy from the English churches. He crossed over London Bridge '. . . Rydynge in redde Chamlett wyth hys Cardenalles Hatte uppon hys hedde . . . wyth two sylver-gilt Pyllars borne before hym . . . greate Lordes and Knyghtes and alle the Parsons and Preystes in London . . . wearynge theyr Copes and carryinge Censers . . .'. Four years later, the bridge witnessed an even greater spectacle when the Emperor Charles V – the greatest potentate of his time – came to plan with Henry VIII a joint war against France. Before crossing the bridge he asked 'that all prisoners in the Marshalsey and Kings Bench should be released' – an excellent piece of public relations – and the King acquiescing he then crossed over London Bridge 'with a sumptuous cavalcade which beggars description'.

In the same year, however, was the much more romantic occasion when the young Edward Osborne, apprentice to a rich clothier, Alderman William Hewett, living on the bridge, jumped into the river to save his little daughter Anne. This pretty little girl

Edward Osborne jumping off London Bridge to rescue his employer's little daughter: when she grew up they were married. He later became Lord Mayor of London.

grew up to be a much-courted beauty, her father becoming lord mayor in 1559. The young couple fell in love and, although there were many more eligible suitors, when Edward asked for her hand, Hewett replied, 'Osborne saved her and Osborne should enjoy her!' In 1575 Edward became sheriff and in 1583 lord mayor, being knighted by Queen Elizabeth. The couple's ultimate successors became dukes of Leeds.

In 1519 the King ordered Cardinal Wolsey '. . . to purge London and Southwark . . . all brothels to be entirely suppressed [being only] for unclean persons unfit to associate with honest men'; for good measure, '. . . none shall keep houses for dicing or unlawful games . . .'. Wolsey's sweep took about fifty persons, male and female, including one of the King's own personal servants. The move was not so much anti-sexual as political, since there had been simmering unrest ever since the death of Henry VII, and the number of homeless and unemployed had grown enormously, leading even to a bread riot when the sheriffs and constables had to rush to Mile End to protect the Stratford bakers who were bringing much-needed bread into the City, breaking the monopoly of the bakers' guild in the process.

Symon Fysshe, in his *Supplycacion for the Beggars*, petitioned the King about the abysmal poverty of his subjects, especially that the women were being driven into prostitution: 'Who is shee that wil sett her Handes to worke to gett three pence a-daye but may have at leaste Twenty Pence a daye to slepe an houre with a Friar or a Monk or a Preeste . . .' and why should a labourer sweat for a groat a day when he can be a pander to the same and get 'at leaste Twelve pence the days'?

In 1535 Henry issued his famous Acte for the punnysshement of the Vice of Buggerie', making it a felony punishable by death instead of what had been for centuries just an ecclesiastical offence. To justify it, he had officials probing into innumerable cases of sodomy amongst the clergy and, in passing, the even greater number who kept concubines or regularly committed fornication.

About this time there were many complaints about the vile treatment meted out to prisoners by gaolers, who would not only grossly overcharge them for rooms and food but sometimes force three persons to share a bed, although they had all paid separately for single beds, or fetter them together at night, 'in batches of four or five'. These were all 'franchise prisons' supposedly under royal supervision, but almost all officials were corrupt.

Henry's solution to the terrible problem of vagabondage was simple: in 1545 he ordered 'All Vagabonds to the Galleys' –

The Great Gate of Old London Bridge with its grisly fringe of traitors' decapitated heads. The last head was that of Venner, leader of the so-called 'Fifth Monarchy Men' in the reign of Charles II.

pressganged for his warships for a projected war; moreover, four months later, when the army was encamped in Boulogne, he ordered his commander '. . . to rydde alle Harlottes and Comon women out of Bullen'. Next year, in April, he closed all the Bankside stewes, although, as Ben Jonson later remarked, 'a damned crew of private ones' took their place. Henry also forbade bull- and bear-baiting, but the ink was hardly dry when he allowed one of his own Yeomen of the Guard to own a baiting-pit on the Bankside, 'notwithstanding the Proclamation'. Soon afterwards this tyrant died in agony of syphilitic periostitis in a stupor; he was only fifty-six.

His young son, Edward VI, ascended the throne in January 1547. In confirming his father's draconian laws, he made a slight amendment to the law on sodomy, inasmuch as the executed sodomist's estate could now go to his surviving family. Although the King was constantly harangued by Bishop Latimer about the now closed stewes (Latimer said they had been shut down but the vice still continued), eventually in 1550 he allowed them to be opened, but with whited walls and their signs painted on them, so as not to confuse the whorehouses with taverns which had hanging signs – '. . . so that they be known for what they are'. The damage had been done, and from that time many of these conveniences were turned into inns and taverns and theatres. They were quite extensive properties with very large gardens and several also had ponds.

Still there was plenty of whoredom in London – Latimer picked out St Martin-le-Grand and made particular reference to 'houses with walled gardens where men and women perform their filthie ceremonies . . . with manie light lewd harlottes', but, more sinister, in 'these howses, there were . . . seditious and mutinous

The Protestant martyr Anne Askew being burnt to death on 16 July 1546 together with her associates John Adams, John Lascelles, and Nicholas Belenian, for heresy. She insisted that 'she would not sing a new song to the Lord' and refused a pardon.

talkinges . . . openlie . . . to the depravinge of Religion . . . the advancement of Poperie and Popish practices . . .'. The other danger was that, as regards fashionable dress, the courtesans were the leaders. Bansley's *Pryde and Abuse of Women* (1550) spelt it out:

> . . . the Citie of London
> For therein dwell prowde wycked ones
> The Poyson of all this Region.
> For a stewed Strumpette can not so soone set up
> In lyght lewde Fashyon
> But every wanton *Jelot* wyll lyke ytt well
> and catch it upp anon.

(Jelot – jilt, a young flighty maiden.)

The fears about religion were not unfounded: priests were now not highly regarded and often had to be protected from jeers, insults, even assaults; in 1550 many churches were plundered and their silver stolen and melted down.

The young King died untimely in 1553 and was succeeded by his sister Mary, a religious bigot determined to restore Roman Catholicism to its former power. She revoked all her father's ordinances, restoring all the properties taken from the Church and inaugurating a reign of terror against Protestants and especially Protestant divines. London, which was a Protestant stronghold, nevertheless submitted to the new rule, with real dissent driven underground but still being organized.

The Queen ordered that cages, pillories and stocks be set up in all parishes in London for the punishment of religious dissenters and also sexual offenders. In November 1555 '. . . the Ill-woman who keepes the *Greyhonde* was carted abowte the Citie', 'A Gentilmanne, Master Manwarynge, with two whores from *The Harry* [a whorehouse in Cheapside] were carted to Aldgate for baudry and hordome' (one of them was a goldsmith's wife!). The woman '. . . who kept *The Bell* in Grassechurche Street was carted as a bawd' – this was a long-established house of whoredom; it was also one of the first 'messuages' to be used as a theatre within the City's boundary. in 1557 'Jon a Badoo [Bordeaux] a Bawd and hys wyff, also a bawd, were arraigned . . . shee was wyppyd at the cart-arse . . . the odur woman beynge a nold harlott of three-score and more was ledd the horse lyke a nold hore . . .'. Sodomy was no longer punishable by death or forfeiture of estates; it went back to being an ecclesiastical matter punishable by fines and penance.

There was great excitement in the summer of 1554 when the future King Philip of Spain came to marry the Queen. The State

The Caidge on London Bridge, one of many ordered by Mary I in 1559 'in every parish' for malefactors, although mostly they were used to punish 'recalcitrant women' and petty criminals.

Entry at London Bridge on Sunday 19 August was so lavishly and expensively arranged that the contemporary chronicler Ralph Holinshed remarked that it was 'a vaine ostentation of flatterie'. Philip was an unwilling bridegroom, quite unenamoured of his bride – the dreadful stench from her rhinitis, a gift from her father's syphilis, was enough to put him off, and her subsequent flights of fancy about her spurious pregnancy are proof that she was also mentally unstable.

In 1558 her sister Elizabeth came to the throne; now it was the turn of the Catholics to be the 'hereticks' and to be punished with the same degree of brutality. Once more the spikes over the Great Gate of London Bridge were full to overflowing. She completed the disestablishment of the monasteries and sequestration of their possessions, although there were now immense complications about ownership.

Elizabeth reverted to her father's laws on whoredom and buggery, and sexual sin was to be punished as of old. In December 1559

Henry Machin noted in his diary, '. . . dyd a woman ryde a-pone horsebacke with a paper on her hedd for bawderie wyth a bason ryngeynge', and some days later, '. . . dyd ryd a carte a-bowte Lundun the Wyff of Harry Glyn a Goldesmyth for beynge baud to her owne dowgther . . .'. However, at Bridewell '. . . dyvers gentyllmen and their servyngemen . . . began a tumulte and affraye . . . they wulle have certayne women owte of the Brydewel and they drew their swordes and began muche beseness [business] agaynste the Aldermens Deputies who hadde been sent for . . .'. Moreover, they got away with it!

'Masteress' Warner, wife of an ex-serjeant of the admiralty, was arrested in 1560 for prostituting both her daughter and her maid,

A felon being 'whipped at the cart-arse': a regular punishment in Jacobean days, usually from the prison to his residence and back, sometimes with a stop at a pillory for an hour or more. Both men and women were to be whipped 'till the blood flowed' on their naked backs; if they collapsed, they were put on the cart until they recovered enough for the process to be repeated.

both now pregnant; she was also indicted as a 'hore'. At the same time a licensed waterman was whipped for 'utterynge opprobrious wordes agaynst the Citie magistrates', and a great many women and men were sentenced for 'nasty lyvynge' – bawdry, all of whom had their heads shaved and were whipped and sent to Bridewell.

However, not only harlots were castigated. Henry Gosson in *The Devills Dreame* (1560) indicates one of London's attractions:

> The Dames of the Citi came hither with spede –
> Your Merchants' wives pretty, wolde seal to this deed.
> To live with a Lover and never to die –
> Where Courtezans hover, this Bargain to buy.
> Wives Widdows and Maydens to the Devill did hie
> Brave Lasses and Ladyes – these Bargains would buy!

Three years later, in the City's *Letter Books* dealing with 'Priests Taken in Adultery', there is a gem. It concerns George Barton, who in 1561 had already been deprived of one living:

> Ye 26 of JUNE was a Mynyster, a Parson of Sent Marie Abchurche of Sent Martyns in Yronmonger lane and other Benefice . . . taken at Dystafflane usynge an other mans Wyffe as hys own whiche was the dawghter to Ser Miles Partridge and Wyff to Wyllyam Stokebregge, Grosar, he beynge taken in ye dede (haveynge a wyff of hys owne) was caryed to Bridewell thrughe all ye stretes hys Breeche hangynge abowte hys knees hys gowne and hatte borne affter hym . . . but hee lay nott long ther but was delyvered withowt punnyshment and still injoyed his Benefices. They were greatlie blamed that committed hym.

In that same year, 1563, the plague struck again and every householder was ordered '. . . TO LAY OUT WOOD and make Bonfyres in the Streetes and Lanes to consume the corrupte Ayre whych otherwyse woulde infect the Citie . . . three tymes the weeke . . .'.

That the Queen was not immune to Cupid's darts is evidenced by the hilarious account of a clandestine meeting with her favourite, the Earl of Leicester, who came down to St Swithin's churchyard with an entourage of 700 'Lordes Knyghtes and Pensioners and Gentylmen' where he had an appointment with Queen Elizabeth, '. . . who hadde secretlie com to Sothewarke takynge a whirry . . . rowed over to ye Three Cranes in ye Vintrie where shee entered a coche covered with blewe . . . and rode to meet ye Erle . . .'. By some mischance they missed each other in the maze of alleys, eventually meeting after crossing the bridge, near Greenwich: '. . . shee cam owte of hir coche in ye high waie & imbrased ye Erle & kyssed hym thrice & they rode togyther to Grenewyche'.

Of much greater interest to Londoners was the installation in 1581 of the first water-pumping station under London Bridge by the Dutch engineer Pieter Mauritz. The first regular supply was pumped 'to those householders who could afford it'; it was later extended over two, then three, arches until it was destroyed in the Great Fire of 1666. Six years later the bridge was to be thronged by thousands of pleasure-seekers on their way to 'the Swanne' – a very low-class theatre, and 'The Rose' and 'The Globe' on the Bankside. The Queen, however, preferred the bear-baiting and the bull-ring and the cockfights.

A more important event, to have a very much longer and more profound effect on London, was the erection in 1565 of a 'Bourse' as a meeting-house for bill-brokers.

> The 22nd day of February being Friday the houses neare to the Conduit in Cornhill about the number of sixty households poor and rich were Cryed by the Bellman . . . to be sold to them that would give the most for them and remove them from thence that in the place thereof the Merchaunts might build their Bourse.
>
> Those houses were cried out divers times and at the last sold and they began that same day . . . in the pulling down divers persons were hurt and in great peril of hurt. . . .

Sir Thomas Gresham's Bourse, opened later by the Queen, became the Royal Exchange. It was then a noisy and violent place frequented by 'such as Ratcatchers and Dog-sellers and Court-ezans' who thronged the maze of alleys which soon became known by their brokers – Grocers Walk, Silkmens Walk, Druggists Walk. Alongside was an arcade, 'The Pawne', with shops selling luxury goods; it quickly became the haunt of prostitutes and catamites, the latter much in demand by 'respectable' merchants of Chepe and Cornhill. Indeed, there was so much sodomy about that the justices of the peace were empowered to hear such cases, 'because buggery provided a powerfully damaging charge'; because of the death penalty, the courts leaned over backwards not to convict. Only if 'penetration' was found could a verdict be reached – otherwise it was just common assault, meriting a fine. The area known as 'The Stocks' (today's Mansion House) was the rendez-vous of 'sexual deviants'. A yeoman from Hoxton was executed for buggery.

Sin and vice were still running strongly in Trimill Street – although it seems to have been better known as Turnbull Street.

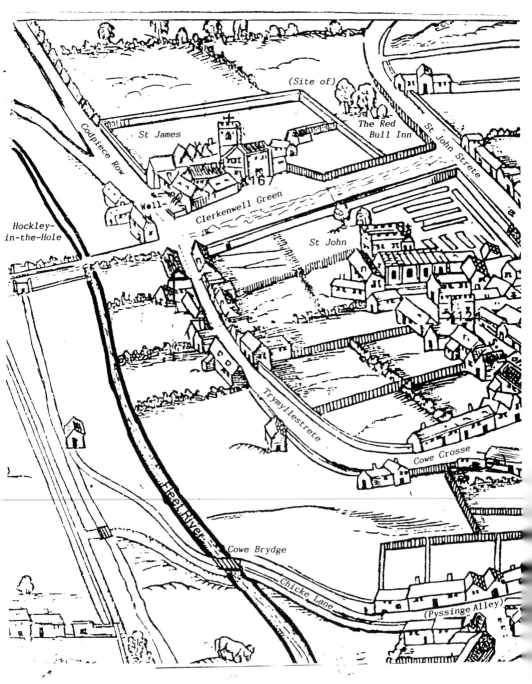

Turnmill Street and district c. 1500 *showing the site of the later* Red Bull *theatre. Cow Cross Street was later extended to the bridge. Based on Agus' map, 1563.*

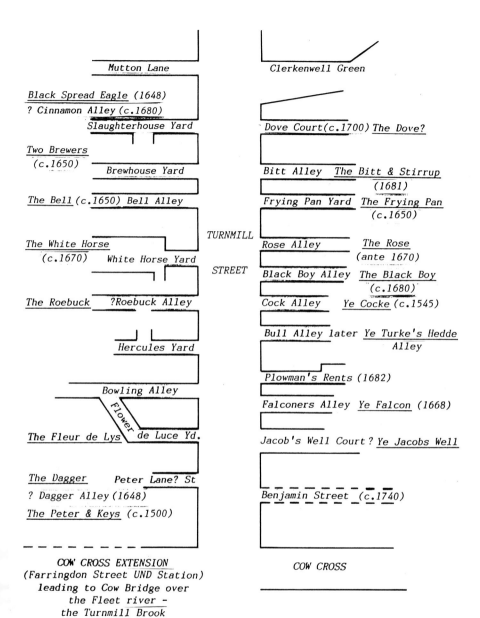

Mutton Lane

Black Spread Eagle (1648)
? Cinnamon Alley (c.1680)
Slaughterhouse Yard

Two Brewers
(c.1650)
Brewhouse Yard

The Bell (c.1650) Bell Alley

The White Horse
(c.1670)   White Horse Yard

The Roebuck   ?Roebuck Alley

Hercules Yard

Bowling Alley

The Fleur de Lys   Flower de Luce Yd.

The Dagger   Peter Lane? St
? Dagger Alley (1648)
The Peter & Keys (c.1500)

Clerkenwell Green

Dove Court(c.1700) The Dove?

Bitt Alley   The Bitt & Stirrup
(1681)
Frying Pan Yard   The Frying Pan
(c.1650)

TURNMILL   Rose Alley   The Rose
(ante 1670)
STREET   Black Boy Alley   The Black Boy
(c.1680)
Cock Alley   Ye Cocke (c.1545)

Bull Alley later   Ye Turke's Hedde
Alley

Plowman's Rents (1682)

Falconers Alley   Ye Falcon (1668)

Jacob's Well Court ? Ye Jacobs Well

Benjamin Street (c.1740)

COW CROSS EXTENSION
(Farringdon Street UND Station)
leading to Cow Bridge over
the Fleet river -
the Turnmill Brook

COW CROSS

'Now Farewel to Turnbull Street. For that no comfort yields.' (The Merrie
Mans Resolution) c. 1600.
Author's reconstruction of Turnmill Street's warren of alleys and inns,
taverns and whorehouses, collated from available sources. All these alleys
were choked with jerry-built tenements where the poorest prostitutes lived
cheek-by-jowl in dirty and insanitary conditions: a short life and not a very
merry one.

The Cocke Tavern was then, in 1585, owned by Henry Stokes who had willed 'One Pound the yeare for the repaire of St James' Church in Clerkenwell to be paid from the rent of his house in Turnbullestreet . . .'; these payments were made regularly until they fell in arrears in 1833.

In 1577 there was a property in Jacob's Alley (properly Jacob's Well Alley), then nicknamed 'Jack's Alley', and a Greek, Constantine Bennet, '. . . left a number of houses . . . that in Turnbull Street . . . to distribute at Christmas among poor people of Clerkenwell parrish from the rents and revenues . . .'. 'The Jacob's Well' in the alley of that name was in 1661 owned by 'Old' Bess Blundell: it was a 'house of ill-fame' of some repute, mentioned in *The Wand'ring Whore* in three editions. In 1585 the street was reported to be 'full of Theeves and thieverie [with many] harborynge howses for Maisterlesse menne and suche as lyve by thiefte and suche lyke . . . and Places of Resorts . . .'. Both Thomas Nashe and William Shakespeare attest the street's notoriety. In *Pierce Pennilesse hys Supplycacion to the Devill*, Nashe commended 'oure uncleane Sisters in Shordyche and Turnbulle Streete . . . hopynge You wyll speedily carry them to Hell', and Shakespeare in *Henry IV* (Part 2) has Falstaff remark of Mr Justice Shallow, 'This same starv'd Justice boasts . . . of Feats he hath done in Turnball Street.'

One of Falstaff's own gallantries was in the Rose Tavern in the infamous Rose Alley in Turnmill Street, then managed by John Sleepe for the Trapp family. In the 1590s Hugh Trappe owned both the Rose and the even more notorious Blue Axe in the yard of that name, which was still open in 1620 when John Lee, who had paid £80 for the lease, defaulted and was 'emprisoned for debt' and the parish took it over.

At this time too, a Roxburghe Ballad refers to '*Le Fleur de Lys* in Turnbull Streete' where a whore and client made an assignation. Fleur de Lys Alley is often mentioned in contemporary broadsheets for its vicious inhabitants. In 1592 Henry Chettle, in *Kinde Hartes Dreame*, mentioned Turnmill Street in which landlords charged '. . . forty shillings yearly for a little Room with a smoky chimny . . . where several of these venereal virgins are resident [the victims of] suche fynes, suche tributes, suche Customes as poore Soules, after seven yeares Service in that unhallowed Order they are fayne to leave . . . seekynge harboure in an hospitall . . .'.

Even greater sinfulness was to be manifested with the coming of the theatres. Hitherto itinerant groups of mummers had performed on any open space they could find – in front of town halls, churchyards or barns, but especially sought-after were inn-

A bilker being chased out of a brothel.

yards, particularly those where carriers were wont to gather. These open yards with galleries attracted the more affluent and were used for the spectators. The stables were used as dressing-rooms, and a temporary 'stage' (usually just a platform) was erected in the yard. *Hoi polloi*, the standing customers, surrounded the platform, usually so thickly that the actors would have to force their way through. The actors did not mind, because they could gather 'pence, groats and twopences' as they passed through.

At first a few of these 'inn-playhouses' were tolerated, especially if 'the Quality' were sponsors. The earliest were the Cross Keyes in Gracious Street (Gracechurch Street) in 1552 and the Bell in the same street in 1560; then the Bull in Bishopsgate and the Belle Sauvage* on Ludgate Hill in 1570.

After 1570 some of these groups formed 'Companies of Players', playing in inn-yards regularly. This disturbed the Common Council, which in 1574 decreed 'That no innkeeper or tavern-keeper . . .

---

* It was still standing in 1777, when Parson James Woodforde was 'bit terribly by Bugges in the Nighte'.

within the Liberties of this City shall openly show or play . . . within his house-yard . . . any play etc., . . .'.

The Bull was then hosting 'fencing contests, the Bell playing *Cutwell* (for which the royal master of the revels paid 10 pence to have some scenery sent to St John Street). In June 1579 the famous actor James Burbage was arrested for a debt of £5. 13s. 0d. as he went down to the Cross Keyes 'to take part in a play'. At this time the Bull was playing *Ptolemy* and *The Bell Savage* (sic), *The Jew* 'neither having amorous gestures or slovenlie talke to hurte the Eares . . . of chaste hearers . . .', but other taverns were not playing fair, so that in 1580 the Privy Council instructed '. . . to thrust out the Players from the City, pull down the playing and dicing-houses within the Liberties', because '. . . the presence of private Rooms led to immorality gambling, intemperance, gathering of Vagrants and masterless Men, Theaves, Horse-stealers, Cozeners, practisers of Treason . . . leading to drunken affrays and bloodshed and [riots by] . . . Apprentices and Factions . . .'; 'unchaste or seditious matter' was also forbidden. The over-riding consideration was then, as in the past, the fear of insurrection by the starving or homeless and very little to do with the fact that tavern landlords had 'greatly profited by letting rooms to dubious couples'. In 1569 there was 'a plague of beggers' against whom special armed marshals were recruited.

The numbers of prostitutes increased mightily, as also the numbers of catamites. The Queen's cousin Henry Carey, Lord Hunsdon, kept 'a bawdy-house of Beasts' in Hoggesden (Hoxton), then a salubrious suburb. Philip Stubbs mentions that one punishment for whores then was 'drawing the whore, bound hand and foot, with a rope round her Necke, behind a rowing boat along the Thames . . . a soft punishment almost as a ducking . . .'. He favoured letting them drown!

The frankest expression of contemporary harlotry is in Sam Rowland's *The Courtezan*:

Tudor Cheapside. On the left is the Crown Seld – *a gallery from which royalty could watch processions: then the belfry of Bow Church and the prestigious row of goldsmiths' shops which was the street's hall-mark! St Paul's is at the rear. In the centre is the Standard or Great Conduit and further up the Great Cross erected in 1290 by Edward I in memory of his Queen Eleanor. The seld (originally 'shed') was erected by the Mercers in 1398).*

H.W. Brewer. ino. et del.

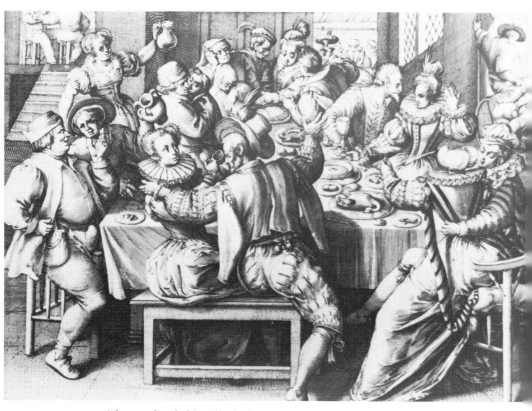

A luxury brothel in Elizabethan times with good food and drink and lovely girls catering for the comfortable bourgeoisie. In London these were appearing around Lincoln's Inn Fields and Lewkenors Lane between Chancery Lane and St Giles.

I am a profest *Courtezane*
That lives by people's Sinne.
With half-a-dozen *Punckes* I keepe
I have greate coming-in.

Her clients include 'a great store of Traders and Gallants . . . Courtiers and rustique Clownes'. She has a coach and 'blew-coated serving-men' and even her own wherry. She will take all who come, at varying prices. In short,

Thus I fitt Fooles in humoures still
That come to Mee for *Game*.
I punnishe them for *Venery*
Leavinge their Purses lame!

In his *Merrie Ballad of Nashe his Dildo* the poet describes his adventures in a 'House of Venery'. Going to his usual place, he found that the object of his desire had been 'removed to another Ground by good Justice Dudgeon'. He asked the 'three-chinn'd Dame' for a substitute, was shown upstairs and given a drink, and asked for 'gentle Mistress Frances'. However, the Dame warns him that '. . . shee is very expensive . . . her Ruff and her Periwigg cannot be kept for half-a-Crowne a Day'. When Nashe says he will pay 'in Gold', the delectable girl is brought in. He describes her 'delights' in great detail – and then, to his horror, 'his Worme failed'. Although she succeeded, after a long time in resuscitating him, she had to go, as 'she had other customers awaiting' and could no longer wait for him to perform his functions. Whereupon he, in depression, dilates at great length on the merits of a 'dildo' 'which never droops'.

This Tudor period was one of great prosperity: building was unchecked, fuelled by the enormous amount of land freed from the paralysing hand of the Church and by the great flow of loot from the New World and legalized piracy. Stubbs recorded that trade flourished as never before:

> . . . within forty yeeres there were nott these *Haberdashers* that selles Frenche or Milland cappes; glasses, knives, daggers, swordes, gyrdles . . . there were nott a dozen in alle London.
>
> Nowe, from the Tower to West Mynster everie streete is full of theym and their shoppes glitter and shyne of Glasses – both drynckynge and lookynge . . . Ladies despise any Thing that was not far-fetched [imported] and deere . . . all gaze on them and buy somewhat even tho' it serve no purpose. . . .

Stubbs accused the merchants of making 300–400 per cent profit, using false weights and measures and creating artificial shortages, while vintners adulterated the wines and gave short measure to boot. He observed that the 'Great Guilds' were 'squeezing-outt' the journeymen and that the Common Council '. . . tended to neglect the upkeepe of the Towne . . . to the greate discommoditie and Annoyaunce of Neybors and Travelers . . . which (streetes) hadde beforehande been well mayntayned . . .'.

The streets were still mainly unpaved, the 'kennels' still full of dirt and excrement – the stench from dunghills and 'previes' and unwashed bodies was horrible. Besides the noise of the new-fangled coaches and the incessant screeching of hucksters, of cooks crying-out 'Hott Pyes! All Hott!' and wives and daughters of the shopkeepers (now with glazed windows lit, in the evenings with

The Bread Street Sheriff's Compter, c. 1550, showing the halberdiers of the Watch with a 'myslyver' about to be carted, the 'minstrels' awaiting their signal to start playing. The rats signify either the state of the prison or the fact that there were witches about, rats being regarded as their 'familiars'.

candles in glass globes) shouting and importuning customers because the loudest voice often attracted the most passers-by, there was now the rumble of heavy coaches, with the coachmen swearing at anyone or anything that impeded progress. Innkeepers would cry out the offer of 'free wine' with the roasts, and itinerant hatters would sell you back your own hat at the other end of the street. From time to time the streets would be cleared for some very important personage or for a pageant, or even for a March of the Watch. And at all times, even late into the night, there would be pimps and panders and ambulant whores.

Manners matched morals in coarseness: there were lavish dinners and suppers and banquets, with men and women beastly in their gluttony, drinking, belching, farting and quarrelling with the servants. In 1542 Dr Andrew Boorde said that, '. . . their talk is so savoureth of scurrility and ribaldry', and Sir John Harington said of the Court that behaviour there was 'ill-breeding and ill-feeling' and that it stank. Even high-born ladies were froward and outspoken in sexual speech and behaviour, although the daughters of the newly affluent middle-class were enjoined to genteel behaviour and chastity – they were, after all, a valuable property and a good investment. Many of them could even read and write.

The lavish displays of food led to great waste, but the leavings were for the servants and sometimes the poor who clustered around: '. . . the poore wulde think themselves happy if they mighte have a mess of pottage or the scrapings from the rich mans table two or three hours later . . . the rich greedy-guttes fill their backs and bellies . . . giving the poor nothing but rebuke . . . yea! chiding them most uncharitably . . . they are driven almost to despair . . .'.

A pair of Watchmen in Elizabethan times. They were usually unarmed, patrolling in pairs with lanterns and bells to warn of their approach to night-walkers and other felonious elements. Sometimes they might 'call the hour'. They were not of high calibre and usually useless in any fracas. By Georgian times they were known as 'Charlies'.

An ever-present danger was highwaymen – they once held-up the Queen on a visit to the village of Isledon, and the streets were full of violence, every man usually carrying a sword or a dagger 'which worked mischief in many a drunken affray', especially at night. Some of the highwaymen were '. . . Gentlemen impoverished by extravagance: some were employees earning insufficient Money: others discharged soldiers without pensions and professional criminals linked with inn-keepers . . . all undeterred by the savage penalties . . .'.

Even in the homes of the comfortable there was still not great luxury: a few chairs and a table, two or three cupboards to display silver plate or china-ware; in the bedroom a roomy four-poster with a feather mattress and a blanket or quilt – and they still slept naked

In January 1557 Alderman Christopher Draper of the Cordwainer Ward employed the first bellman. His bell was to warn local citizens to 'have a care of their lights and fires, to help the poore and to praye for the deade'. There had been a great many fires caused by carelessness. However, watchmen had carried bells for centuries prior to this, although that was to warn people to keep off the streets after nightfall.

except for the night-cap. (Only late in the Queen's reign was a nightdress introduced from France, and the only underwear was a petticoat under the ornate dresses, and a 'corsage' leaving the breasts almost bared.) Many of the larger mansions were ornately carved outside in the Tudor style now occasionally seen, and these would be furnished in the French or Italian manner: on the walls tapestry and paintings, usually of the lord and master and his wife and family.

The greatest and most terrible danger was from fire, although this was to some extent limited because there were still large gardens. Nevertheless, 'Altho' men be aware, they cannot avoyde theyre Neybore's negligence . . . whenne the wynde aryseth & bloweth the flakes from howse to howse . . . whiche sodenlye kindle all over the Citie . . . beyonde all expectacion . . .', although every house was supposed to have a barrel of water, a ladder and some buckets ready outside the front door, a relic of Edward I's time.

This was the London of Shakespeare, with 'the wondrous enlargement of the suburbes' accomplished under the Tudor dynasty.

9 'Sweetehearts and Good-wenches'

When, in 1603, James Stuart, King James VI of Scotland, was informed by the English envoy Sir Anthony Weldon that he was to be King of England as well, he could hardly believe his luck. To be translated from 'lowsie Edinborough' (Sir Anthony's description) after having escaped two attempts at assassination was a very inviting prospect. England was peaceful and prosperous, and its nobility, in contrast to his tetchy and plain-spoken Scots compeers, were servile. Above all, to a man accustomed to penny-pinching to make ends meet, there was lots of money.

James was a cynical man, withal. During his journey south he observed '. . . that if he had shown his bare arse to the people they would still have cheered him'. Physically he was not a very prepossessing character. He was 'corpulent, in dishevelled clothing – although with a steel doublet against would-be assassins underneath, the weakness of his legs making him ever to lean on other men's shoulders and always fiddling with his codpiece'. These idiosyncrasies led to his nickname 'the Bandy-legg'd Presbyterian' and to the canard that he was a homosexual, since he was always seen to be lovingly hugging stalwart young men. The Stuarts were a randy lot. His grandfather, James V, had been castigated by Sir David Lindesay of the Mount as 'Aye fukkynge lyke ane furious fornicateur', and his beautiful mother had been much criticized for her amoral behaviour.

He loved gambling and dancing and wenching, for much of which latter pastime he frequented the famous Hollands Leaguer

A bilker is chased out by the cheated whore, the Madam inveighs in the doorway and the miscreant has a chamberpot emptied over his head. This must have been a very frequent happening at all periods.

in Old Paris Gardens, enjoying the favours – so she claimed – of the fair Elizabeth Holland herself. He lacked kingly dignity, mixing frequently with the most disparate characters. He was also very mean – 'He was verie liberal of what he had not and would rather part with an hundred pounds he never had than one twenty-shilling piece in his own hand.'

Nevertheless, his advent proved of great advantage to England, and to London in particular, where the *magnificos* queued up to buy the peerages and knighthoods which he was selling quite cheaply. His Court was famous for its frivolity and extravagance – although cleanliness was not *de rigueur* (one countess complaining that she always returned home lousy).

From such a monarch, brothels and brothelry had little to fear. After all, Edinburgh was noted for the number of its whorehouses and its whores, although Sir Anthony (who must have taken a good look round) observed that the poorest London whore was a 'princess' compared with the Scottish whores. Many of these latter were to make the journey south in due course to leaven the English 'princesses' and add a Scots flavour to the English Court.

Nor was James overly religious. An early Proclamation ordained that, '. . . after Divine Service on Sundays good people be not prevented nor discouraged from dancing . . . or other harmless recreations'. It was a wise move to divert discontent amongst ordinary folk whose lives were otherwise drab and dreary.

James and his entourage were also heavy drinkers. At a sumptuous banquet for the King of Denmark, 'Certain Ladies were dressed as *Faith, Hope* and *Charity*: Hope did essay to speak but Wine rendered her endeavours so feeble that she withdrew. Faith left the Court staggering. Charity fell at the King of Denmark's feet . . . she then returned to Hope and Faith who were both sick and spewing in the lower Hall. . . .'

Under James' rule, 'Sweethearts and Good-wenches' could be found at any tavern and ale-house. The magistrates' courts bulged with stories of whorings from all over the City. Men and women were 'synfully lusting even on the Sabbath Day'. Abortions were rife in many brothels, and buggery flourished. Lord Hunsdon's Hoxton 'House of Beastes' was busy – one Alban Cooke was taken *in flagrante delicto* with a man under twenty years of age therein. (Although many distinguished sodomites, such as Sir Francis Bacon and Sir Walter Raleigh, were never discommoded.)

In 1608 Emma Robinson '. . . sat at her door till eleven or twelve at night to entertain lewd Persons'. Ellen Allen was 'a bad Woman who had inticed a Dutch man to lewdness'. In Elizabeth Basse's

Ducking was an ancient punishment for scolding and errant women. The ducking-stool was usually in a fixed position by some nearby water – a pond or a stream – although they were often mounted on a 'tumbrel' and moved to the scene. Sometimes a ducking was made a great public occasion with 'minstrels', conjurors and buskers to enliven a procession.

bawdy-house '. . . it was so rowdy that murther was like to be committed'. In 1611 Beaumont and Fletcher, in *Scornfull Ladies*, say: 'We have liv'd in a continuall Turnbull street' and refer to 'your swaggering cheating Turnbull Street Rogues'. Thomas Middleton, in *Anything for a Quiet Life*, has a French whore referring to 'la Fleur de Lys en Turnbul Street', giving the impression that it was a centre for French whores.

A little earlier Bishop Hall had written '. . . of broken *nuns* [whores] who have to frequent the stewes to raise the lewd rents demanded by rapacious landlords . . . who were turning dye-howses into whore-howses . . . exorbitant rents demanded for the smallest attics . . . the poorest had to go weekly to the pawn-shops to pawn their clothes to pay the rent . . .', and Thomas Dekker wrote in 1612 'of the open doors of carted bawdes   all daye and nyght . . . with a appaire of Harlots in *Taffata* Gownes' beckoning to the customers.

In February 1609 George While, a butcher, was taken by the constable from a 'notorious bawdy-house' in Cripplegate, '. . . swaggering drunke all night . . . and still abusing the Constable in the morning'. In 1610 John Burgoyne, likewise of Cripplegate, was charged '. . . that he not only received people sick of the Plague . . . but also another sycke of the French poxe . . . who liveth there incontinently with Fayth Langley a whore . . .' In 1611 Joan Woodshore of Clerkenwell was charged that '. . . she was a noted Whoare . . . who sold Tobacco [without a licence] . . . and with running at two sea-faring Men with a Spitt or Rapier . . .'.

In 1613 the courts were very busy. In February Anne Wright was found hiding, dressed only in a sheet, in Mrs Crabbe's brothel in Clerkenwell. (In December Mrs Crabbe was to be 'whipt and carted' for keeping the brothel.) Anne Robinson of Aldgate was sentenced for being a 'notorious Queane' who sat at her door until midnight 'to entertaine lewd Perssons that resortes unto her'. Joan Cole, already in the Bridewell, was further sentenced to be carted and whipped 'with papers on her head and a Bellman before her ringing his bell', and three other 'Turnbull Street Whoares must accompany her', including Helen Browne, who had been found lurking 'in a lewd house in Turnbull Street in a dark cellar'. It is curious that Turnmill and Turnbull – which was a nickname – are found interchangeable even in official documents.

William Sowthe and his wife kept 'a house of Mis-rule in Cow Cross in which verie sinfull Lust and Carnal behaviour' took place, but worse still, 'one Shercoe' confessed that he 'had had the use of Isabel Sowthe's bodie on the Sabath day when they shulde all have been in churche', so there was adultery into the bargain. George Maine, a barber-surgeon, a guildsman, kept a bawdy-house in nearby Clerkenwell Green and was sent to the pillory; but a licensed scrivener, Roger Williams, and his wife Margaret were carted from Newgate to their own house, shamed and returned to prison.

Sam Rowlands, in his '*A Crewe of Kinde Gossips* (1609), dealt with the absent husband syndrome:

> There are kind Gentlemen, some two or three
> and they, indeed, my loving Kinsmen be,
> whiche will not see me want. I know that, Ay! . . .
> Two of them at my house in Term time lie
> and comfort me with Jests and odd Device
> Whenas my Husban's oute a-nights at Dice.

These absent husbands posed a more serious problem to their wives. In the broadsheet ballad 'A Marry'd Woman's Case (1609) one verse reads:

> A Woman that's to a Whoremonger wed
> is in a most desperate Case.
> She scarce dares to perform her Dutie in Bed
> with one of Condition so base:
> For sometimes he's bitten with Turnbull-street Fleas –
> the Poxe or some other infectious Disease
> and yett, to her Perill, his Lust she must please,
>   Oh! Thus lives a Woman that's married.

While a number of 'respectable' brothels existed catering for both husbands and wives, the latter were warned to be careful 'not to barter their favours without securing some advantage' and to be careful at some houses in Moorfields wherein they might be surprised by unexpected visits from the lord mayor's constables 'with a Drum', and end up in the local cage. In 1614 the Clerkenwell cage had been pulled down because '. . . it was muche decaied . . . but it was sett uppe agayne under the bricke Wall at the ende of the Cuckynge-stoole'. This was situated down by the Fleet 'ditch', not far from the newly built Hicks Hall, the first to have cells in its cellars for bound-over malefactors.

In 1615 the number of sexual misdemeanours was so large that the keeper of the Bridewell refused to accept any more 'Clerkenwell Whores' because he had no more room. Later a new 'House of Correccion', the Clerkenwell Bridewell, was built to accommodate the hordes of whoredom. John Taylor, 'the Water Poet', in The Praise & Vertue of a Iayle and Iaylers (1623) warbles:

> In London and within a mile, I ween
> There are of Iayles & Prisons, full eighteen:
> and sixty Whippynge Postes & Stockes and Cages
> Where Sin & Shame & Sorrow hath due Wages.

Physical cleanliness was also not highly regarded. In 1607 the annual wardmote of the Vintry complained to the mayor and sheriffs 'that the City had failed to provide a Lanthorne and Candle' according to the regulations, 'outside the Longhouse [the communal privy for men and women set up by Dick Whittington] whereby manie inconveniences have happened'. These 'inconveniences' included failure by the gong-farmers to clear away the dung and also frequent flooding at high tide of the River Thames, and the lack of illumination caused many a stumble. In 1691 the wardmote noted that '. . . it had made the same complaint for eighty-two years and nothing had been done'. Moreover, the Cripplegate wardmote complained in 1607 that '. . . divers Persons dwellynge in severall allies do dayly brynge their nyghte soile and other unfitt Excrementes and lay them in the open streetes to the greete common Annoyaunce to the Dwellers and Passers-by . . .', and they too were still complaining in much the same terms in 1647.

Illiterate and corruptible constables and beadles were the law-enforcement officers: '. . . the Constable is a *Vice-roy* in his streete . . . his jurisdiction extends to the neareste Stocks and he is a *Scare-crowe* to that ale-howse where he drinkes not his Morning draughte . . .'.

Times Whistle (1614) mentions that '. . . sodomy and incest were rife at Court . . . protected by the Most Powerfull' – meaning the King himself.

In 1622 James issued an ordinance 'Touching upon Disorderly Houses', aimed principally at Saffron Hill, in Farringdon Without, '. . . which of long time hath been pestered with divers immodest lascivious and shameless women . . . common whores . . . in divers howses for base and filthy lucre's sake, ackrewyng to the benefitt of Landlords and Tenants . . . women who sit usually at the doores . . . shamefully allure . . . suche as pass by . . .'. Added to this was a warning to corrupt headboroughs and beadles who might try to cover up or warn such miscreants. (A headborough was a superior constable). Every part of the City was now 'infected'.

The places raided were Cowcross Street, Cocks Lane, Smithfield, St John Street and Clerkenwell – all in Farringdon ward; the liberty of Norton Folgate and Shoreditch – outside Bishopsgate; Petticoat Lane in Bishopsgate Without; the Charter-house Liberty, and Wapping (which was outside the City's juris-diction). None of the bawds and whores now arrested were to be released on bail unless a real surety was found – a substantial citizen. Saffron Hill, however, was still a liberty outside the City.

The presence of the Fortune Theatre in Golden Lane added not only to the gaiety but also to the roughness of Cripplegate Within. In 1624 the well-known astrologer and abortionist 'Dr' John Lambe, whose special *forte* was the supply of young virgins to elderly aristocratic lechers, was mobbed when coming out of the theatre and 'hys braines were bashed out'. He had procured and seduced little Joan Seger, a virgin aged eleven, raping and bugger-ing her and infecting her with venereal disease. He was arraigned

Drowning of a witch, c. 1600. Her house burnt down, her cart broken and her horse driven away, the supposed witch is dragged through the mill-race. The boar is her 'familiar'.

and found guilty but by the intervention of George Villiers, Duke of Buckingham, was set free. Lambe was much esteemed at Court apparently for his prognostications as an astrologer but actually because of his skill in abortions for unwanted aristocratic pregnancies. He died of his injuries soon afterwards, whereupon Buckingham protested to the King, who instructed the City Corporation to pay a fine of £3,000 'for their negligence in arraigning his *protégé*, and to uphold the prestige and power of the monarchy. This decision caused further riots in the City – although assuredly Dr Lambe should have prognosticated his own demise?

In 1624 John Sleepe of the Rose in Turnbull Street comes alive again, being described as 'a wideawake man in Mirth and Pastimes'; his son owned the Whelp and Bacon by Smithfield Pond, as well as the William and Mary in the Bartholomew Fair grounds until he died in 1702.

In 1624 James was compelled to re-enact his 1622 ordinance, this time adding Turnmill Street to the list, following a report the previous January '. . . that manie lewde Persons in Turnmillestreete . . . keepes common brothell houses and harbour divers impudent Queanes . . . murders were committed there . . .'. In the course of these raids one William Poole was indicted 'for the murther of hys Wyff Elizabeth by stickinge a Knife in her Belley'; he was duly hanged. Well might the writer of 'The Merrie Mans Resolution', a very popular contemporary ballad, say after his London-wide peregrination.

And Farewel to Turnbal streete
for that no comfort yeildes,

although he found many 'strapping Lasses . . . who were Wenches lyke unto *Feyries*' in Clerkenwell. It is possible that William Poole was related to that John Poole who in 1636 'kept a howse in Two Brewers Alley in Turnmill Street' and who had rented the premises to Thomas Christie with the proviso that '. . . he shal give a shilling for Bread to the poore every Sunday' out of the rent.

Another charitable action was that of William Anderson, lessee of the Bitt Tavern, whence Bitt Alley got its name. (It is thought to derive from the 'Bit and Stirrup' for horses.) On his death in 1649 he devised the rents from his tavern 'for the poor of Andover and Clerkenwell, in equal parts'. Likewise 'the eminent Brewer' Giles Russell, owner of the well-known tavern the Swan, bequeathed 'his lands for the maintenance of eighteen children in several parishes including three in Turnmill St . . . on his wife's death, all to go to the Bridewell'.

In 1626 at least one highly respectable character lived in Turnmill Street: this was Dr Thomas Worthington, famed translator of the Douai Bible, 'who had lodgings there'.

These alleys have, with a couple of exceptions, all disappeared. Broad Court was 'a nest of squalid human kennels . . . reeking yards overflowing with filth from waterless privies without seats or doors'; Frying Pan Alley '. . . was only 2'6" wide and 20ft long . . . there was not room to get a coffin out without turning it on edge'. The famous Black Eagle Alley, named after the hostelry of that name, was 'noysome'. In all these alleys the tenements were literally stacked with poor prostitutes struggling to make a living but sometimes earning just enough for some bread and a drink of ale. To be called 'a Turnbull whore' was the greatest insult that could be thrown at any 'venereal virgin'. Sam Pepys in *Penny Merriments* (1668) mentions 'The Olde Pye House in Turnmill St where women brawl: and in the nearby *Three Tuns* the slogan was "No! No! No! Money, No Cony."' By 1659 (*vide* Chettle) the influx of Huguenots and Welsh, establishing small workshops and schools, began to change the general ambience of Clerkenwell. Several breweries were set up, the waters from the wells being deemed very pure. There was an advertisement in *The Daily Courant* in 1714: 'A house to be lett in Turnmill Street . . . with a common sewer and a good stream running by it . . . to turn a Mill to grind *Haire Powder*, or Liquorish or other Things. . . .'

In 1732 the famous Whig politician John Wilkes, who was born in

Clerkenwell, rented a house in Turnmill Street, on the west side (by the river), two doors away from Bell Alley. It was probably for one of his many amours – he was not squeamish: any time, any place and any whore would do.

In 1748 the famous printer and publisher Edward Cave bought a printing press 'to be powered by the Turnmill Brook', while in 1768 'A Blackfriars Waterman took his boat to Turnmill where he plied, removing the Inhabitants who could not leave the houses because the Water was more than four feet deep. . . .'

Turnmill Street exists to this day, a dull, respectable row of undistinguished commercial offices along the east side confronting a long blank wall behind which runs the Metropolitan Railway and Farrington Street Station. There is no sign whatsoever of its former frailties.

King James I died in 1625 'of Bright's Disease, bleeding Piles, Stones in the Bladder, Arthritis and Dental caries' but before doing so he warned his son, soon to be Charles I, that, 'Homosexuality is one of the few horrible Crimes that a King, was bound in Conscience never to forgive!'

10 Of Rogues, Plumers and Cloaktwitchers

In sharp contrast to his father, Charles I was a man of moral rectitude. His begotten sin was a belief in the Divine Right of Kings, which by this time was somewhat shopworn, although he refused to admit it. It was the eventual cause of his downfall. His reign opened with an inauspicious omen – one of the worst outbreaks of bubonic plague throughout the kingdom. This boded ill for the other plague, that of bawdry, and by his first Parliament in 1625 he directed the Lord Chief Justice 'TO TAKE SOME PRESENT ORDER for the reformation of Places of open Bawdry in Clerckenwell, Pick-thatch, Turnmill Street, Golden Lane and Duke Humphreys at Blackfriars'.

The Pickthatch (or Pickhatch) was an undefined area around Aldersgate and Clerkenwell which was a nest of low-class whore-dom. The 'pick-hatch' referred to the metal grill set in the heavily barred door enabling the resident to see who was demanding admittance – a necessity in that very rough area. The 'hatch' was the description – as in escutcheons – of crossed metal lattices. Almost every whorehouse in the area had one; hence the general name.

Golden Lane had become a problem area after the Fortune Theatre had been built there in Queen Elizabeth's day: it had become very rough indeed. Clerkenwell itself was a comparative newcomer to bawdry, since before the sequestration of the monasteries by Henry VIII in 1539 it had been within the priory of St John

The Fortune Playhouse in Golden Lane. The only one in the City. Built in 1600 for Philip Henslow and Edward Alleyn, it was burnt down in 1621 and rebuilt. Closed by the Puritans in 1642, the Fortune continued with illegal performances until demolished by Cromwell's Ironsides in 1649. The illustration shows the second theatre.

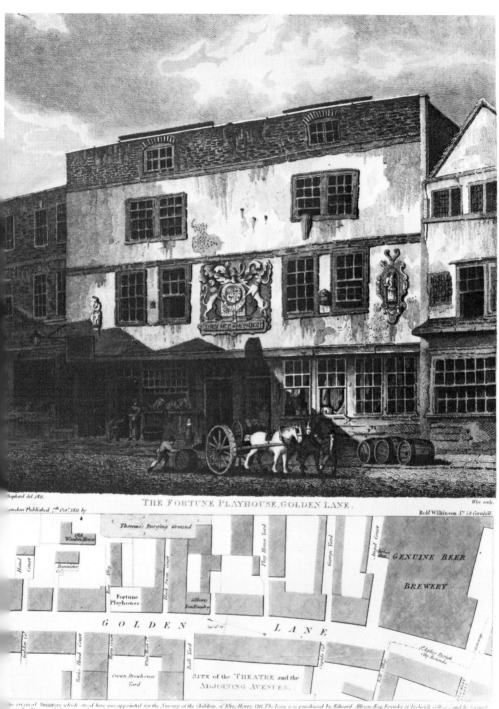

Shepherd del. 1811.   Wise sculp.

THE FORTUNE PLAYHOUSE, GOLDEN LANE.

London Published 7th Oct. 1811 by   Robt. Wilkinson No. 58 Cornhill.

he original Structure which stood here was appointed for the Nursery of the Children of King Henry VIII, The Lease was purchased by Edward Alleyne Esq. Founder of Dulwich College, and he turned it into the Theatre which he denominated "The Fortune" and finished it in 1599. In 1649 the whole Building and the theatrical Property were destroyed by Fire. After being rebuilt it was offered for Sale in 1661 ... d there was sufficient Space to allow twenty three Tenements and Gardens, and a Street now called Playhouse Yard which at present exhibits a scene of Poverty and is an Avenue from Golden ... to Whitecross Street.

The procession of Marie de Medici on her way to Whitehall to visit her son-in-law Charles I in 1638. It was of surpassing magnificence and cost, but the picture does not show the rioting crowds who threatened to lynch her all the way to the palace.

of Jerusalem and partly within the soke of the kings of Scotland; but its near neighbour, Turnmill Street, helped give it a bad name.

This ordinance was just as ineffectual as all the others before it. Moreover, it could now be circumvented by the great corruption in the administration of justice, where it was said that the local constable was effectively judge and jury. A key man was 'the justice's clerk' who could get a case dropped or mislay essential papers or even pass on part of the bribe to the magistrates – these were, of course, 'tradeing justices' who lived on the revenue generated from plaintiffs and defendants; some were therefore more 'flexible' than others. Cases are on record where the magistrate actually had shares in a brothel. A bawd could be back in business the quicker she paid the bribe; she was responsible for her girls and could bail them out or let them rot in gaol.

Charles clearly failed to follow the great changes taking place 'below' – he ruled without a parliament from 1630 to 1640, when he was compelled to recall 'these cursed aged Cats' and found himself faced by one Oliver Cromwell and like-minded 'puritans'. This parliament, *inter alia*, abolished torture and reduced prostitution from a felony to 'a nuisance if committed in public', the penalty being a ducking or a whipping and a short spell in Bridewell. Simple fornication earned a penalty of three months in a 'House of Correccion'. Adultery, however, was still punishable by death – although during the Commonwealth period following the execution of Charles I in 1649 no jury would convict in such cases. The attempt to stop ill-treatment of prisoners was often frustrated because most gaols were still 'franchise gaols' – places of profit for the keeper, who still got paid for putting on or taking off 'irons' (gyves and fetters). The first enactments against cruelty to animals were made by banning bull- and bear-baiting and cockfights, albeit these 'sports' were still carried out more or less clandestinely.

The Commonwealth affirmed the right of all men to have a say in their government but was not prepared to risk God's wrath by enfranchising their helpmeets – even though women were the mainstay of the Cromwellian order. Cromwell was not a social leveller: his savage suppression of the Levellers and Diggers – both equalitarian sects – proved that, as did his murderous actions against the Irish 'rebels'. He really had no understanding of the problems of the really poor, let alone women's special problems.

The cucking-stool and the cage were kept busy, although there were slight alleviations. A harlot could be respited a ducking 'as long as she doth behave herself', and the hanging of women as 'vagabonds' was ended.

In 1645 the Book of Common Prayer was replaced by the *Presbyterian Directory*. Marriage was no longer a sacrament, although 'to marry in the Lord' had still to be done by a minister. In 1653 it took the solemnization of marriage out of the hands of the clergy into the hands of the magistrates, with a new official, the parish registrar, to record it. There was, as early as 1650, an act for 'suppressing the abhominable sins of Incest Adultery and Fornication'. It had little effect.

To maintain discipline in the army, in 1642 'any girl who consorted with a soldier' was 'suspected of incontinency' and frowned upon; but an act of 1650 dealing with the death sentence for adultery exempted 'women whose husbands had been missing for three years'. The records are surprisingly explicit in sexual matters. In a case when a woman saw a young man put his hand up her daughter's dress and expostulated, he replied, 'I will fuck thee and thy daughter before I go home . . . I have fucked ten women in this parish.' In another case the excuse was 'She was a handsome wench and would fuck well!' Very often the 'invitation' was by the lovers' 'usually putting out their privy member'. There were 'vagrant whores' and 'village whores' at inns, fairs, markets and even crossroads.

There were many cases of sodomy. A twelve-year-old apprentice told the Court: 'I have lain with Meredith Davy, my master's servant since Easter last year . . . he hath used to take me in his arms [after they were in bed together] . . . and hath put his prick

. . . until he hath wet it . . . [usually] on Sunday and Holyday nights when he had been drinking . . . last Sunday others heard and told the Dame. . . .' In another instance a yeoman's son went into a field to ease nature and '. . . when he had untrussed himself one Downey . . . came up behind and offered his privy Member to have entered his fundament . . . he entreated the lad to stay still' so he could bugger him. There is also the matter of one Dowdeney who '. . . twenty or thirty times when alone with the blacksmith . . . had taken his privy member . . . and suggested that they might go to some private place . . . that he might bugger him . . . .'.

Most curious of all is the report about bestiality involving this same Dowdeney, who just before Christmas 1645, while the blacksmith was shoeing his mare, suggested that '. . . they close the stable door so that he could bugger William Hucker's mare then in the stable . . .', but this time the blacksmith thrust him away, saying, 'Tho' you take this course to hang yourself you shall not take any course to hang *me*!'

Male attitudes demonstrated little regard for women: many could not understand why women got so upset about rape – 'it was such a small matter'. In part these attitudes were encouraged by the replacement of the king's jurors by the jurors of the lord protector who consistently refused to pass 'guilty' verdicts for adultery, because it '. . . might mean hanging a man for a human frailty'. Many a prostitute's life was saved thereby, one being Damaris Drye, later Damaris Page, 'the Great Bawd of the Seamen' and *protégée* of King James II. Only two executions were actually carried out, one being that of Ursula Powell, 'wife to Robert Powell for whoredom with a man unknown'. She 'pleaded her belley' and indeed was pregnant, so the merciful court allowed her to be hanged for her adultery 'after the accouchement'. Thereafter most were given a 'Protector's Pardon' by Oliver Cromwell and then his son.

There were nevertheless many gaps in the Commonwealth's pretensions to humanitarianism. There was the case of Anne Biddlestone who in 1648 '. . . was drove through the streets by an Officer, holding a Rope in his Hands at the other end fastened to an *engine* called *The Branks* like a Crown of Iron muzzled over her Head and Face with a great *Tongue* of Iron forc'd into her Mouth which forc'd the Blood out: which is the Punishment the Magistrates do inflict upon chiding and scoulding women . . .'. At the same time, '. . . men were drove up and down the streets with a great *Tubb* or *Barrell*, open in the Sides with a Hole at one end with their Heads put through so covering their Bodies down to the small of their

Mrs Anne Biddlestone being marched with her head in the vicious mouth-piece, The Branks, *which depressed the tongue and could tear the mouth. Originally a punishment for scolds it was also applied to witches. c. 1648.*

Leggs: and then close the same calling it the *New-Fashion'd Cloak* . . . the Punishment for Drunkards and the like . . .'.

The worst was the treatment of witches. A 'witch-finder' was paid 25 shillings 'a piece for all he could condemn as witches'. The magistrate would then send the bellman out, crying, 'All people that would bring any Complaint against any woman for a Witch –

they shall be sent for and try'd by the Person appointed.' One witch-finder later confessed that, '. . . he knew women as witches by their looks'. When pointed out, they were '. . . stript, and Pinns thrust in their Bodies'. He had 'picked-out no less than twenty-seven', none of whom confessed but were hanged. Later this man was condemned as a villain, confessing on the gallows that, '. . . he had been the death of above two hundred and twenty women in England & Scotland for the gain of Twenty shillings apiece: and beseeched forgiveness . . . before he was executed'. Neither the judgments nor the executions were questioned: all they wanted to know was '. . . by what Law the magistrates could try women for witches and by what Law pay men twenty-shilling apiece: and by what Law men are hired to give evidence to take away people's lives?'. All that the eventual enquiry ordered was: 'The Lord Protector commands all Judges and Witnesses to appear, execute justice and give evidence *gratis.*'

In June 1652 there was the uncommon case of 'Mary Neale, commonly called the *Queen of Morocco* taken in a Bawdy-house as a suspected Whore . . . she weares rich clothes and cannot give good accompte how shee cometh by them or how shee gets her living . . . shee says her mother's name is Stuart and shee lives in Moor Fields . . .'. This sobriquet was usually given to a black or coloured woman, and it is the measure of the popular contempt for the monarchy that she adopts the name of Stuart! At the same Sessions Mary Neason, servant to Mrs Susan King, '. . . drew men into her mistress' house, the same being a Bawdy-house . . . she was sent away because she hath the Poxe. ORDERED. That she be sent to Bridewell', which is curious, because there were no medical services in any prison at that time and certainly not for treatment of venereal disease. Constant thrashing or slitting the nose was the accepted cure for such diseases.

Not that all was well in the prison service either. A complaint was made to the Middlesex magistrates in April 1646 by George Dodson, keeper of the New Prison at Clerkenwell, who was supposed to pay rent 'from the fees and fines'. His revenues were being greatly reduced because headboroughs and constables of other prisons '. . . secured the transfer of his prisoners, without Warrants from the Justices, to their prisons "because they take the considerable fees" and so he could not pay his rent. The Bench "understanding his predicament" gave him time to pay . . .'. There is no record that anything was done about such fiddles, which were being practised from judges down to the lowliest prison tapster.

The New Gate as it was in 1666: the upper part was used as a prison although Newgate Prison was actually nearby. It was taken down in 1765 to clear Newgate Street, for the increasing traffic.

Then a little xenophobia emerges, when John Greene was '. . . charged with keeping a notorious Disorderly House keeping Wenches at his Dore to beckon in Flemmings and other lewd Persons . . .'. For centuries Flemings and Picards had been lusting after British maidens, and they were still at it. Then in 1653 James Stuart, a 'Napper' took lewd women to Adam Wallis' house 'to be *napped*'. His companion Richard Dawson had a 'Napping House' in St Martin-le-Grand in which men and women were found 'in very uncivil postures' and the women were even found 'dancing with gentlemen at Night'! Two pimps ('seductioners') were also taken.

There was also a host of obscene publications. The two official licensers, John Rushworth and Gilbert Mabbott, were financially and sexually corrupt, so that they were breaking their own rules. One man, John Crouch, was able to publish in 1660 a mountain of pornographic material. This occasioned such rude ballads as 'Bum Fodder – to wipe the Nation's Rump' – a reference to the Rump Parliament, when even lowly street urchins chanted

> Old Noll, when we talked of *Magna Carta*
> did prophesie well, we should all smart-a
> and now we have found this Rump's *Magna Farta*
>   Which Nobody can deny!

Cromwell's own love-affair with Bess Dysart, his 'Bess o my Heart', was no secret, nor were the Roundheads the joyless Puritans they are thought to have been – the elite Ironsides were real puritans. Indeed most of the 'Great Bawds' of Charles II's era were already practising in and around Farringdon and Cripplegate in the 1650s. During Oliver Cromwell's lifetime Henry Marsh published *The Crafty Whore*, or 'The Mistery & Iniquitie of Bawdy-houses', accurately describing the situation in Commonwealth London: 'They are houses full of Rogues, Plumers, Fylers and Cloak-twitchers . . . Warehouses for all Thefts and Fellonies . . . to save the Whores the labour of caterwauling at midnight under *Bulks* or at Street-corners with a large *White-apron* . . . in poor tottering houses in the suburbs . . . the Bawd being . . . a Cunny-woman. . . .'

After Cromwell's death in September 1658, it was said that, 'Its a poor Kin that hath neither Thief nor Whore in it!' Nevertheless, with all its shortcomings, the Commonwealth manifested greater humanity than any previous rule. Sinfulness and coarseness were now to have a free reign in the capital.

One of the greatest beneficiaries was to be the revival of one of London's oldest sin-centres, the 'smoothe-feilde' or Smithfield which in 1102 had been 'a moorishe grounde and comon laystall for excrementes voyded oute of ye citie'. In the following year it was granted to the monk Rahere 'to buylde a churche and an hospital to the glory of Sent Bartholomew', with a licence to hold a fair for three days at St Bartholomew's-tide to provide an income. Rahere was the first prior and is reputed to have built the church with his own hands.

In 1113 Henry II renewed the charter, granting the privileges of the fair, especially for 'the Clothiers of all England and the Drapers of London . . . and for Debts and Contracts, the Court of *Pie-poudre* . . .'. This court settled complaints by 'outsiders' – the name is said to come from old Norman-French recalling the dusty feet of visitors from afar – *pieds poudrés*. In 1174 William FitzStephen said it was a place of recreation for all London's citizens, with a horse-market every Friday. In the middle was a large 'Horse-pool' or pond, later to be used as a ducking-pond, and nearby a grove of elm trees, later the place of execution of alleged noble traitors. There were also some sheep-folds and cattle-pens. The hosiers were grouped together in a part still called Hosier Lane. The nearby Long Lane, leading to opulent Beech Street, was soon filled with inns, taverns and 'houses of Resort'. Similarly with Duck Lane – to be gentrified into Duke Street and centuries later the starting-point for several famous procuresses, particularly Madam Britannica Hollandia of 'Hollands Leaguer'.

In 1200 the City laid down its 'Custumes of Smythefeld' regulating prices and weights and the rake-offs for the bailiff, and in 1241 designating the adjacent Cock Lane as an 'assigned place' to which City whores were to be exiled. This was a precinct owned by St Paul's Cathedral and probably governed by much the same rules as the Bankside *stewes* of the bishop of Winchester. However, the area was already a 'red-light' district, since most of the lanes leading down to the Turnmill brook were warrens of whorehouses.

When Edward I celebrated his great victory over the Scots in 1293, '. . . all the Citizens according to their Trades celebrated . . . the Fishmongers with four silver-gilt *Sturgeons* mounted on four gaily-caparisoned Horses and four silver *Salmons* on Horses and forty-six armed Knights and a thousand horsemen . . .'. In 1305 this king celebrated the capture of the brave Scottish hero William Wallace by having him barbarously executed on Smithfield, 'amid the plaudits' of the crowd. Throughout the medieval period there were tournaments and great jousts as well as many 'triumphs'. In 1357 and in 1362 the jousts lasted five days. In 1381 Mayor William Walworth killed Wat Tyler there, at the parley with Richard II. In

1375 there was the Great Tournament with Dame Alice Perrers as 'Lady of the Sunne', and in 1394 the ward of Farringdon Without was created which included Smithfield in its area, although the City's influence was constrained by the charter.

Because the whole area was near to the 'Shambles' where meat was slaughtered (today's Newgate Street) it was a very rough neighbourhood, lending itself to every sort of unseemly behaviour, keeping the hospital busy all the time. In 1421 the great Richard Whittington 'repaired' the hospital and also the gate 'of olde tyme called ye West Gate' in addition he built a public 'two-holer privy' near Cock Lane.

Malefactors were usually hanged 'twixt the horsepool and the River of the Wells' but special criminals, such as 'hereticks' and witches, were burned. In 1530 Henry VIII legalized 'boylynge in oyle', originally meant for women who had poisoned their husbands. However, the first to suffer this dreadful end was Richard Roose, a cook of the bishop of Rochester: 'He was publicly boiled to death at Smithfield in a huge cauldron made of Iron suspended from a massive iron tripod set over a pile of Logs . . . he suffered for more than two hours before he died. . . .' In 1535 the unlucky Carthusian monks were all boiled to death: a contemporary illustration shows that some were trussed up like chickens, thrust into cold water and boiled. Others had been partially dismembered beforehand. In 1538 the prior of Greenwich, John Forrest, 'was encaged and roasted alive' for refusing to accept King Henry's 'supremacy', and many women were burned there for adultery. In Queen Mary's reign (1553–8), no fewer than 200 fervent Protestants died by this means, and the burning of witches went on even in Commonwealth times. On 10 May 1652 John Evelyn, passing by Smithfield, '. . . saw a miserable creature burning who had murdered her husband'. (After 1700 women were strangled before being burned.)

Favourite drinking-places were the Ram Inn, the Rose Inn, the Bell, the Three Foxes and the Adam and Eve, all now covered by the meat market; most famed 'for goode cheer' was the Kings Arms on Snorrehyll (Snow Hill), a narrow, winding lane leading down to the Turnmill brook.

The fair was sometimes called 'the Cloth Fair' – the street of that name still runs by the side of the church parallel with Long Lane, which dates back to 1249 and commemorates William le Long de Portpool, a 'fripperer' or cloth-broker. At the Bartholomew Fair the famous 'Bartholomew Babies' – gingerbread dollies – were sold. (By Jacobean days the 'Babies' were the ambulant poor whores whose customers queued up outside the temporary tents or sat on a bench outside awaiting their turn.) The constables were constantly complaining about the open copulation in the narrow alleys.

In 1641 there was a penny broadsheet ballad *Room for Company at Bartholomew Faire* which described the mixture of participants:

> Cutpurses and Cheaters, and Bawdy-house Keepers
> Punckes, Aye! and Panders and casheered Commanders . . .
> Alchemystes and Pedlars, Whores, Bawds and Beggers
> In Bartholomew Fair.

John Marston, in *The Dutch Courtezan*, praised the Bartholomew Babies: 'They will bestow upon you that which will stick by you as long as you live. They are no ungrateful Personalities – they will give you *quid pro quo*. . . . Do you give them French Crowns they'll give you the French Poxe . . .', and Ben Jonson had called attention, in *Bartholomew Fair*, to the bawd Alice berating Judge Overdo's wife, complaining that, '. . . the poor whores can have no Traffic [business] because of the rich Private Whores whose Capes and Hoods and Velvets call away our Customers and lick the Fat from us!'

The Great Plague of 1665 caused an exodus of citizens of every

Wenceslas Hollar's dramatic picture of the destruction of London in the Great Fire of 1666.

degree from London, and the Great Fire of the following year completely altered the aspects of the City. Both the hovels and tenements of the poor and the houses of the wealthier inhabitants had been destroyed; moreover, a great many business premises had been burned down. The King's requirement that all new buildings must be of brick and that certain streets had to be widened, with the consequent obliteration of many property boundaries, meant that rents escalated, so that smaller businesses could no longer trade profitably – indeed, a great many had been ruined.

Former extra-mural suburbs, Smithfield, Farringdon, Cripplegate, Bishopsgate and the Tower, now became urbanized. There were, of course, still some brothels and Mollies Houses which had been rebuilt about the Royal Exchange, but the homosexual 'Houses of Resort' now ranged from a cluster around the pleasant suburb of Beech Lane to another, less salubrious cluster around Fetter Lane in Holborn.

From the time Charles II came to the throne in 1660, there was a marked laxity about sexual misbehaviour – what was good for the Court was good for the commonalty! Smithfield was still a place for great relaxation and enjoyment for those looking for sexual outlooks. Sam Pepys 'went alone to the Fair' on 7 September 1668 and '. . . beckon'd a Wench into his Coach and gave her a Shilling for her Services'.

The King himself occasionally adopted the Haroun al Raschid tactic of mixing incognito with his subjects, in his guise as 'Old Rowley'.

On one memorable occasion Lord Rochester and the Duchess of Cleveland cozened him into a local bawdy-house, arranging to have his pocket picked. When the King had finished his sport, he found he had no money and had to ask the bawd to allow him credit till next morning, but she refused because she did not know him. He then pulled a ring from his finger and told her to call a jeweller to value it. The jeweller, after examining it, remarked that, 'There is only one man in the kingdom who can afford to wear this ring and that is the King himself', whereupon he fell to his knees and apologized, what time the bawd trembled too. However, with his customary aplomb Charles made light of it – but nobody knows what he said to his two friends later! He was, of course, not very particular about his sexual partners.

The broadsheet *Strange Newes from Bartholomew Fair* (1661) tells the story of 'Bonny Bess of Whore and Bacon Lane neere unto Pye Corner . . . and Merrie Moll of Ducke Street [respectively Hosier

The Sheriff's Compter in the Poultry after rebuilding in 1667, the original prison having been burnt down in the Great Fire of 1666.

Lane and Duke Street] . . . who satt at the wayside with their Leggs spreade wide crying "Here's your Ware, Boys!"' Business was very bad, and they sighed because '. . . they had neglected the *Chuck-Office* and the Half-crowns earned thereby as practised in *Jack-a-Newberries Sixe Windmills* . . . itt woulde have broughte them Custom enough!'

Thomas D'Urfey in 1701 lamented the plight of these Bartholomew Babies:

> At ev'ry Dore lies a Hagg or a Whore –
> and in Hosier Lane, if I'm not mistaken
> Such plentie of Whores, you'll have a Paire
> to a single Gammon of Bacon!

Complaints were often made about drunken cattle-herders who ill-treated their animals, which would then stampede through the neighbouring stalls and shops – the origin of the phrase 'A bull in a china shop' – and even as late as 1789 cattle were being driven through Sunday church congregations!

One very welcome occasion was in 1686 when Smithfield was packed to watch the death of the public hangman, Jack Ketch. After his appointment in 1663 he had been responsible for the most barbarous practices at his executions. In 1683 he had hanged Lord William Russell and two years later had executed the King's own nephew – and putative king – James, Duke of Monmouth, after which he boiled the heads of thousands of Monmouth's supporters in cauldrons of pitch before they were broadcast all over the kingdom. But in 1686, it was reported: 'Jack Ketch, the Public Hangman, hanged himself at the Wrestling Places backsyde of Clerkenwell . . . the Sunday of Bartholomews-day and two others for robbynge about the Bartholomew Fayre, at which 20,000 persons were present.'

In 1691, when William of Orange was on the throne, there was a spate of publications giving information to would-be lechers. There was *A Catalogue of Jilts, Cracks & Prostitutes, Nightwalkers, Whores, She-friends, Kind Women & others of the Linnen-lifting Tribe.* This listed twenty-one women who could be found 'in the Cloy-

'London, thou art the flower of cities all!'
William Dunbar (1465–1530)
Wenceslas Hollar's *magnificent panorama, 1666.*

160

sters' of St Bartholomew's Church during the fair, 'between eight and eleven'. There was a brief description of their age, size and shape and particular specialities. For example: 'Mary Holland, tall graceful and comely, shy of her favours but may be mollified at a cost of £20. Elizabeth Holland [her sister] . . . indifferent to Money but a Supper and Two Guineas will tempt her.' Dorothy Roberts was fond of 'usquebaugh' (whisky), so could be had for a bottle of wine. 'Posture Moll', a flagellant, wanted only half-a-crown for 'her raree show'. Mrs Whitby 'who formerly refused Five Guineas' will now take up with 'any ordinary fellow for Ten shillings' – she having been mistress to a high-born colonel. Most interesting in this particular list is the inclusion of two black women, 'Bridget Williams, a pretty little Negress . . . not yet mistress of her profession so can be offered half-a-crown . . . and bullied out of her money again . . .' and 'Mrs Sarah Heath, a Negress . . . her Fee is higher . . . more experienced . . . will make no concession about fee . . .'.

There are also some curious broadside sheets issued in July 1691, one being

MERCURIUS MATRIMONIALIS
or
A CHAPMAN for Ladies only
lately offered for SALE
by Way of AUCTION.

It is a list of women and the type of gentleman they'd like to be knocked down to. On the obverse is *A Catalogue of Batchelors* (obviously a spoof). There is another of the same date:

BY CONSENT
Characters of some Young Women belonging to
the 'CHANGES' who are to be dispos'd of
by Way of AUCTION on July 6.1691

with a *caveat*: 'No Man should Bid unless he is able to maintain any of the Ladies in a Proper Style.' Number one on the list is 'One very pretty Proper BLACK Gentlewoman . . . something superannuated but so fast FIX'd that nothing but a Coach and six Horses can drag her out. Worth at least £40.0.0.'

So widespread had become the sins and villainies that in 1692 the London Society for the Reformation of Manners was established – a group of vigilantes employing paid informers to report on breaches of the peace and morals. During its existence its members hounded poor prostitutes to death or transportation, in the end earning the condemnation even of people who supported their moral views. Their efforts, needless to say, had little effect on the sin business, although they did compel much harsher punishments to be levied.

One curious case was that in May 1693 when Sarah Stratford, '. . . a Woman of Ill-fame procured Elizabeth Farrington for 20 Nobles. SENTENCE. To stand in the Pillory for an hour between 9 a.m. and midday for three days at Cow Cross and then at *The Fountain Tavern* in the Strand with a Paper on her Breast . . . then three Months in Newgate Prison without Bail or Mainprize . . .'. (The sum of money is also curious: a 'noble' was worth 6s. 8d. – (three nobles to a pound – and why the fine should be expressed in an even then obsolete currency needs some explanation.) Cow Cross was at the end of Turnmill Street. The Fountain in the Strand was also known as a haunt of homosexuals all through the eighteenth century.

A contemporary poem 'In the Long Vocation' (the long vacation of the law courts) describes the situation in the City 'when Business was scanty but Cherries and Whores extraordinary Plenty':

> When the Cits did retire to their Countrey Houses
> Leaving servants at Home to lie with their Spouses:
> When Wives too, would junket while their Cuckolds did sleep
> and spend more in a Night than they got in a Week . . .
> When *Sodomites* were so impudent to ply on th'Exchange
> and the Theatre *Jilts* would swive for a Crown
> and for want of brisk Tradeing, patroll round the Town . . .'.

It went on to describe how 'proud Drapers' would bugger their apprentices when the shops were shut, mentions the 'Blue Aprons' (poor prostitutes) and ends the recital with details of how one bilked some poor girl and fled to Finsbury Fields because '. . . the Reckoning was too high and my Pocket too low!'

From this time there was a tremendous upsurge in sodomy, involving many hitherto highly respectable City worthies whose attendance at many a local 'Mollies House' was observed. One of the nearest and best known was the Horseshoe in Beech Lane (now Beech Street), which was a pleasant, tree-lined thoroughfare with many fine mansions standing in their own grounds. Prestigious inhabitants were the gallant Prince Rupert, whose house in 1663 was run by 'Mother' Daniels, and General Monck, later Duke of Albemarle, who set King Charles II up on the throne. Mother Daniels had an extensive clientele among the nobility and gentry.

A very curious recreation in that area, noted by Ned Ward about 1680, was the Farting Club in Grub Street which had been '. . .

established by a Parcell of empty *Sparkes* about thirty years since at a Publick House in Cripplegate Parish and meet once a Week to poyson the Neighbourhood, and with their Noisy *Crepitations* attempt to outfart one another'.

As early as 1559 there was a Mollies House opposite the Old Bailey, and in 1661 there was the Three Potters at the 'Armitage' (Hermitage) in Cripplegate Without.

The greatest scandal of all was the raid on a 'Sodomites Club' in the City in 1707. It netted no fewer than forty men, who included a highly respected Cheapside mercer, Jacob Ecclestone, who was taken from the Wood Street compter to Newgate, where he committed suicide. A respected Cheapside draper, William Grant, hanged himself there, and the curate of St Dunstan's-in-the-East, Mr Jermain, cut his throat with his razor, as did another merchant, Mr Bearden. Several others committed suicide before the case was heard. All frequented the alleys around the Royal Exchange for 'HE-Concubines': at this time there were more than twenty 'Houses of Male Resort' in London patronized by Buggerantoes'. (Incidentally, Ecclestone was a known visitor to the Horseshoe in Beech Lane run by Mother Daniels.)

Pope's-Head Alley next the Royal Exchange was most notorious for catamites, and there was a Mollies House in Camomile Street, Bishopsgate (the manager was known as the Countess of Camomile'), and in Sweetings Alley, also near the Royal Exchange, where 'breeches-clad bawds' congregated.

Many were there just to blackmail likely innocents. On 19 September 1724 a young man was stopped by a man 'with his privities in his hand', who seized the youngster, crying, 'A Sodomite! A Sodomite!' He was terrified. A passing gentleman advised the young man to give the blackmailer 5 or 6 guineas, but he said he had 'not so much money in the world!'. They followed him to his place of employment, intent on extorting more money, but a man working there, knowing the boy's impeccable character, drew his sword, and the miscreants ran off, 'leaving the boy prostrate with shock'.

In 1722 there was a spate of prosecutions. In April one John Dicks picked up a young boy '. . . took him to several ale-houses and plied him with drink', then buggered him in the yard behind the Golden Ball in Fetter Lane. A pot-boy ran out to see what was going on and Dicks tried to bugger him as well, what time the landlord hearing the boys' cries ran out and caught Dicks 'in the very act of sodomy'. In a panic Dicks besought the landlord not to report him '. . . for if you swear against me you swear away my life!' Despite all this testimony Dicks was only found guilty of 'attempted sodomy', fined twenty Marks and stood an hour in the Temple Bar pillory, then two years in Newgate.

In October Thomas Rodin was indicted for buggery in Mrs Peter Wright's *Mollies House* and brothel in Long Lane Smithfield upon a complaint by one Clayton who alleged that Rodin had said:

> . . . that he took more Pleasure lying with a Man than with the finest Woman in the World, and had not toched his Wife this nine Months!

It then transpired that Clayton was 'a pimping Perjuror' and that Rodin was a 'poor honest but ignorant man'. He was duly acquitted.

The magistrates were always insisting on proof of actual 'penetration' to try and avoid the death penalty, so that many were only charged with the lesser crime of 'attempted sodomy' punishable by fines and imprisonment. Moreover care had to be taken when there was so much blackmail of honest men by criminals for even the threat could drive many a man to suicide. Just a few weeks previously '. . . a man found with a Catamite in an ale-house in Rosemary Lane in Tower Ward . . . went into the Privy and cut his throat, he being a well known Butcher, highly esteemed . . .'

In January 1725 two men were found guilty of 'threatening to swear an attempt to sodomy against a young Man in the City to extort Money from him'; his parents took them to court, and they were sentenced to 'two hours on Tower Hill Pillory, two hours on the Cheapside Pillory, a fine of Twenty pounds and six months in Newgate'.

In 1726 'Mother' Margaret Clap's Mollies House was '. . . a Place of Rendezvous for Sodomites . . . she had provided Beds in every Room . . . there were commonly thirty to forty *Chaps* every Night – and even more – especially on Sunday Nights . . .'. It was raided after having been visited by 'informers' of the Society for the Reform of Manners. They found 'a company of Men fiddling dancing and singing bawdy Songs' in 'Thomas Wright's *Mollies House* in Beech Street, Barbican' and recognized several of the men at Mother Clap's. One of them testified that he had been buggered by Jacob Ecclestone; and a catamite named Newton also testified against him.

One Peter Vevican was found guilty of buggery with John Brailsford 'in the open Pope's Head Alley next the Royal Exchange'; they got away with the pillory, a fine of 5 marks and six months in Newgate. Two men caught *in flagrante delicto* in St Paul's Cathedral denied 'penetration' and were sentenced to an hour in the St Paul's pillory, fines of £40 each and six months in Newgate. St Paul's precincts were favourite haunts of prostitutes of both sexes.

Not only orthodox religious citizens found all this abhorrent: there was an angry response from the *Venus' Vultures* – a contemporary nickname for whores – at this flourishing competition, which occasioned a counterblast:

> How Happy were the good old English Faces
> 'til *Mounsieur* from France, taught *PEGO* a Dance
> to the tune of *Old Sodom's Embraces*.

> But now *WE* are quite out of Fashion.
> Poor whores may be *NUNS*, since *MEN* turn their *GUNS*
> And vent on each other their Passion.

> But now, we find to our Sorrow we are over-run
> By the Sparks of the *BUM*
> And Peers of the Land of Gomorrah!

Daniel Defoe in the pillory in 1713. In contrast to most others, the mob pelted him with flowers and put garlands around the base to demonstrate their support for him against the government.

The pillory was then a very dangerous experience. On 9 October 1764 *The Public Advertiser* reported that:

> . . . a bugger aged sixty was put in the Cheapside Pillory . . . the Mob tore off his Clothes, pelted him with Filth, whipt him almost to Death . . . he was naked and covered with Dung . . . when the Hour was up he was carried almost unconscious back to Newgate.

Notwithstanding all this public 'shame' there were no executions for this felony in London between 1731 and 1756.

The most famous *cause célèbre* was that involving William Beckford, son of a Lord Mayor of London and William 'Kitty' Courtenay, later ninth Earl of Devon. Before he died in 1816 Beckford sent a letter to *The Times* apropos the hanging of some poor sodomite, concluding with the words, 'The Danger must be very great indeed and everyone in the Country must be running the Risk of having his Arse exposed to Fire & Slaughter!'

In 1829 the new Crimes Against the Persons Act abolished the death penalty for almost every crime except buggery! The last two men to be hanged were John Smith and James Pratt in September 1835; but not until 1861 was the death penalty finally expunged from the law of this land.

11 The Wand'ring Whores

The flagrant examples of sexual and financial corruption at the Court of Charles II could not be hidden from the commonalty: the Court and the King were vulgar in speech and behaviour, using many vulgar expressions and gestures – Lord Rochester's works are crammed with the common four-letter words. There were now innumerable broadsheets satirizing in the crudest terms almost every courtier and courtesan. The first 'gossipy' newspapers appeared about 1680 – the earliest ones were concerned mainly with politics and money.

Pornographic literature became popular: sets of albums of erotic pictures were imported from China as early as 1570. Most purported to be translations of foreign works, such as Pietro Aretino's *Puttana Errante* (1534) and the French *L'Escholle des Filles* (1655), which Pepys thought 'the lewdest book I have ever read . . . rather worse than the *Puttana Errante*, so that I am ashamed of reading it!'. (It did not stop him going back later and buying it and hiding it at home.) Public imagination was caught by the so-called 'Aretinian *Postures*' of Giulio Romano, depicting varied gymnastic complications to make fornication more interesting – and certainly more tiring if attempted by normal human beings. All these 'postures' in fact came from the erotic murals at the House of the Vetii in Pompeii; they were later engraved by Marcantonio Raimondi, constituting the first 'feelthy postcard' type of pictures.

La Puttana Errante was published in an English translation 'adapted for a colder climate' by John Garfield in 1661, under the title *The Wand'ring Whore*: it included a list of procuresses, ambulant whores and pimps – the procuresses in hierarchical order.

L'Escholle des Filles, first published in Paris in 1655 by Michel Millet and Jean Ange, was adjudged obscene, and these authors were hounded and punished. It was a dialogue between an experienced young lady and her innocent teenage friend, and has some pretensions to elegance in speech. Not so the English version of 1658, entitled *The School of Venus*, which is in coarse and crude language including all the four-letter words. The London book-sellers were harassed by the official licenser's 'messengers'. What really upset the Establishment were the opening words of the knowledgeable young lady, Fanny, in reply to a question from the innocent Katy, '. . . whether this Pleasure could be partaken of by others than Maids and young Men?': 'All people of all Ranks and Degree participate therein even from the King to the Cobbler, from the Queen to the Kitchen-wench. In short, one half the World fucks the other!'

Several of the words alluding to the penis, then thought very coarse, are unknown today: a 'yard' – a rod or staff; 'tarse' – to tear or rend; 'pintle' – a pointer; 'pricke' – from *prican*, to pierce. The word 'cunt' – originally *kunte* – was freely used in ordinary conversation, often referring more to the womb than the vagina. These became 'dirty words' only when the middle-class gentrification of the language started, about 1790.

As to manners, taking Samuel Pepys as *l'homme moyen sensuel* and prototype, a not very appetizing creature appears. He was a sycophantic penny-pincher, not very clean in his personal dress and habits, a bully to his servants, unfaithful to his pretty young wife, with furtive amours with servants and frequent trips round the red-light quarters, and a lavatorial sense of humour. He frequented ale-houses, joining in the singing of bawdy songs – one favourite being a ballad, with every verse ending 'Shitten-come-shite the way to love is!' He was so much taken with it that he mentions it several times in his diary. He was not even gracious to the women who 'obliged' him – he resented their 'impertinence' in asking for small sums or even for paying for snacks or a glass of cheap wine.

He expresses surprise that his wife wears 'closed Drawers' *à la français* which were drawn down for urination or defecation; the Court ladies wore 'split Drawers' buttoned at the rear to be let down to permit easier evacuation. Such manœuvring had hazards, and the petticoats were all too often 'beshit and bepissed'. In dire need Court ladies just went to one side and urinated in the passage where they stood, if they could not quickly get one of the silver pisspots supplied by royalty.

Most of Pepys' acquaintances were of the same stamp. The wonder is that, with such off-hand promiscuity, they were not every one of them poxed up, the more so since the 'condom', although invented in 1564 by Gabriel Fallopio Frascatori as an anti-syphilis 'engine' was seldom used. Its contraceptive possibility was realized only much later, when Rochester lauded it. (It is possible that Lord Rochester invented the name, since there is no record of a Colonel Conton or Condon, as alleged.)

One consequence was the immense spread of venereal disease. Dryden averred that Charles II got it from Lady Shrewsbury, who got it from Dick Talbot. Louise de Quérouaille ranted at the King that she had got syphilis from him. She was ill for a long time, but there is no record that the King had it. Gonorrhoea was an accepted hazard and regarded as a great nuisance but not as a deterrent. Dr Alexander Frazier, physician-in-ordinary, could easily cure that, and Pepys mentions that he '. . . was helping the Ladies at Court to slip their Calves, and Great Men of their Claps'. There was also Dr Florence Fourcade a French 'chirurgeon', skilled in treatment of venereal disease and in 1678 appointed chirurgeon-general to the forces, with special regard to 'cases of venereal sickness'.

Madame Fourcade ran the famous Mercury Sweat Baths in Leather Lane to which all noble – and wealthy – sufferers from syphilis were directed. Henry Saville, writing in 1668, informs his friend Rochester: '. . . had he known what tortures he would be undergoing there he would have turned Turk!' (Their shared concubine, Jane Roberts, '. . . endured sufferings that would make a damn'd Soule in Hell fall a-laughing . . . it will make youre Hayre stande on Ende . . .'). Similar establishments were run by two quacks, 'doctors' Barton and Ginman, and yet another by the staunch Cromwellian Dr Marchamont Needham, with Dr Thomas Jordan, until they decided that the mercury treatments were useless and closed down.

Small wonder then that the 'unmentionable Vice' also flourished. Rochester's play *Sodom* (1674) covered every aspect of buggery, leaving nothing to the imagination.

There were Mollies Houses in Farringdon and Cripplegate and a very well-known one in Beech Street, within the City's walls. A contemporary tract satirized '. . . the effeminate Clothing worn by *Fopps* . . . making it difficult to distinguish a Gentleman from a Servant . . . [the author felt ashamed] to see them aping their Servants with vulgar Apparrell in verie bad Taste & with their Haire brush'd high over the Forehead and drawne back with a Comb like a Woman's *coiffure*. . . . Master *Molly* will pass for a Ladye. . . . Powder & Painte was as muche used by our Man as by any French Woman. . . . Catamite Prostitutes offer their perverse Services openlie in the Streete. . . .'

The theatres were also blamed for this increase in buggery: in the savage *Satire on the Players* (1681) several actors were attacked. Cardenall Goodman, later to be Lady Castlemaine's paramour and the father of her last child, was described as a thief (as well as a member of the syphilitic No Nose Club) and James Nokes the famous 'comoedian' was called 'Buggering Nokes' and attacked:

> Ye smock-fac'd Ladds, secure your gentle Bums
> For full of lust and Fury, see – he comes.

A scabrous poem 'On the Ladies of Honour' gave the names of every maid-of-honour at Court, and attacks John Bromley, Lord Montfort:

> Thrice fortunate Boy
> who can give double Joy
> Behind and Before
> To delight My Lord and My Lady!

Some of the men named were compelled to flee to Paris and exile.

Most information about conditions at the lower end of the social ladder comes from John Garfield's *The Wand'ring Whore* (1661), detailing whoredom in the Clerkenwell, Cripplegate and Moorfields area, with a long list of procuresses, about 200 whores, some with locations, and many pimps and 'Bandstring-sellers'. (A 'Bandstring-seller sold maidenheads, pandering to the 'defloration mania . . . an old English Vice', *vide* Ivan Bloch.) There is also a comprehensive list of 'Pickpockets, Nightwalkers, Decoys, Hectors & Trapanners'. All these bawds started their careers in the Commonwealth period in or near these locations – all were well established by 1660.

Garfield soon landed up in Newgate, not for pornography but for failing to pay the 4 pence stamp duty. Someone had grassed on him to Mr Forrest the 'intelligencer', who had already raided a number of whorehouses and taken bawds and girls to prison. While in prison Garfield managed, in November 1661, to publish *A Strange & True Conference*, purporting to be a report of a meeting in Newgate of the three foremost bawds, Mrs Cresswell, Mrs Page and Mrs Fotheringham. Then he published *Strange and True Nevves from Jack-a-Newberry's Six Windmills*, being a history of Mrs Fotheringham's bizarre establishment. In this he mentions that *The Wand'ring Whore* had been very successful because '. . . there had been more Tradeing in one day than they had seen in a whole Month before!', although he complained that now '. . . the Privat Whores have got the knack of it'.

Then, in 1663, still in Newgate, he published *The Sixth Part of the*

Wand'ring Whore Reviv'd, which was a rehash of old stuff. Simultaneously John Crouch (*Mercurius Democraticus*) published *The Wand'ring Whores Complaint for Want of Tradeing*, with candid descriptions of many whores and their pimps. There is another 'Queen of Morocco', a Mrs Honor; Mistress Westover, 'Bandstring Seller to the Law Office' in Chancery Lane; and Fair Rosamund Sugar-Cunt whose pimp was Mr Howard. (She was operating thereabouts as a 'poor whore' some twenty years later.)

A fifth issue of *The Wand'ring Whore* was published but Garfield, still in prison, repudiated it: it was a collection of smutty jokes. In 1663 came *Strange and True Nevves from Bartholomew Fair* and *The Wand'ring Whore's a Dice-Rogue*, the content of which is unknown because no copy has survived. Hundreds more were published which have not survived – a great pity, because they would have shed light on the phenomenal increase in this 'tradeing'.

Curiously enough, there is no mention in any of these effusions of buggery or 'Mollies Houses' – perhaps because they were unwelcome competitors?

In every generation there is a 'Mother Cunny' as a premier bawd, although it is very difficult to know who is so named. In the same way each generation produced its 'Queen of Morocco', even though her birthplace might be no further than Moorfields. Some bawds of importance are mentioned: 'Old Bess' Blundell owned three whorehouses in the Covent Garden area but also a busy one the Jacob's Well in the alley of the same name in Jewin Street, Cripplegate. There was also a Jacob's Well in Jacob's Well Alley in Turnmill Street at this time, likewise a house of ill-fame. Mrs Frances Sands ran the Ragg'd Staff in Chiswell Street, hard by Mrs Fotheringham's establishment. Mrs Habbiger ran the Turks Head in Turks Head Alley off Grub Street. Bawd Paskins ran the Armitage in St Giles, Cripplegate.

On 25 July 1664 Pepys was looking around for a prostitute but noted 'only loathsome people and houses' and went home, but on 4 July 1667 he referred to 'a group of young lads plotting arson . . . in a bawdy house . . . called *The Russia House*, the Mistress of which is always seen in her shift'. There was a multiple-house old bawd, a Mother Cunny, whose principal establishment was in St Martin-le-Grand; she had three others in Farringdon Without.

Some were just houses of assignation for Court and City wives. Pepys noted on 15 April 1666 that, 'The wife of the King's Physician, Dr Timothy Clarke had picked up a Gentleman at Westminster Hall and took him to a blinde little bawdy-house at Moorfeildes.' John Evelyn remarked that, 'Ladies of Rank now frequent

The coach terminus in Wood Street, hard by the Compter, where the incoming country women and girls were met by London bawds and gulled into prostitution. Here the vicious Mother Needham is cozening an innocent for her client, the evil Colonel Charteris in 1730.

Taverns in which no Courtesan would even set foot!', although the pamphlet *The Parliament of Ladies* spread abroad 'the dangerous and abominable Doctrine that it was far safer and cheaper to lye with Common Wenches than with Ladies of the Quality'. In 1681 the poem *'Utile Dulce'* discloses:

> . . . or when at *Potter's* Bawdy House, renowned
> As any of that quality in Town,
> I hear how Ladyes, bred in Godly way
> Have oft of late been known to goe astray!

12 Farringdon – That Vaste Estate of Lecherie

The twin disasters of the Great Plague and the Great Fire, with the consequent exodus of a large part of the population, turned the old ward of Farringdon-extra into a teeming urban district. Amongst the refugees were very many light ladies and their manageresses who set up in business. There was plenty of room for expansion and improvement – it is from this time that more elegant whore-houses, with 'all mod. cons.', are described. Most expansion was to the north-west, because eastwards the way was blocked by the walls of the Tower of London, although Bishopsgate Without and Wapping, up-river, also became 'whores-nests', being managed by expatriates from Farringdon-extra!

The original Farringdon ward was named after its very rich alderman William de Farindon and is the only City ward to be known by its founder's name. The Farringdon family were goldsmiths, the aristocrats of the guilds. William's grandfather, Thomas, had been a supporter of Wat Tyler in 1381, and it was probably only his immense wealth that saved him from execution; it may even have been his (secret) accolade when in 1394 the extended ward was named Farringdon *Extra*.

The extended ward included many ancient sokes and liberties, some of whose privileges still survived, which accounts for a number of anomalies in government subsequently. One of the most interesting was the liberty of the Fleet, an area on the west side of the 'fleot', the fast-flowing river which from Roman times had marked Londinium's boundary. Indeed, the Roman road led straight up the hill from Ludgate over a little bridge. This road was actually known as 'the strete of Fletebrigge', being called Fleet Street from 1274, when it was celebrated for the number and variety of its inns and taverns and 'the brilliance of their signes'.

However, it was already a rough neighbourhood. In 1228 '. . . it happened that one Henri de Buke slew an Irish labourer with a knife, in the Fleetbrigge strete and fled for sanctuary to St Marie, Suthwerke . . .'. While there he admitted his guilt to the City chamberlain, Gervase le Cordewaner, and the two sheriffs, after which 'he abjured the realm'. However, these officials, 'having allowed him to go free out of their own Liberties', had contravened a royal ordinance 'thereby contravening the Crown and Dignity of his Lordeship the King', Henry III, who was no friend of the City. They were fined.

Even in the time of Edward the Confessor (r. 1042–65) the wealthier London merchants had built 'commodious' houses on the slopes of the River Fleet, the road on the ridge being known as

A Fleet wedding in 1747, in the Old Fleet Market, near the infamous Pen in Hand Tavern, where marriages were performed by 'disreputable clergy' importuning passers-by. In this scene a young sailor is marrying a harlot.

> *Jack, rich in Prizes, now the Knott is ty'd*
> *Sits pleas'd by her he thinks his mayden Bride:*
> *But tho' a modest Look by Molly's shown*
> *She only longs for what she oft has known!*

Trimill Street. By 1265 there were already complaints that the rubbish and dung thrown into the stream had made it 'foule and noysome'. It was to continue so for some centuries to come!

Down beside the Lud Gate stood the infamous Fleet Prison, first mentioned in 1197 as *'le gailae de Ponte de Flete'*, a gaol for felons and miscreants. Later it was used for 'stern punishments' meted out by the dreaded Star Chamber. From about 1500 it became notorious as a debtors' prison and for the scandalously cruel treatment of prisoners by sadistic and greedy gaolers. Conditions inside were appalling but, because it stood in its own 'liberty', the mayor and sheriffs had little control; even the occasional royal statutes for alleviation were little heeded. Within the liberty and within the prison itself valid marriages could be made until the practice was forbidden in 1711. (The notorious 'Fleet marriages' by unfrocked priests could still be found until 1774, in spite of the Marriages Act of 1754.)

The Scottish traveller John Macky's description early in Queen Anne's reign is interesting – he makes it sound like a 'home from home', although he is clearly describing prisoners with money and not the great majority of the indigent:

> It is a large building . . . like a Monastery . . . you enter the Great Courtyard by a . . . strong Gate kept by two *Turnkeys* . . . four galleries one above another with eight Rooms each side for the Convenience of those Prisoners who . . . cannot take the *Liberty of the Rules* . . . a handsome Chapel where Prayers are said twice a Day & Sermons on Sundays and Holy Days . . . underneath is a large Cellar & Kitchen and . . . a large Garden . . . here there are no bolted Doors nor iron Bars . . . they visit each other promiscuously there be nothing that looks like a Prison but the height of the Walls . . . a Travelling Market every Day . . . with Cries as in the Streets . . . a Prisoner is under no constraint but may send out for every thing . . . such as can give the Warden Security they won't run away have the Liberty of going abroad anywhere [or] Lodging within the Rules which consist of four or five Very Good Streets. . . . They may go where they please if they conceal it from their Creditors. . . .

The 'lodgings' are 'Spunging Houses' in which the keeper would have an interest. Lord Eldon describes a very luxurious one in Tooks Court, Chancery Lane, as late as 1814. (The prison was burned down by Lord George Gordon's rioters in 1780.)

The Fleet Bridge was also a main thoroughfare and a ceaseless hive of activity. There had been a 'stout' wooden bridge there for generations, complete with a customs house to collect import duties and murage. In 1419 '. . . . everie Carte bringinge in Corne

Begging at the Grate. An indigent prisoner allowed by the gaoler of the Fleet Prison to stand outside to beg food or alms from passers-by, while other prisoners may be seen 'at the grate' of their cell. 1730.

into London by Waye of the Flete or Holebourne shall pay One Penny . . . the Carte that brings Nutts or Cheese shall pay Two Pence halfpenny . . . and for every dead Jew buried in London Three Pence halfpenny . . .'.

In 1431 this bridge was 'repaired' by the lord mayor, John Wels; according to Stow it was 'a faire stone bridge coped on either side with Iron Spikes & Lanthornes of Stone to be placed [lit] on Winter evenings'. After the Great Fire in 1666 it was rebuilt in stone 'as wide as the Street, for Coaches and Carts'. Since before 1500 there had been houses and taverns on the bridge: in 1509 the Rose Taverne-atte-Flete-bridge is recorded, and there were at least eight others. The Rose was still standing in 1675. In 1751 the Rainbow Coffee-House was there, but five years later the bridge was demolished.

The Fleet was still subject to flash floods: in 1679 'It bore down upon the back-parts of several wholesale Butchers' houses at Cow Cross carrying away many Cattle alive and dead . . . at Hockley

The entrance to the River Fleet showing the Bridewell Bridge 1756.

several barrells of Ale and Beer and some of Brandy swam about
and were retrieved by an adventurous Rabble. . . .'

In 1710 John Gay, in *Trivia*, recording the filthy state of the
stream, wrote:

> Then, leaning o'er the Rails, he musing stood
> And view'd below the black Canal of Mud . . .
> Who that rugg'd Streete would traverse o'er
> That stretches, O! Flete Ditch, from thy black Shore?

As late as 1763 a barber from Bromley in Kent, who had come to
London to see his children, was found in that ditch standing
upright, frozen to death – he had slipped and fallen in. In 1832 that
'noxious flood' brought the cholera to Clerkenwell. Today the
stream is the main sewer into the Thames.

Clerkenwell gets its name from the ancient 'Clarkeswell': it was
for centuries a quiet, leafy suburb for innocent recreation. It is only
the best known of several springs, mentioned in Domesday Book,
when it was the *'fons Clericorum'*, 'the spring of the parish clerks',
who celebrated every summer with their 'Enterludes' – mainly
Nativity or other religious 'plays'. It was distinguished by being
'curbed about with a square of hard stone', the pure spring water
gushing out of an iron spout continuously, so that all could drink
without hindrance. From the adjacent vineyard (still recalled by
the little Vine Street at the bottom of the green) a rather stronger
drink could be got to add to the gaiety. On Clerkenwell Green *hoi
polloi* could disport themselves, although from time to time more
serious gatherings were to be found, such as Wat Tyler's companions in 1381 and Jack Cade's in 1450, as well as many an apprentices' march in Cromwellian and Stuart days. At the 'Enterludes',
which, apart from the religious plays, were also entertainments by
jesters and the like, royalty and courtiers might be present when
times were not out of joint.

There was the Faggs-well, first recorded as *'super rivulus de
fackeswel'* in 1197, indicating that it fed a brook of that name.
However, the origin of the well, which was said to run 'coloured'
water, must be traced back to Anglo-Saxon times, since in Old
English *fag* meant multicoloured, more usually of pale yellow or
brownish hue, and the spring was known to be chalybeate. Stow
described it as 'a great water', then known as 'Smithfield Pond' but
also known as 'the Horse-pool', because the citizens used to water
their horses there. By Stow's time it '. . . was muche decaied, the
springs stopped up . . . and is but fowle'.

There was the Loddereswel or Loders Well which in 1200 had

The old house of detention, Clerkenwell, c. 1798.

been donated by the Lady Muriel de Montigny to the nunnery of Clerkenwell, 'with a right of way from the Cartulary'; and the Godeswell, which gave its name to the present Goswell Road. The Red Well got its name from one Osbertus of Redwell in Hertford-shire, who presumably had land in the Clerkenwell area at that time. There was yet another well in the churchyard of St Giles, Cripplegate, in which in 1244 Anne of Lodberie (Lothbury) was drowned – 'ducked' to death, since Lothbury was a well-known whores-nest off Cheapside.

The oldest recorded is the Skinners Well, dating from very early times, when the fraternity of skinners each year gathered to perform 'certayne Playes . . . of ye Holy Scriptures'. These were Nativity plays and attracted large crowds, which were, sadly, not all religious, since in 1385 they were banned, 'because the plays became so noisome'; indeed, in 1390 it was reported that the site was 'in place where the Wrestlings have of late years beene kept'. However, times must have changed, because in 1409, in the presence of King Henry IV and 'the Nobles and Gentles of England', the plays lasted eight days.

Finally there was a 'chys-wel', perhaps so-called because it sprang from the *chis* (OE, gravel) or gravel soil. This was at the very boundary of the City in Cripplegate Without, giving its name to Chyselstrete up to about 1279, when it became known as Everardeswellstreete (a nobleman Walter de Everard lived there-abouts in 1250), by which name it was still known in King Charles II's reign, when its most notorious inhabitant was Priss Fotheringham (see Chapter 13).

Although itself not too much tainted, Clerkenwell Green was surrounded by the deepest and most profligate areas imaginable. Just across the Fleet was the unspeakable Hockley-in-the-Hole, a most apposite name indeed for the wicked excesses that went on there. Apart from the surfeit of prostitution and brothels, Hockley was the resort of every known type of criminal – no crime was too dreadful to contemplate. In Anglo-Saxon days it was 'Hocca's Leah-in-the-hollow, and when the river overflowed, '. . . itt was verie troublesome to negotiate'. The inhabitants were the poorest of the poor, and the physical situation was summed up by Ned Ward as late as 1717:

> alle the Stinkes that rise together
> from Hockley-hole in sultry weather.

It sheltered thieves, pickpockets and 'infamous women'. In Elizabeth I's time it had a bear-garden which also served for bull-baiting and prize-fighting and 'all sortes of rough games' which attracted great crowds of all kinds: 'Dukes, Lords, Knights & Squires & Butchers and Drovers and the lyke people' – all could be treated alike. The animals were paraded through the streets. John Gay in *Trivia* (1716) described how,

> . . . led by the Nostrill walkes the muzzled Beare
> Behinde him moves majestically dull
> The Pride of Hockley-hole, the surly Bull. . . .

A further elaboration was described in *The Weekly Journal* of 9 June 1716, when a wild bull was turned loose 'with fireworks stuck all over him' and chased through the streets. Spectators were invited to come at about three o'clock, 'because this sport continues long'.

Dog-fights were also a great speciality, but the increasingly popular sport was the 'Tryalls of Maisters of Self-defence' – fist fights without gloves or rules. Richard Steele in *The Spectator*, No. 436, in 1712, said that Hockley-in-the-Hole was a place 'of no small renown for the gallantry of the lower orders of Britons': '. . . a fight between Sergeant James Miller and a soldier Timothy Buck . . . the prospect of maimed bodies did not deter them . . . the crowd placed their bets according to their fortunes rather than their merit, from Pit to Galleries . . . there was much effusion of Blood and their Wounds were sewn up on the Stage . . .'.

'Fencing at Sword for a Half-a-Guinea Hatt' vied with 'Six Men to Wrestle for three Paires of Gloves at Half-a-Crowne a Paire'. One of the principal venues for this sport was Ye Cocke atte Hockley, where perhaps the very greatest attraction was the women wrestlers who fought for prizes or, just as often, to settle a quarrel. *The London Journal* in June 1722 reported: 'I, ELIZABETH WILKINSON OF CLERKENWELL having had some Words with NANN HIGHFIELD & requiring SATISFACTION, DO INVITE her to meet me . . . and Box with me for THREE GUINEAS, each woman to hold a Half-Crown in each Hand and the first that drops her Money to lose the battle. . . .' They 'maintained the battle with great valour for a long time' to the satisfaction of the spectators. More often the women would wrestle with each other, scratching and clawing till they were almost naked and bleeding, the prize being no more than a pair of gloves or a Holland smock – the latter greatly prized by harlots. There were such sports as 'Cudgel-boxing' and, of course, cock-fighting at the Two Brewers Tavern, the prize in 1744 being 'A large sow and Ten Pigs – or the value in Money'. No cock was to exceed four pounds and one ounce in weight.

In the hostelry the Coach and Horses was found 'a small leather *portmanteau* with a cut in the leather R.Tvrpin' – belonging to the famous highwayman who used the tavern for his raids on the highway to Islington. The Coach and Horses still stands on the site, a memorial also to another famous son, the Bow Street runner and thief-taker Jonathan Wilde, later hanged for theft and conspiracy. By 1790 it had been tidied up and named Ray Street, and that in turn disappeared in 1856, leaving the name to a short street off Farringdon Road.

In the clean-up, Codpiece Row was renamed Coppice Row, Cut-throat Lane became Corporation Lane and the site later of the Quakers' workhouse for 'poore decayed Members of the Society of Freindes'.

A few hundred yards from the Green was another source of sinful congregation: the notorious Red Bull in St John Street, a theatre built in 1600 by Aaron Holland, the son of an innkeeper in Grays Inn Road and an associate of Philip Henslowe, the theatre-and brothel-owner of Bankside. It was quickly known as 'a Gaff' – a low-class showplace specializing in strong, gory, rough drama. It was used by the Queen's Company of Players until 1617. It was renovated and roofed over in 1625 and managed to keep open even during the Commonwealth – although on a very low key – until the Restoration in 1660 gave it a new lease of life, albeit the quality of the performances left much to be desired. It claimed, however, to have the first woman actress in England: in December 1660 Andrew Newport mentioned, 'Upon our stages we have women actors, as beyond the seas' – until then, young men had played women's parts. However, on 21 August 1660 King Charles II had issued a Royal Warrant that, '. . . thenceforth only women should play women's parts . . . that plays might be esteemed not only harmless Delights but useful and instructive Representations of human Life . . .'. (In fact Mrs Catherine Coleman had appeared as Ianthe in Davenant's *Siege of Rhodes* in 1656.)

Sam Pepys went there in January 1661, diarizing: '. . . clothes very poor and actors but coarse fellows . . . not above one hundred in the whole house . . . the play poorly done and with much disorder . . . a boy was beaten about the ears on stage . . . which put the whole house in an uproar . . .'.

The audiences were no better than the players: courtiers standing in the pit ogled the ladies in the boxes, and the orange-girls cried their wares incessantly. At best it was noisy; at worst worse than a bear-garden. The most devastating critique came in 1665 from Henry Saville, Lord Rochester's friend: 'Comedy was outspokenly lubricious with Gallants cuckolding or seducing virgins; bedroom scenes with actresses in dress and undress and actors unbrac'd and unbuttoned . . . vulgarity was the Rule . . . spitting coughing nose-blowing . . . wiped on the sleeves – references to bawdry, Close-stools, brothels, famous Bawds, flagellation, venereal diseases and impotence and buggery . . . and such indecent postures as would never be suffered except our stage, which has turn'd the Stomach of so squeamish a man as I am. . . .' Soon after this the theatre was demolished.

There was also the Fortune Theatre in Cripplegate Without in Golden Lane, built in the circular mode in 1600 for Philip Henslowe and Edward Alleyn at a cost of £500, but it burned down the following year and was rebuilt in brick. It also played low-class, lubricious comedies to rowdy, appreciative audiences until it was closed down in 1642 by the Commonwealth, but it carried on with 'illegal plays' until in 1649 a group of Cromwell's Ironsides partially dismantled it. (It was at this time the property of Dulwich College, to which Alleyn had left it when he died in November 1626, although his widow still had a life interest.) In March 1660 representatives of Dulwich College claimed that, '*The Fortune* is in ruinous condition and is to be let for rebuilding.' They sold it to William Beavan for £75 in March 1661, and in March 1662 '. . . the sayde play house is totally demolished'.

But the principal attractions lay just a few hundred yards away, in Cripplegate, where two of the most famous whorehouses in all England were to be found, run by the outrageous Priss Fotheringham and the very Empress of Bawdry, Elizabeth Cresswell.

13 Priss Fotheringham's
Chuck-Office

'Priss' Fotheringham's saga is an account of the lowest depths of prostitution in its time. She was born about 1615 and was possibly of Scots origin but is first heard of at the Middlesex sessions, when on 8 July 1658, as Priscilla Carsewell, spinster, 'late of St Martin-in-the-Fields', she was charged with the theft of some goods belonging to a widow, Ellen Cragg, on 2 June. She was found guilty and sentenced to be hanged but by great fortune was granted a Conditional Pardon by the new Lord Protector, Richard Cromwell, in January 1659.

When and how she became involved with the Fotheringhams is not known – there were very few of that name in London, but one James ffotheringham was living in Emperours Head Lane in Cripplegate Without in 1638. He was a person of some consequence, being then assessed at the considerable sum of £4. A son, Edmund, was born to James and Anne on 13 August 1630 and baptized at St Martin-in-the-Fields. Some time later, as 'Old Bawd Fotheringham', Anne kept a brothel in Cow Lane, an alley off Cowcross Street, dying before 1661. Edmund had served his 'apprenticeship' under his mother's excellent tutelage but how and why he 'married' Priscilla Carsewell is not known: it was most likely a 'Fleet marriage' of mutual convenience, for he was her pimp and was at least ten years younger.

As a young girl Priss was 'a Cat-eyed Gipsy . . . pleasing to the Eye in her finery', but early in her career she became badly scarred with smallpox in one of the recurring plagues between 1640 and 1660. The effects were worsened by the inexpert treatment of a notorious quack, Hercules Pawlet, originally a watchmaker. He also practiced mayhem, being in 1670 charged with robbery but luckily found not guilty, escaping a well-deserved hanging.

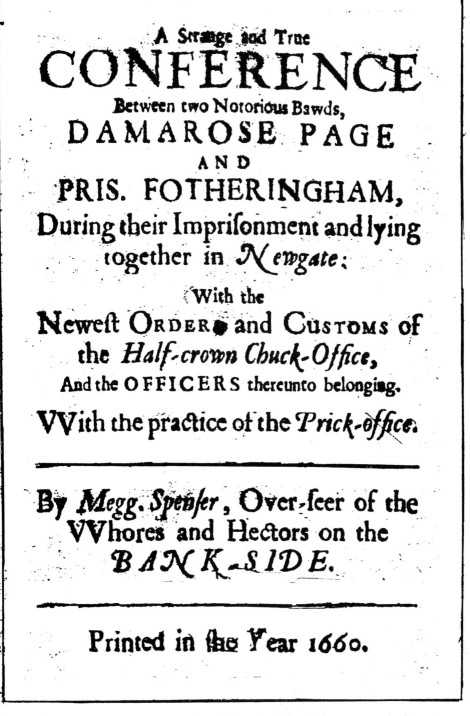

A Strange and True

CONFERENCE

Between two Notorious Bawds,

DAMAROSE PAGE

AND

PRIS. FOTHERINGHAM,

During their Imprifonment and lying
together in *Newgate*:

With the

Neweft ORDERS and CUSTOMS of
the *Half-crown Chuck-Office*,
And the OFFICERS thereunto belonging.

VVith the practice of the *Prick-office*.

By *Megg. Spenfer*, Over-feer of the
VVhores and Hectors on the
BANK-SIDE.

Printed in the Year 1660.

John Garfield's pamphlet, which with his Wand'ring Whore, *gave the first*
details of the bizarre happenings in Cripplegate Without.

To add to her misfortunes, Priss' husband had 'befrenched her' and 'pockified her Bones soundly' – in plain English, he had given her venereal disease, beaten her and treated her cruelly, so that she ran away with a 'poor Sword Cutter', taking with her as much of her husband's goods and money as she could lay her hands on, but after she had spent every penny on this paramour he deserted her. Since *'sine cerere et Bacche friget Venus'* – without food and drink love turns cold' – she had to go back to 'her rotten husband'. In revenge he charged her with theft and embezzlement, for which she was imprisoned in the 'Metropolitan Colledg' (Newgate Prison), where she sat for about a year. It proved a good school, because there she met Damarose Page and Mrs Cresswell, experienced and successful teachers, as well as her chronicler, John Garfield.

Priss' speciality was an arcane aspect of fornication much appreciated in Roman times, known in English as 'chucking'. As a money-spinner it had no equal. An early chronicler reported: 'Priss stood upon her Head with naked Breech and Belley while four Cully-Rumpers chuck'd in sixteen half-crowns into her *Commoditie.'* She performed this feat several times a day. Small wonder then that her brothel, the Six Windmills in Chiswell Street, in Cripplegate Without, attracted a clientele from far and wide.

These windmills, too, have a history. There were a number of dunghills nearby onto which for centuries the gong-farmers of the City had dumped their loads; but in 1563 the lord mayor and aldermen ordered that, 'The filthy dunghills outside Finsburie Court lying in the high-waie be removed and carried away.' On the mounds then left, a windmill was erected. A map of 1563 shows two; another, later map shows four, and Faithorne's map of 1658 shows six, lying upon the line of Hog Lane, leading to Bishopsgate (today's Worship Street). Nearby in 1641 were the King's dog-house and three small tenements, adjoining the first windmill.

The nearest houses were in Everardeswellstreet, later (and still today) known as Chiswell Street. There were some disreputable taverns, one of which, standing on the corner with Whitecross Street, was the Jack of Newbury (referring to John Winchcombe of Newbury, called England's first capitalist, who died in 1520). The earliest reference to the Six Windmills is of a less than glorious episode in 1642, during the Civil War: 'Last Monday sennight early in the Morning before the valiant Prentices came to exercize in the Artillery groundes by Moorfeildes that a crew of these Neuters had planted in the *Six Windmills* six peeces of Ordnance charg'd with White Powder.' By planting these guns in advance with harmless white powder, the apprentices could observe which side was winning and turn their guns accordingly. Hence they were contemptuously called 'Neuters', because in any battle '. . . they coulde wynde themselves to the stronger Side as a Saile turnes in the strongest Wyndes'. The site is today's Artillery Grounds of the ancient Honourable Artillery Company, and it is still in use. A *Surveigh* of 1649 describes each windmill, giving the name of each miller.

Priss drew customers from the George and the White Cross taverns which were her neighbours, as well as from the Ship in Little Moorfields (now Finsbury Pavement), which today is patronized by respectable City gentlemen.

In 1658 there was, next to these windmills, 'an ale-house of ill repute' formerly known as 'Jack a Newbury', '. . . until the Fruits of some abhominable Practices compelled them to take him down for fear of the multitude (of rampaging Apprentices) . . . as if the alteration of the sign of the *Six Windmills* had changed the Nature of these Vultures . . . for it hath undone more Yongsters than half the Houses in the City . . .'. Nevertheless, in 1660 Priss' 'Chuck Office' was known as 'Jack-a-Newberries Six Windmills', for by then the much-pockified Priss had ceased to be a whore and had become the matron, her husband having kept the business going while she was in the 'Colledg'.

In Newgate she had learned of two developments. First, a project for a sort of association for mutual benefit on the lines of the famous Venetian organization, and secondly a suggestion that she should link her 'Chuck Office' with the bizarre Last and Lyon in the liberty of East Smithfield, hard by the Tower, whose speciality was fellatio. Its popular name was 'the Prick Office', and it was owned by Thomas Hammond and managed by a Mrs Jones. The prerequisite for employment there was '. . . That everie one of them must buss the end of his *Trapsticke* as he lyes naked uppon his Bed with his Tarse standinge upwards . . .'. This sexual therapy was, of course, available to his customers, although it was felt by some that it was un-British and Aretinian. (It is the only mention of fellatio to be found in contemporary literature.) Such a *mariage de convenance* would have been mutually profitable.

At this time the keeper of the 'Metropolitan Colledg' was William Deacon, who would do anything for money, so that any well-heeled criminal could do almost anything he pleased. John Garfield published from the prison not only his *Wand'ring Whores* but also in 1660 *Strange and True Nevves from Jack-a-Newberries Six Windmills*, sub-titled 'The Unparralleld Practices of Mrs Fotheringham' He detailed the names of 'whores, hectors and cully-

A contemporary portrait of the beautiful courtesan Patience Russell, who was much esteemed by Lord Rochester and his coterie of aristocratic lechers; she was a protegee of Mother Cresswell and was often to be found in her house.

rumpers' and their specialities, mentioning, *inter alia*, the most famous contemporary bawds Mrs Cresswell, Betty Lawrence, Mrs Curtis, Mrs Smith, Mrs Bagley and Mrs Russell – a very curious mixture given that Patience Russell was Lord Rochester's mistress, Betty Lawrence a low-class flagellant and the mighty Elizabeth Cresswell confidante of royalty.

However, it was a rude and crude time, and all were flesh-pedlars touting business from well-heeled 'cunny-hunters', not too fastidious in their choice. As Dr Johnson was later to remark, 'Were it not for Imagination, Sir, a Man would be as happy in the Arms of a Chambermaid as with a Duchess!'

In the first three issues of *The Wand'ring Whore*, Priss is ranked second to Damarose Page, 'The Great Bawd of the Seamen', in Deacon's list of bawds, so that in her day she must have been considered 'a Great'. He gives a number of anecdotes of activities purporting to have happened *chez* Priss, but although most of them are too scabrous to repeat here, that concerning Moll Savory, who used to dress 'in a rich widdows apparrel', bears repetition. A kind-hearted gentleman picked her up and treated her to 'a glass of Canary wine' in a local inn. She told him she must go before eight o'clock, and he took out his expensive gold watch to show her it was but seven o'clock, calling for more wine. While he was '. . . groping and hugging her she picked his pocket of the watch' and protested that she must go, but he insisted that all she needed was a chamber-pot, which was brought and she secreted the watch, 'thrusting it with the gold chain and key into her Commoditie'. They had spent several hours drinking when, the gentleman missing his timepiece, he insisted that she be searched, but nothing was found and she was about to depart when, '. . . an alarum betrayed her, going dub-a-dub in her Cunte at nine of the clock'. That female thieves used this hiding-place cannot be denied, but an alarm-watch at this time was very rare!

The anecdote about Mrs Cupid is, however, based on fact. She was known as 'the Dutchwoman'; her husband, James, was a well-known licensed victualler and a guildsman whose licence was revoked because he kept a disorderly house in St Giles. Mrs Cupid was an expert in the 'chuck-game', and it was reported that '. . . one evening French Dollars, Spanishe Pistoles and English Half-Crowns were chuck'd in as plentifully pour'd in was the Rhenish Wine . . . the Half-Crowns chuckt into her Commoditie doing lesser harme than the Wine . . . for its smarting and searing quality . . .'. Garfield remarked that in Priss' case only the best Sack was allowed because it smarted less. This particular 'sport' is recorded from time immemorial, and its residuary legatee is the pouring of champagne into ladies' slippers. The incident prompted Garfield to exclaim that 'A *Cunny* is the deereste piece of Flesh in the World!'

As for the proposed sorority – which may have had some basis, it contained some very sensible ideas about mutual help, especially against venereal disease, contraception and abortion, as well as the 'restoration of virginities'. There is no mention of cundums, possibly because they were only imported from France and were terribly expensive. Against syphilis there were Dr Fourcade's mercury baths in Leather Lane and innumerable quack remedies offered by French and Dutch quacks who disappeared with their fortunes, leaving a mass of suffering females behind them. One of the best known was Madame Agnodice, whose shop was at the Hand and Urinal in Moorfields; there was a similar establishment nearby called the Ape and Urinal – although this was probably the nickname for a tavern. Madame Agnodice was also a beautician, offering 'Exotic Italian *Washes* to remove skin blemishes . . . the *Spanish Roll* to conceal pock-marks, and a prescription against venereal disease *Venus' Scorpion* . . .', the latter being based upon a secret prescription made for the goddess when she had been bitten by a scorpion. It was no more useless than Fourcade's mercury-baths, and certainly much less painful. There is mention of 'Venus' Pocket Pistol', vulgarly 'Pegoes Nightcap', something made of leather, which may conceivably be a reference to a sheath but could not check '. . . the yett still corrupte & uncurable Disease'.

There was also an appointment of a barber to the sorority for depilation, 'according to the Spanish mode of shaving-off alle the Haires off a Wenches *Commodities*', for which an extra fee was payable. It was not a male monopoly; there were five women barbers in 'Drewery Lane' in 1653 who operated a curious moral code. If a married woman gave 'a dose of the clap' to a neighbour's husband, they whipped her and shaved off her pubic hair, 'demonstrating that she was a whore'. The daughter of one of them, Anne Weaver, married a Roundhead captain, George Monck, who became that General Monck who handed back the throne to Charles II in 1660 and was created Duke of Albemarle for his service. Pepys described her as 'illiterate homely and dowdy . . . with less wit and no beauty'.

There was also a 'limner' – a painter, ordinarily a portraitist whose sitter's picture would be hung on the wall for potential customers to see and choose. Limners were also to paint indelicate pictures *à la Aretino* – or rather, Giulio Romano – to leave nothing to

Not only prison gaolers were harsh towards their inmates: most other officials
were hated for their behaviour towards accused persons. The scene is at the
Mint Prison:

'Behold, a Bailiff is a Villain bred
Alive he's hated: damn'd when he is dead!

c. 1750.

the imagination, since these customers were not connoisseurs of art and needed only something simple to grasp immediately (although Alleyn's Bankside brothels were luxurious enough to contain many genuine Old Masters which now grace the art gallery of Dulwich College). In the case of Priss' 'chuck Office', the limner was to paint 'their principal beauties as well as their Faces'.

The clerk to the proposed sorority was to be Elizabeth Lawrence – presumably she was one of the few who could read and write; but three years later she is advertised for her flagellation brothel – it was stated to be 'her predeliction'.

Priss was already in bad health when released from Newgate, and it was not improved when she went back to her brothel, which (*vide* Garfield) was in '. . . an area full of noysome alleys and the stinke of stifled buyldinges . . . of unsavourie Breath, sultry Venom . . . she was overgrown with Age and oversworn by her former all-too-frequent embraces . . . so she . . . kept the profits made by the exertions of her pupils . . .'. Her husband, 'rotten with syphilis, was shortly [in 1663] to be put into the *Bill of Mortality*'.

The terrible bubonic plague of 1665 devastated Cripplegate and Moorfields, aggravated by the immense 'laystall' (dunghill) almost opposite the Six Windmills which fouled all the waterways runnels and ditches. In July, August and September no fewer than 6,640 men, women and children died in Cripplegate Ward alone. The wealthier inhabitants had all fled, including the vicar of St Giles', Dr Prilcott, who never returned to his parish from his safe country retreat. The churchyards were so full that another had to be opened in Moorfields and (*vide* Walter Bell, the historian of the Plague) '. . . it was rare to find the word "Gent" against the names in the Register . . . there was barefaced concealment of the actual number of deaths . . .', although William Baghurst, a nearby apothecary, remarked: 'While fresh young bodies of men and girls suffered from the Plague the common prostitutes in the back streets and alleys, foul as they were with the Itch Scabbe and Sores were scarcely even struck' – a canard expressed as early as the time of the Black Death 300 years earlier. It was firmly believed that copulation with whores, when coupled with the contracting of a venereal disease, gave one immunity from the plague.

Priss was also one of the victims of the terrible Shrove Tuesday apprentices' rampage of 1668, when her establishment was threatened with destruction, being caught in the cross-fire between the rebellious apprentices and the Duke of York's Redcoats. The rebels demanded that the captain tell them whether the Duke (later James II) was present '. . . and came up to the Six *Windmills* flinging Stones . . . saying they would be with us ere long at Whitehall . . . crying "Hey! Now or Never!"'. Even after their leaders had been arrested, they forced the Keeper of Finsbury prison to release the prisoners, throwing brickbats and shouting, '. . . if the King did not give them Liberty of Conscience then May Day must be a bloudy Day . . . they had been Servants and now they would be Masters . . .' Cromwell's spirit was still astir in the breasts of the City's proletariat, which caused shudders at Court.

Soon after all this Priss died, but her memory was enshrined in the hearts of the locals, whose encomium was: 'In the practice and Proficiency of her Profession she hath outstript the oldest Beldam in man's memory.' The lubricity of her Chuck Office was remembered in ballad and song, but her most fitting epitaph was the unforgettable aphorism 'Money and Cunny are Good Commodities!'

14 Mother Cresswell's Saga

Very rare are the instances where professional bawds, successful in their profession, get involved in national politics. Bawdry is a full-time and worrisome occupation, beset with troubles and even physical danger; strong nerves are needed, as well as business acumen and a flair for flattery and diplomacy. It requires a real knowledge of men's weaknesses and a (well-concealed) contempt for them, especially the pretensions of aristocrats and politicians. In Elizabeth Cresswell's own words, 'If Privy Councillors, Judges, Aldermen, Doctors, Dukes, Lords, Colonels, Knights and Squires may be made into Beasts by stupid *Jades*, how thinkest thou such *Cullies* can be handled by women of *Sense* and *Understanding*?' She went on to say, 'A man will pay as for a *Dutchess*, yett all the while he embraces in Reality a common Strumpett.' This was the key to her success and riches.

She came from a respectable middle-class family of Protestant stock in Knockholt, Kent, who were related to the well-known Percival family, one of whom, Anthony, was knighted by Charles I in 1641, and there is a connection with the famous Cresswells of Tonbridge. Sometime after Elizabeth was born, in 1625, the family moved to the salubrious suburb of Camberwell, only a couple of miles from the lively Bankside pleasure haunts and Whitehall. It was a 'good address' for Robert Cresswell, Gent., of Grays Inn, a property-owner in Leigh near Tonbridge, who married the maiden Anne Gourlay on 14 June 1607 at St James', Clerkenwell. Their son Robert, citizen and merchant taylor, residing in St Botolph's parish, Aldgate, married Isabella Oram, spinster of that parish, in October 1625, and their daughter Elizabeth was baptized soon after. She was stated to have been a lovely little girl of great charm and attraction.

Quite how she became a prostitute operating in Aldersgate, Shoreditch and Clerkenwell is unknown, but in July 1658 she was

A contemporary portrait of Mother Elizabeth Cresswell by M. Laroun.

already a bawd: she was described as a 'Spinster', but in February 1659 she is described as 'a Widdow', and as there is no record of deaths, it is most probable that she had had a common-law husband. A possible explanation for her career is that when Elizabeth Cresswell was born, Elizabeth Holland was the veritable Queen of Bawdry at Hollands Leaguer, and when it was stormed she was about six years old – this incident would certainly have been discussed in Camberwell. By the time she was sixteen, young Elizabeth may have decided to follow this path to fame, fortune and riches. By this time too, the centre of bawdry had shifted to Farringdon Without.

In July 1658, 'considered a Bawd without rival in her wickedness', she came before the magistrates in Hicks Hall, Clerkenwell. The constable, John Marshall, testified: 'Elizabeth Cresswell living in Bartholomew Close was found with divers Gentlemen and Women in her House at divers times: some of these women were sent to Bridewell. . . .' She had, in fact, made a grievous mistake – she had tried to bribe this honest puritan constable with 'four pieces of gold . . . to forbeare to disgrace her and her House'.

It was clearly a superior brothel, and she was trying to protect some eminent clients: none of the gentlemen was named, and no more is heard of the matter – probably because the justices' clerk had been squared. But in the following October, after she had moved to St Leonard's, Shoreditch, she was up before the Westminster bench when a large number of hostile 'informants on Oath' declared '. . . THAT ELIZABETH CRESSWELL *alias* CRESWORTH late of Bartholomew-the-Great & nowe of this parish . . . did entertain divers loose Persons, Men and Women suspected to have committed bawdry . . . the said Elizabeth having lately taken a House . . . for which she paid £100 for a Fine and a Rent of £40 per annum, whereunto many Persons well-habited have resorted by Day as by Nyght . . . continued Drinking, Ranting, Dancing, Revelling, Swearing . . . demeaning themselves as well on the Lord's Day and Fast Days . . . the said Elizabeth refused to give admittance to the Constables and Headboroughs . . .'. She must have been very sure of the protection of her well-dressed clients to have refused admittance to the Law, but the witnesses testified that many times they had seen men and women, '. . . the Woman having stript to her Bodeys & Petycote going into a Room where they have shutt the Casement & lockt the Dore . . . on the Lords Day at noon some Company drunk about a Dozen bottels of Wine AND FURTHER that divers Women suspected of Lightnes have . . . declyned the way to the House at the fore-gate when Neighbours lookt on . . . .

making a great bustle and compass . . . and did surreptitiously slip in at a back gate whereby much Infamy is brought upon the Place . . .'.

Worse was to come: '. . . in the Habitt of a Gentlewoman [one of the whores] began to propose a Helthe to the Privy Member of a Gentleman . . . and afterwards drank a Toast to her own Private Parts . . .'. This was going too far. Some of the neighbours were ready to move away, because '. . . their Daughters and Maid-servants were often taken for Whoares by the Men who frequent that House'.

Elizabeth Cresswell was sentenced to the 'House of Correccion' and 'sett to Hard Labour', provided that she was well enough – a clue to her future 'hacking cough'. It is very unlikely that she ever did any hard labour, having certainly given some 'Golden Oint-ment' where necessary, but in February, with one Elizabeth Sherlocke, she was up before the magistrates and sent back to the prison. It is then that she is described as 'a widdow'.

Meanwhile there had been tremendous changes. Oliver Crom-well had died in September 1658, his son Richard had succeeded him as Lord Protector (handing out many pardons to lucky whores) and by April 1660 Charles II was back on his throne. At this time she was operating from a house in Whetstone Park, Lincoln's Inn Fields (outside the City jurisdiction), selling 'Strong Waters and fresh-fac'd Wenches to all who had *Guineas* to buy them with', although her principal establishment was in Back Alley, off Moor Lane in Cripplegate (Moorgate Underground Sta-tion stands on the site). It was a substantial and well-appointed residence, described in some detail by Richard Head in 1663. He was the rakehell son of a London chaplain, sent down from Oxford and in London becoming a part-time con man and fiddler, as well as an incorrigible wencher.

Head and a companion went to 'Mother' Cresswell's, '. . . famous for the good Citizens' Wives that frequented her house . . . she still rode Admiral over all the other Bawds in Town'. On entering they were conducted into a fine, handsome room, and a manservant brought them bottles of French Wine and some 'salt meats', and then the 'Old Matron' came in, greeting them by chucking them under the chin. When she had seen the colour of their money, she sent in a 'nice young girl', but they could not agree a price, so another was sent in, 'a raving Beauty', explaining that she was 'of superior birth serving only Persons of Quality'. She asked for a guinea; he drunkenly offered half-a-crown, and she accepted half a guinea.

Mother Cresswell and her establishments benefited also by the greater use of coaches, which could bring the wealthy to her doors, although it was said at the time that, 'Poor Whores are whipt while rich ones ride in Coaches!' The mistresses of rich merchants now demanded a 'coach and livery' as part of their settlement – the livery often being that of a nobleman.

By 1668 Elizabeth Cresswell was riding high. Indeed, to para-phrase the Psalmist, 'Seest Thou a Woman diligent in her Business, she shall stand before Kings.' In fact, according to the Chevalier Phileas de Chasles, 'His Majesty Charles II personally honoured her with his Presence and deigned to inspect her House . . . he saw that she had established a sound Organisation which administered a Network of Emissaries and Spies in England . . . as well as France. . . .' She had a sort of *pied-à-terre* in Millbank, near Whitehall, employing a couple of nubile 'secretaries' to advise and arrange the despatch of suitable ladies to exigent noblemen, safe from interruption from bailiffs, constables and importuning creditors.

She had survived both the Great Plague and the Great Fire and by 1666 was emotionally involved with Sir Thomas Player, the city chamberlain and also a member of parliament. This friendship stood her in good stead – although eventually it was to bring about her ruin. In the City she maintained a 'House of Assignation' for lustful City wives and daughters, and she also recruited 'Ape-Gentlewomen' – women who sought amorous dalliance for money but wished to pass as amateurs and not be classed as common whores. They operated about the Royal Exchange, which was booming as a result of the immense rebuilding of the City, and there were rich pickings. She also had an agency for supplying concubines who were recruited from the 'Town Misses', often called the 'Countesses of the Exchange' and popularly as 'side-pillows', serving as gentlemen's helpmeets additionally or in place of a wife. These women operated from the alleys round Gresham's Royal Exchange, then known as the Old Exchange, the New Exchange being in the Strand where now Coutts Bank stands. Of these ladies it was sung: 'They Master your *Britches* and take all your Riches!' They usually consorted with two or three men 'desirous of buying her *Commodity*'. Many were recruited from Cavalier families who had been ruined in the Civil War.

In 1668 Elizabeth was involved, with Damarose Page and other madams, in the so-called and highly seditious pamphlet *The Poor Whores' Pettition to Lady Castlemaine*, ostensibly a cry for help from ruined London whores to the Great Royal Whore. (The author is thought to have been John Evelyn, who detested Barbara Palmer, Lady Castlemaine.) Mrs Cresswell is reputed to have assisted in the widest distribution of this effusion. It was headed 'THE POOR-WHORES PETTITION TO THE MOST SPLENDID ILLUSTRIOUS SERENE & EMINENT LADY OF PLEASURE, the Countess of Castlemayne etc., the HUMBLE PETITION of the Undone Company of poore, distress'd Whores, Bawds, Pimps and Panders etc.'. It asked for help because Barbara Castlemaine had great experience in whoring, had arrived at great estate thereby and was fully aware of the distressful situation into which her poorer sisters had been thrown by the great apprentices' riots on Shrove Tuesday, when their houses had been pulled down and set on fire. It then listed all the principal centres of whoredom in London on 25 March 1668. These included Saffron Hill, Chiswell Street and Moorfields, as well as Ratcliffe and Wapping.

The next reference to Mrs Cresswell is on 3 April 1670 in a note sent by Dr John Hawkes to the lord mayor. Coming through Finsbury Fields the previous evening, he had been threatened 'by a Gang of fourteen Youths' who in the confrontation had said that, '. . . on Monday next they would assemble the rest of the Apprentices with Swordes and Lances and raze the Brothell House where the Murder was committed and as well one Howse opposite occupied by Mrs Cresswell . . .'. The lord mayor immediately told the governor of the Tower of London, who sent some militiamen.

Between 1670 and 1680 Mrs Cresswell's wealth and influence grew apace, as also did her intimacy with Sir Thomas – who was sometimes called Sir Thomas Cresswell! A contemporary Roxburghe Ballad notes: 'Old Player's grown Rampant, pick'd up with a Woman!' He was a rabble-rousing anti-Papist, nicknamed 'The Rabshakeh', frequently visiting Mrs Cresswell's country house in Camberwell and giving stupendous parties for political cronies which often turned into sexual orgies. In the ballad 'Oates' Boarding School in Camberwell', describing a fund-raising function for Titus Oates, is found:

There shall all Provision be made
to entertain the *Best*.
Old *Mother* Cresswell of our *Trade*
For to rub-down our Guest.
Three hundred of the briskest *Dames*
in *Park* or *Fields* e'er fell
Whose am'rous *Eyes* shall charm the *Flames*
of the *Saints* at Camberwell

An old and very large Tudor building in a narrow passage off Grub Street which might well have been occupied by Mother Cresswell. It was still standing in 1860.

To gather 300 girls from Whetstone Park, Lincoln's Inn and Moorfields was no mean achievement and demonstrates her powers of organization and the wideness of her contacts. However, Sir Thomas was using public funds to support the ineffable Oates – presumably under the heading of 'Business Entertainment'. It was also remarked that some of the guests wore 'Clokes of *Geneva Cut'* – identifying them as zealous Puritans.

Mrs Cresswell's name now appears in many ballads and plays. In *Gallantry à la mode* (1674), at Cresswell's 'precise Damsels doe appear': she supplied only 'the best Commodities solde at the dearest Rates'. In Elkanah Settle's farce *The Empress of Morocco*, a parody of Shakespeare's *Macbeth*, Hecate and the Witches sing:

> A Helthe, a Helthe! to *Mother* Cresswell
> from Moorfields fled to *Millbanke Castle* . . .

Millbank being a euphemism for Whitehall.

Meanwhile Sir Thomas was supporting the legitimacy of James, Duke of Monmouth (bastard son of Charles II and a fervent Protestant), in the succession, which angered and frightened the rabid Catholic heir, James, Duke of York; and his support for Titus Oates was landing him in deep waters. He was now borrowing large sums from his paramour. In the end it was Oates and his 'Popish Plot' which ruined both Sir Thomas and his friend, in the vicious campaign against Catholics which hounded to death or beggary many innocent people. It was alleged that Captain Thomas Dangerfield, the 'scoundrelly double-agent provocateur', had visited *Maison* Cresswell once or twice for amorous purposes, but he was involved in the 'Meal-tub Plot', which involved Elizabeth Cellier, the 'Popish Midwife'. The inference was that Mrs Cresswell was covering up a treasonous plot.

Mrs Cellier, a licensed midwife and impeccable Protestant, had had the misfortune to fall in love with Dangerfield when he was in Newgate, and she became a devout Catholic in January 1679. Dangerfield requited her love by involving her in his villainous activities, of which she was quite unaware. He instigated a raid on her home, where papers were found at the bottom of a meal-tub, being alleged plans for the overthrow of Charles II and the restoration of the Catholic religion.

Mrs Cresswell was quick to dissociate herself from this *imbroglio*, but from this time her decline may be noted. Oates was pilloried at Tyburn in 1685, and Dangerfield was 'whipt almost to death', dying soon afterwards of an injury to his eye. Mrs Cellier was

Mrs Elizabeth Cellier, The Popish Midwife *in the pillory for her part in the* Meal-tub Plot. *Much public indignation was manifested because she had secured a shield to protect her face.*

vindicated and lived for many years, sponsoring, *inter alia*, the first association of midwives.

Mother Cresswell was still rich and influential, protesting that only pure Protestant bawdry was carried out in her brothels. Still, in the ballad 'A Narrative of the Old Plot (1686) there is mention of 'flogging at Cresswell's in Camberwell', which implies the attendance of 'Posture Girls' who were experts in this *genre*.

One of her regular visitors was Sir Anthony Ashley-Cooper (later Lord Shaftesbury), a close confidant of the King who was a known homosexual but who kept a whore around him to 'prove' that he was heterosexual. In Thomas Otway's *Venice Preserv'd* there was a vicious attack on him:

> A *Senator* that keeps a Whore
> in Venice, none a higher Office bore –
> To lewdness ev'ry Night he ran:
> Show me, all London, another such Man –
> Match him at Mother Cresswells if you can!

Hitherto Mrs Cresswell had backed the winning side, but now Charles II (who had kept his own Catholicism secret, and also his subvention from the King of France) decided after all that his brother James should be his successor, although he was a Catholic. This was bitterly resented by the great mass of Protestants, particularly that Protestant stronghold the City of London, which favoured the Duke of Monmouth. There were riots and tumults, aggravated by James' assertion that he would rule as an absolute monarch, in the inflammatory words, 'I will make no concessions! My father made concessions and he was beheaded!' This made all parliamentarians angry to boot. The rashly outspoken Alderman Sir Thomas Player attacked the Duke of York, saying, 'The City would raise no more Money to pay the Whores at Whitehall . . . and not for arbitrary government . . . the Crown was at the disposal of the Commons, not the King!' The King sent a warning shot by arresting Sir Thomas' servant but still had to temporize and sought other means to damp down his opposition.

Mrs Cresswell was the first to feel the draught. *The Imperial Protestant Mercury* (November reported: 'The famous Madam Cresswell was, on Tryall of *Nisi Prius* at Westminster convicted after above thirty years practice Bawdry . . . some of her Does most unkindly testifying against her . . . to receive sentence at the next Sessions. . . .' It was a shrewd blow aimed at a steady financial supporter. She remarked later that, '. . . a malignant Jury . . . had dispossessed her of her lovely Habitacion . . . which I have many years kept in Moorfields to the Joy and Comfort of the whole Amorous republic'. It would not have been difficult to get her 'does' to testify against her; many would have harboured grudges for one or other reason, others would have been coerced. They knew that *in extremis* they would go to Bridewell, while she would be able to bribe her way out of trouble.

She was soon back in trading, but in the meantine the King had appointed a new lord mayor and routed his detractors. This débâcle was celebrated in John Oldham's *Satyres Vpon Jesuittes* (1683):

> Presto Popola Pilkington:
> Shit upon Sheriff Shute;
> Cuckolding Clayton no less ill . . .
> Sir Thomas has gone to Cresswell
>   and Somebody has the Gout!

Alderman Thomas Pilkington and Alderman Samuel Shute had been ousted; ex-Lord Mayor Sir Robert Clayton had trimmed his sails. Pilkington was imprisoned from 1682 to 1686 and, when James II was ousted, became a member of parliament and lord mayor. Sir Thomas Player died in 1686 but Sir Robert Clayton grew richer and richer and died in 1707.

Sir Thomas' misfortunes were linked directly with Mrs Cresswell in a *Pasquinade, The Last Will and Testament of the Charters of London* (1683), as being the last bequests to the chamberlain of London: 'TO SIR THOMAS PLAYER. I LEAVE all the Manor of Moorfields with all the Wenches and Bawdy-houses thereunto belonging, with *Mrs CRESSWELL* for his immediate Inheritance to enjoy and occupy from the Bawd to the Whores downward. . . .'

The next blow was a demand for £300 for a bond for Sir Thomas 'as an unpaid debt', which was bruited in Nathanael Thompson's *Loyal Song*:

> Bobbing about in Kent and Camberwell
> For which thy Stock lay waiting;
> Where's all that Money now, Can'st tell?
> If not, thou'rt near to breaking! . . .
> Not being paid, the worn-out Cresswell's broke. . . .

She had guaranteed a bill of exchange for her paramour, and because she had already contributed so much to his political activities, she was now short of cash and could not meet this comparatively small obligation: the charges were meant to embarrass her trading. She was hoist with her own petard, since one of her fixed precepts to her 'daughters' was, 'Never get involved in politics or religion, and never lend a Penny to a friend!'

She was also now an ailing woman – the 'hacking cough' was undoubtedly consumption coming to a head, and a spell in the notorious hellhole of Newgate certainly aggravated it. Even by her bribery of the prison-keeper and his minions the surroundings were horrible, and by this time in 1684 she would have been sixty. She died in prison, but there is a small mystery as to whether it was Newgate or Bridewell. On the approach to death she is reputed to have reverted to piety. James Grainger, in his *Biographical History of England* (she is the only bawd therein mentioned), relates:

> She desired by her Will to have a Sermon preach'd at her Funerall, the Preacher to have Ten Pounds but only on this express Condition that he was to say nothing but what was *well* of her . . . a preacher was found with difficulty to undertake this Task. He preached on the generall Subject of *Mortality* [and] concluded with saying: –
> By the WILL of the deceas'd it is expected that I say nothing but well of her. All that I shall say therefore is this: She was *born well*, she liv'd

well and she *died well* for she was born with the name Cresswell, she liv'd in Clerkenwell and she died in Bridewell!

It would be fitting, although the story is a little suspect, because much earlier, in 1625, John Marsten in *The Dutch Courtezan* has his bawd Cocledemoy's soliloquy on whores end: '. . . 'tis moste certayne they must needes both live well and dye well since they moste commonlye live in Clearkenwell and dye in Bridewell'.

Elizabeth Cresswell died sometime in 1685, and her will shows that she was still a wealthy woman despite her wails of ruin and poverty through a 'malignant jury'. She desired 'a Decent Buryall in the Parish Church of Nockholt in the County of Kent accordynge to the Manner of the Church of England', claiming to be of 'Sounde and Perfecte Minde and Memorye, Prayse be to God'. She left many substantial legacies to her Percival cousins, a gold watch to her 'lovynge Freinde Margaret Clarke the Elder', and 20 shillings to the poor of Nockholt. Two of her 'girls' were given three years to pay off their debts to her in six-monthly instalments, and the residue of the estate was to go to the little daughter of her 'kinsman' John Smale of Nockholt, to be 'broughte upp and educated accordynge to the discretion of Margaret Clarke', and all the moneys were to be held in trust for the child during her minority. However, she was not buried in Knockholt, nor seemingly in prison, for the register does not, as usual, make the special mention of those who died in a prison. She was not soon forgotten.

George Shell's *The Whores' Rhetorick* makes it clear that his book is dedicated to 'Lady Creswel . . . because of her recent Misfortunes', and when it was reprinted in 1685 it bore the sub-title *Mrs Cresswell's Last Legacy*. It is effectively a manual of instruction for would-be whores. There was also a book *La Vie de Maman Cresswell* quoted by de Chasles, probably a translation of an English book – neither of them can now be traced: a great pity, because she was undoubtedly a powerful personality and the only bawd to meddle in high politics. By the time she died the immigrant Huguenots had transformed the Clerkenwell area into a puritan stronghold, and high-class bawdry had moved westward to the purlieus of Covent Garden.

15 Banking Beats Bawdry

For most of its existence London was protected by the Roman-built but oft-restored twenty-foot-high wall, and while it remained, the City's authorities could, by exhortation and threats, control in some measure the houses of sin and the generality of sexual sinners. (The final weapons were the pillory, the thew, public carting and shaming, prison and then banishment to an extra-mural 'assigned place'.)

A *murage* (wall tax) was levied from time to time to keep the wall in good repair, although these moneys were often embezzled by impecunious monarchs or dishonest City oligarchs; wear and tear and frequent fires encouraged philanthropic citizens to pay for essential immediate action in default of royal or public funds. In 1257 Mayor Ralph Hardel, draper, when having the walls repaired, paid for 'new bulwarkes' (barbican towers), and in 1282 Edward I ordered a complete overhaul which was not completed until 1311, in the reign of his successor. In 1387 King Richard II, '. . . fearing invasion by the French pulled down houses about the walls and cleaned the ditches' – the wide moat which circled the walls. The eventual 'enemy' was not the French but Sir John Oldcastle's Lollards, 'who assembled a great power' outside the walls in 1413 before he was overcome and executed.

It was, however, the expanding needs of commerce which required in 1415 that Mayor Thomas Falconer should pierce the wall with a new gate, called Moorgate, '. . . so that the citizens could reach the villages of Isledon [Islington] Clerkenwell and Hoggeston [Hoxton] . . .'; as an extra convenience 'a new latrine' was built a couple of years later. The very ancient Crepelgate

A boisterous scene in a coffee-house cum brothel c. 1760. The whore in front is picking the cully's pocket. Drinking, smoking and whoring were equal sins! The figure in the conical hat is the Devil egging them on.

206

postern nearby – known in King Aelfred's time as Cithilgate (the gate to the forest) – was now a source of obstruction, because '. . . at either end there was a door which must be shut in the nighte season . . .'; the room above was 'in olden time used as a prison' for nightwalkers. In 1672 Moorgate had to be 'widened and high-ered so that the City *Train Bands* could march through with their pikes erect', although the present Moorgate Street was not built until 1845, 'for easy access to London Bridge'.

In the aftermath of the Great Fire of 1666 the walls were restored, but the migration of the population was never stemmed, and the sin-palaces began to migrate to the peripheries of the extra-mural wards, into such adjacent liberties as the Fleet, the Temple, Saffron Hill and Hockley-in-the-Hole in the west, and Bishopsgate and the Tower Liberties in the east.

Many clandestine small brothels still remained within the walls, a great many around Sir Thomas Gresham's magnificent new Royal Stock Exchange. Prostitutes and catamites swarmed around the busy brokers and rich merchants in Silkmen's Alley, Grocers' Alley and Sweeting's Rents, and especially around the ancient Pope's Head Tavern in the alley of that name.

In 1652 Pasquale Rosee's Coffee-House, the first in London, opened in a shed in St Michael's churchyard, serving 'that bitter blacke drincke' observed by Pepys, which Evelyn described as being sold in 'obnoxious . . . places of subversion'. Moreover, *The Women's Petition Againste Coffee* (1674) claimed that, '. . . it made Men as Unfruitfull as the Desert whence that unhappy Berry . . . is bought'. Next to open was the Sultanesse' Head in Sweeting's Rents, and in short order Jonathan's at No. 20 Exchange Alley and Sam's at No. 14.

But it was at the Pope's Head Coffee-House in the alley of the same name that sinfulness was most evident. In that alley the famous Sally Salisbury, that 'beautiful little Wenche that sells

Plus ça change, plus c'est la même chose! 1790–1990

During a heated debate in Parliament when many new taxes were proposed, such as a 10% property tax and taxes on servant maids and beer as well as a window tax the 'People's Friend' Charles Fox sarcastically remarked that in order to avoid being crushed by these taxes it might be necessary to move from the first to the second floor and even to the attic, but if someone already occupied the cellar 'then where to go?'. Gillray seized on this to attack Fox, who is here portrayed with his supporter Lord Henry Petty urging John Bull already forced almost into bankruptcy, to find the money to pay taxes. a travesty of Fox's attack on the Government's proposals.

pamphlets to schoolboys and 'prentices . . . obliging the 'prentices at half-a-Crown for half-an-hour', began her meteoric career when a rich Dutch merchant took her under his wing until she went 'up West' to fame, glory and a sad death.

Hereabouts were the catamites who tempted Cornhill and Cheapside merchants into 'Mollies Houses' in Beech Lane, Cripplegate, and Fetter Lane, Farringdon, and to shame and suicide – or to Mother Cresswell's luxurious whorehouse off Grub Street. After her death they had even greater choice in Lewknors' Lane and Whetstone Park at the City's fringe about Chancery Lane.

While the intra-mural citizens were moving to the more salubrious suburbs, the areas outside the walls were filling up with hard-working, God-fearing, sober-minded immigrants, bringing old and new crafts and industries into their new homes, incidentally reinforcing the 'puritanical' attitudes of true Londoners. Huguenots colonized Spitalfields, outside Bishopsgate; the Welsh congregated around Clerkenwell, setting up schools and chapels; the Italians turned Saffron Hill into Little Italy. Dutch, Spanish and Portuguese Jews had settled from Cromwell's time around Bevis Marks, and the later influx of European Jews brought many new industries into the Portsoken. None had great interest in whoring or sexual aberrations.

In 1760 London's walls and gates were all taken down, and with the new roads and better means of communication the centre of political and social life shifted to Westminster, leaving the City to become the powerhouse of banking and commerce and less and less a residential area, although the streets were crowded by day and night, particularly the brightly lit main thoroughfares of Cheapside, Cornhill, Eastcheap and Bishopsgate. One bright spot of amusement, however, was lacking – there were no theatres within the walls. Not until 1959 was permission reluctantly given for the Mermaid to be erected at Puddle Dock, at the very fringe of the City in Blackfriars, thus reducing the chances of moral pollution spreading inwards. (The theatre at the Barbican is likewise on the fringe!)

The City's power also stopped the railways from breaching its walls, so that every morning and evening there is a great migration in and out; it also stopped the Victorian tramways at its borders! In consequence the number of actual residents declined enormously, so that today the City streets swarm busily from nine till six and thereafter are as quiet as a morgue; and, almost incredibly, on any Saturday morning these days, every shop on the famous

Cheapside is closed! It is extremely unlikely that there is a single whorehouse anywhere within the City's extended walls.

Thus, without any fuss or trouble, Commerce and Banking have ousted Venus' servants. London is no longer a – sexually – Sinful City. Other sins, like Greed and Envy are rife – but the streets and lanes are clean!

Bibliography

BM – British Museum

Abbott, George, *Tortures in the Tower of London*, David and Charles, 1986

Alexander, Boyd, *Life at Fonthill* – William Beckford (1957)

Anon., 'A Diurnal of Dangers' (1617) in *Notes and Queries*, Vol. 149, p. 374, 21.11.1925

Anon., *The Craftie Whore*, 'The Mystery of the Bawdy Houses', 'for Henry Marsh' (1658; BM E 1927)

Anon., *The TRYALLS of SUCH PERSONS as under the NOTION of LONDON–APPRENTICES were Tumultuously Assembl'd in Moorfieldes and Other Places on EASTER HOLIDAYS last under Colour of Pulling down Bawdy Houses*, 'At the Sessions in the Old-Bailey on Saturday April 14.1668. Printed for Robert Pawlet and are to be Sold at *The Bible* in Chancery Lane neare unto Serjeants Inn' (London, 1668)

Anon., *The Two-Penny Whore* or 'A Relation of a Two Penny bargain' ('Printed for W. Thackeray, T. Passinger and W. Whitwood', 1670)

Anon., *The Women's PETITION against COFFEE* 'by A Well-Willer. The Humble Petition of thousands of Buxsome Good-Women languishing in Extremity of Want' (1674)

Anon. (Daniel Mallet ?), *Gallantry à la Mode*, A Satyricall Poem (1674)

Anon., *The Last Night's Ramble* (BM: Harley MS.7316, *c.* 1678)

Anon., *The Bridewell Whores Resolution* or 'The Confession of the 24 Backsliders'' 'With allowance Rob.L'Estrange' ('Printed for F. Coles, T. Vere, J. Wright and J. Clarke', *c.* 1680)

Anon., *Utile Dulce* (BM: Harley MS.7319, *c.* 1681)

Anon., *A Pasquil or Pasquinade*: 'The Last Will and Testament of the Charters of London', (1683) See also Scott, ed

Anon., *A Satyre upon the Players* (BM: Harley MS 7319, *c.* 1684)

212

Anon., *The Court Diversion* (BM: Harley MS 7319, *c.* 1685)

Anon., *A Catalogue of Jilts, Cracks and Prostitutes* (1691)

Anon., *College Wit Sharpen'd* ('Printed for J. Wadham', 1739)

Archenholz, Baron Johann Wilhelm von, *The British Mercury* or 'Annals of History Politics and Manners' (Hamburg, 1787–92)
> *Pictures of England* (first German edition 1770; trans. 1788)

Bagford Ballads, The – see J. B. Ebsworth ed.

Bailey, Derrick S., *Homosexuality and the Western Christian Tradition* (Longman, 1955)

Behn, Aphra, *The Town Fopp*, a Comedy (1677; BM 11774)

Bloch, Iwan, *Sexual Life in England*, trans. H. Forstern (Arco, 1958)

Brown, Thomas, *Cheats of the Town* (1776; GH, Bay H.5. No. 19)

Brown, Thos (pseudonym), *The Midnight Spy* ('Printed for J. Cook at The Shakespeare Head in Paternoster Row', 1766; GH)

Burford, E. J., *Queen of the Bawds* – Madame Britannica Hollandia and her House of Obsenitie (Neville Spearman, 1973)
> *The Orrible Synne*, London Lechery from Roman to Cromwell's times (Calder & Boyars, 1973)
> *Bawds and Lodgings*, A History of the Bankside Stewes. *c.* 100 –1675 (Peter Owen, 1976)
> *In the Clink*, England's Oldest Prison (N.E.L., 1977)

Bryant, Arthur, *Man in the Making* – Samuel Pepys (Collins, 1959)

Chamberlain, John, *Letters* – see N. E. McClure, ed.

Chasles, Chevalier Phileas de, *Le 16ème Siècle en Angleterre* (Paris, 1846)

Chester, Jos. Lemuel, *London Marriage Licences 1521–1689*, ed. J. Foster, (Quaritch, 1887)

Cohen, Jeffrey, 'Jewish Prostitution' in *Jewish Chronicle*, 26 March 1976

Corrie, E., ed., *The Sermons of Bishop Hugh Latimer* (The Parker Society, Cambridge, 1884)

Cranley, Thomas, *Amanda, or the Reform'd Whore* ('Printed at and are to be sold at *The Golden Key* against the Middle Temple Gate', W. Haywood 1 July 1635)

Crossley, J., ed., *The Works of John Taylor, the Water Poet* (The Spencer Society, Manchester, 1870–71)

Dekker, Thomas, *The Belman of London* (Butter, 1608)
> *The Bel-mans Nighte Walkes*, whereunto is added *O per se O* (Creed, 1612)

Dictionary of National Biography

Dryden, John, *Satyre on the King and Duke* (BM: Harley MS 7319, *c.* 1675)

Dunton, John, *The Phenix* (B. Bragg, 1707)

Dunton, John, *The HE-Strumpet*: A Satyre on the Sodomites Club (1707)

    The Whipping-Post: A Satyre on Everybody with The Whoring-Plaquet or 'News of the Stallions and Kept Misses' ('B. Bragg, at the Black Raven' Paternoster Row', 1706)

D'Urfey, Thomas, *Pills to Purge Melancholy* (1709)

    Collin's Walke through London: a Poem in Burlesque ('Jno. Bullord at the *Olde Blacke Beare in* St Pauls Church Yard', 1690)

Ebsworth, J. B., ed., *The Bagford Ballads* (Ballad Society, Hertford, 1876)

Ebsworth, J. B., and Hindley, Charles, *The Roxburghe Ballads* (Ballad Society, Hertford, 1877)

Evelyn, John, *Diary*, ed. William Bray (Dent, 1951)

Filip, Jan, *Celtic Civilisation and its Heritage*, trans. R. F. Samson (Czechoslovak Academy of Science, 1960)

Finch, B. E., and Green, Hugh, *Contraception through the Ages* (Peter Owen, 1963)

Foster, J., ed. – see Chester, Jos. Lemuel

Foxon, David, *Libertine Literature in England in the 17th and 18th centuries, 1660–1745* (1963)

    (article in the *Book Collector* Vol. XII, No. 4, pp. 26 ff.)

Fuchs, Emil Eduard, *Illustrierte Sittengeschichte von Mittelalter* (Munich, 1909)

Gardner, R. S., *Reports of Cases in the Court of Star Chamber* (Camden Society, NS, 1875)

Garfield, John, *The Wand'ring Whore* (1660)

    The Wand'ring Whore's Complaint for want of TRADEING ('Printed for *Mercurius Democraticus*, J. Jones', 1663)

    A Strange and True Conference etc. by *Megg Spencer* (1660)

    Strange Nevves from Bartholomew Fair or *The Wand'ring Whore* DISCOVERED, by Peter Aretino, translated by *Theodorus Mirrorismus* (1661)

    Strange and True Nevves from Jack a Newberry's Six Windmills by Peter Aretino, Cardinall of Rome (1660)

Grainger, James, ed., *Biographical History of England* (Baynes, 5th edition, 1824, Volume IV, p. 219)

Grose, Francis, *Classical Dictionary of the Vulgar Tongue* (reprint of 1931)

Gwillim, John, *The London Bawd*, With her Character & Life, Discovering the various Intrigues of Lewd Women ('Gun Yard in Bishopsgate', 4th edition, 1711)

Hall, Bishop Joseph, *Virgidimarium, or Satyres* (1597; Harrison, 1602)

Bibliography

Harben, H. A., *A Dictionary of London* (Jenkins, 1918)

Hardy, J. W., ed. – see Middlesex Sessions

Harvey, A. D., Prosecutions for Sodomy in England' in *Historical Journal*, 1978, Vol. 21, No. 4, p. 939 ff.

Head, Richard, and Kirkman, Francis, *The English Rogue* (Hy. Marsh, 1665)

Holloway, Robert, *The Phoenix of Sodom* or 'The Vere Street Coterie' ('6 Richmond Bldgs, Artillery Lane in Tooley Street'; J. Cook, 1813)

Inderwick, A. C., *Calendar of Inner Temple Records*, (1600–01), (Henry Sotheran, Oxford, 1896)

INDEX of Inhabitants of the City of London, 1638 (OUP, 1888)

Jeaffreson, J. C., ed., *Middlesex County Records* (1888)

Journal of the Common Council of the Corporation of the City of London, 1618–19, Vol. XXX, folio 382

Mackay, Charles, ed., *Songs of the London Prentices* (Percy Society, 1841)

McKerrow, E. B., ed., *The Works of Thomas Nashe* (Sidgwick & Jackson, 1910)

Marshall, Dorothy, *The English Poor in the 18th century* (Routledge, 1926)

Mercurius Democraticus – see John Garfield

Mercurius Philalethes (Roger L'Estrange), *Select City Quaeries* or 'The Discovery of Cheates, Abuses and Subtilities of the City Bawds and Trapanners' (1660)

Middlesex Sessions Books, Calendar of, ed. J. W. Hardy: 1689–1709 (Middlesex Committee, 1905) and 1612–18 (Middlesex Committee, New Series, 1935–41)

Middlesex County Records 3. Edward IV – 4 James II, ed. Jeaffreson, 4 vols, (Middlesex Committee, 1888–92)

Mirrorismus Theodorus – see John Garfield

Morrison, J. H. ed., *The Prerogative Court of Canterbury* – Births, Christenings, Wills (British Records Society, 1893–1901)

Nashe, Thomas, *Nashe his Dildo* (c. 1600; Bodleian Library: Rawlinson MS Poet 216)

Old Bailey, *Secret Trials for Murder, Rape, Sodomy, coining, etc.* (1734–5), 2 volumes

Oldham, John, *Satyre Vpon Jesuittes* – 'Satyre and Song' (1683)

Otway, Thomas, *Venice Preserv'd* (1682)

Pepys, Samuel, *Diary* (various editions, including R. Latham and W. Matthews, USA, 1970–76)

Pink, W. J. and Wood, E., *History of Clerkenwell* (Chas. Herbert, 1890)

Rae, James, *Deaths of the Kings of England* (Sheratt Hughes, Manchester, 1913)

Reich, Emil, *Woman Through the Ages* (Methuen, 1908)

Reynolds, Robert, *The Ape-Gentlewoman* or 'The Character of an Exchange Wench' (Pye, 1670)

Reynolds, Rowland, *The Character of a Town Miss* (1680)

Riley, H. T., ed., *Liber Albus* (Griffin, 1861)

Rochester, Earl of – see John Wilmot)

Rollins, H. E., ed., *Pepys Ballads* (Harvard University, USA, 1922)

Rosenbaum, Julius, *The Plague of Lust* (Carrington, Paris, 1901)

Roxburghe Ballads – see Ebsworth, J. B.

Rye, William B. ed., *England as seen by foreigners in the days of Queen Elizabeth* and *King James the First* (J. A. Smith, 1865)

Scott, Sir Walter, ed., *A Collection of Scarce & Valuable Tracts of Lord John Somers*, 'Civil Tracts' (Cadell & Davies, 1809–13)

Sellars, H., 'Italian Books printed in England before 1640' in *The Library*

Settle, Elkanah, *The Empress of Morocco*, a Farce (Scenes 4, 1924, Volume 15, pp. 114–15) (1674)

Speed, Sam, *Fragmenta Carceris*: the 'King's Bench Litany', the 'Legend of Duke Humphrey' (1675)

State Papers (Domestic), Calendar of, ed. J. W. Hardy (Records Commission, 1856–95)

Stow, John, *Surveigh of London*, ed. C. L. Kingsford (OUP, 1908)

Stow, William, *Remarks on London* (St Aubyn, 1722)

Taylor, John, 'The Water Poet', *A Vertuous Bawd, A Modest Bawd* (H. Gosson, 1635)

    A Common Whore (1622)

    In Prayse & Vertue of Iayles & Iaylers (1623)

Tempest, Pierce, *The Cryes of the City of London*, 'by M. Lauron, drawn after the Life' (1688)

Thompson, Paunde, ed., *The Letters of Henry Prideaux to John Ellis*, 1675 (Camden Society, 1875)

Thompson, Nathanael, *A Choice Collection of 180 Loyal Songs* (1685)

Thompson, Roger, *Unfit for Modest Ears* (Macmillan, 1979)

Uffenbach, Zacharias von (1683–1734), *London in 1710*, trans. W. H. Quarrell and M. Moore (Faber, 1934)

Ward, Edward (Ned Ward), *The London Spy*: including 'A History of the London Clubs' (G. Sawbridge, 1709)

Weldon, Sir Anthony, *The Court and Character of King James the First* (privately printed, 1817)

Wilmot, John, Earl of Rochester, *Satyre: Against Mankind* (Bodleian Library, Oxford, n/d, MS Firth, c. 15)

Poems of the E of R, (1722)

Selected Poems, (1732)

The Lady's March, (attrib.; BM: Harley MS 7319)

Poems for Severall Occasions, (1732)

Wilson, J. H. ed., *A Choyce Collection* (of MSS: Ohio State Library)
  The Rochester-Saville Letters, (Ohio University Press, 1941)

Winstock, Lewis, ed., *Marches and Songs of the Cavaliers and Round-heads* (Lee Cooper, 1972)

Wood, Anthony à, *Life and Times*, 1664–81 (Oxford Historical Society, 1892)

Wright, Thomas, *Vocabulary of Anglo-Saxon English*, (1884) London 1672

Wycherley, William, *The Plain Dealer* (play; 1672)

Yearsley, P. McLeod, *Le Roy est Mort*, (Heritage, 1935)

Index

Index

Index

Ducke Lane, 155, 158, see Duke Street
Ducking-stool, 21, 32, 148, 155
Duke's Place, Aldgate, 66
Duke Street, 155, 158, see also Ducke Lane
Duke Humphries' Rents, 146
Dulwich College, 183, 192
Dunghills, 56, 57, 99, 131, 192, see also
    Gong-farmers, Laystalls, Sanitation
Dung-rakers, 50
Dunstan, Archbishop, 28
D'Urfey, Thomas (1653–1723), 159
Dutch beer, 59
Dutch Courtezan, The (1625), 205
Dwellings/Housing, see Building
Dysart, Lady 'Bess' (–1687), Duchess of
    Lauderdale, 154
Dystaff with towen, 93

Eadgar's Laws, see Edgar, King
Ealdgate, see Aldgate
Earls, 32, 41, 50, see also Aldermen, Jarls
East Anglia, 7
Eastcheap, 58, 98, 210
Eastfield, Alderman William, 54
Eastern Vice, 16, 38
East Saxons, 25
East Smithfield, 29
Ebbgate, 56, 99
Ecclestone, Jacob, 163, 164
Echevins, 48, see also Commune
Edgar, Aetheling, 40
Edgar, King (959–75), 29, 30, 32, 36
Edith, Princess of Scotland, 40
Edward the Elder, King (–899–925), 28
Edward the Confessor, King (1042–65),
    33, 50, 174
Edward I (1239–72–1307), 54, 69, 70–79,
    86, 107, 155, 206
Edward II (1284–1307–27), 54, 79–81, 94
Edward III (1312–27–77), 81–8
Edward IV (1442–61–83), 55, 105–8
Edward V (1470–83–83), 108
Edward VI (1537–47–53), 51, 117–19
Edwy, King (–955–9), 28
Egberht, Archbishop, 23
Eightpence, Osbert (Huitdeniers), 41
Elms, The (place of execution), 155
Elias *le Mire*, physician,
Emma, Queen, 32
Emperour's Head Lane, 184
Empress of Morocco, The (1674), 201
English tongue (1362), 32
Enterludes, 178
Eowende (Penis), see Castration
Ephraim ben Jacob, Rabbi of Bonn
    (1113–1200), 43
Equestri, 13
Erkenwald, Archbishop (–693), 23
Essex, 19, 20, 24
Ethelburga, St, (–676), 23
Ethelred 'the Unrede', King (–979–1016),
    30, 32
Ethelredeshithe, 24, see also Queenhithe

Eulagium, The, of Malmesbury (1362), 87
Evelyn, John (1620–1700), 156, 172
Everardeswellestreete, 67, 180, see also
    Chiswell Street
Evil May Day, 1517, 114
Exeter, Bishop of, 80, see also Stapledon
Exsoletum (Catamites), 9
Eyre, Alderman Simon, 54

Fagges Well, 178
Fair Rosamund Sugarcunt, 165, 171
Falconer, Alderman Thomas, 55, 206
Falstaff, Sir John, 126
Famine, 80
Farringdon wards, 51, 86, 97, 100, 142,
    154, 156, 158, 169, 173, 198
Farting Club, The, 162, 163
Faunus (god), 10
Fellatio, 41, 187
Fetter Lane, 83, 158
Fetters, *see* Irons
'Fiddles', see Cheating
Figges (venereal sores), 21
Fires, 55, 135
Fishmongers and Fish Street, 30, 33, 53,
    91, 93, 104
FitzAilwyn, Henry (c.1150–1212), 47, 49,
    52
FitzOsbert, William, 48
FitzStephen, William (c.1120–1190), 41,
    42, 155
FitzWalter, Hubert, portreeve (–1205), 48
Fitzwaren, Sir Ivo, 52
Flambard, Justiciar Ranulf (–1128), 38, 40
Flavinius, Lucius Quintus, 16
Fleet Marriages, 175, 184
Fleet River and Street, 3, 36, 56, 68, 79,
    85, 95, 173, 174, 175, and *passim*
Flemings, 37, 57, 87, 101, 154
Fleur de Lys, Le, 126
Floralia, 10
Folksmoot, 21, 24, 25, 50, 65
Fons Clericorum, 178, see Clerkenwell
Forestallers (Retailers), 50, 68
Forlicghers, 21, 69
Fornication, 13, 14, 27, 28, 29, 32, 69, 71,
    72, 102, 116, 148
Fornixes, 14
Fortune Theatre, 142, 143, 146
Forum, 8
Fotheringham, Priscilla, 179, 180, 184–93
Fountain Tavern in-the-Strand, 162
Fourcade, Dr Florence, 169
France/French, 27, 29
Franks, 21
Frascatore, Gabriel (1630–81), 168, 169
Fraternities, 50, 53
Freemen, 13, 20, 22, 25, 50, 60, 65, see also
    Folkmoots
Frey with the Phallus (god), 30
Freya (goddess), 19
Fricge (god), 19
Frisians, 21

221

Index

Index

Malpass, Alderman Philip (–1468), 104, 105, 114
Manners and Morals, 132, 133, and *passim*
Marching Watch, 64, 132
Marriage Act (1754), 175
Marry'd Woman's Case, A (1609), 141
Marshalsea Prison, 114
Marsten, John, 205
Masons, 43, 55, 95
Masters' Side, 107
Masons, 43, 50
Mayors, 47, 50, 51, 63, 71, 80, 91, and *passim*; see also Lord Mayors
Maypoles, 33
Meal Tub Plot, The (1684), 201
Mercers, 53
Mercia, 21, 25, 33
Merciless Parliament, The (1381), 93
Mercurius Democraticus (1661), 171
Mercurius Matrimonialis (1691), 161
Mercury Sweat-baths, Leather Lane, 169
Merrie Mans Resolution, The (1630), 143, 144
Metamorphosis of Ajax, The (1590), 57
Metrapolitan Colledg (Newgate Prison), 187
Middlesex Sheriffwick, 40, 46, 62, 152
Middleton, Thomas (1570–1627), 139
Mihindelane (Pyssynge Alley), 75
Milk Street, 30
Millet, Michael, 167
Milliners, 58
Minstrelsy, 93, see also Carting
Mint, 21
Mithras (god), 8
Mollies Houses, 158, 162, 163, 164, 169, and *passim*
Monck, General George, Duke of Albemarle (1608–70), 162, 190
Monmouth, James Stuart, Duke of, 160, 201
Moorfields/Moorgate, 42, 55, 141, 190, 204, 208, and *passim*
Moots/Moot-worthy, 36
Morbis Indecens aei Cunniensis, 81
Morbis Turpis, 81
Mortimer, Roger, Earl of March (1231–82), 80
Murage (wall tax), 67, 175, 206
Murrain of Kine (1315), 80
Mutinus (god), 12
Mysteries, 30, 50, see also Guilds

Nappers/Napping, 154
Narrative of the Old Plot, A (1686), 202
Nashe his Dildo (1598), 131
Nashe, Thomas (1567–1601), 126, 131
Neale, Mary, 'Queen of Morocco', 152
Necessary Houses, 46, see also Sanitation
Negress, 152, 161
Nest ap Tewdr, 39
Neuters, 187
Neville, Thomas (–1471), 105, 108
Newgate and Prison, 31, 93, 103, 107, 156, 164

Nightdress, 135
Nightwalkers, 72, 91, 208
Nokes, James (1630–1692), 170
No Mony, No Cunny, 144
Nose-slitting, 152

Oates, Titus (1649–1702), 191, 201
Official licensers (1653), 154
Offa, King of Mercia (–757–796), 25
Olaf Trygvasson, King of Norway (–1000), 31
Old Bailey, The, 163
Oldcastle, Sir John (1653–83), 101, 206
Oldham, John, 203
Old Pye-house in Turnbull St, 144
Old Rowley (Charles II), 158
Ordinances and Proclamations in date order
1138 Forbidding Nuns to Wear Certain furs, 69
1161 For the Government of the Bankside Stewes, 44
1189 Of Necessary Chambers in Houses, 46
1189 All Streets and Lanes to be cleansed, 46
1189 Charter of Privileges, 48
1215 Magna Carta, 48
1272 Concerning Person wandering by Night, 71
1272 Of the Cleansing of Streets and Lanes and Against Courtezans and Brothelkeepers, 70
1275 Of Batmen: All boats to be moored at the City side at nights, 70
1282 Forbidding Noise and Tumultes about St Paul's and against use of sea-coals, 65
1284 Of Thieves and Courtezans, 72
1290 Enforcing Knighthoods, 74
1307 Concerning Whores and Procuresses, 74
1320 Forbidding Bailiffs to harass Merchants, 81
1320 To employ Rakers . . . with sufficient rakes, 81
1327 That the Liberties of the City be not taken away, 84
1347 Leprous people to be voyded out of the City, 87
1351 The Statute of Labourers, 86
1352 Whores must wear hoods of striped material, 87
1381 To arrest all women Nightwalkers, 91
1384 Common Whoremongers to be removed from the City, 93
1385 As to Street walking by Night, 95
1399 Turnmill Brook to be cleansed, 101
1417 For the abolition of all Stewes within the City, 98

224

225